W9-DEP-073

Hunters, gatherers and first farmers beyond Europe

[ESN]

Hunters, gatherers and first farmers beyond Europe

An archaeological survey

Edited by J.V.S. Megaw
Professor of Archaeology, University of Leicester

Leicester University Press 1977

0823685   124901

First published in 1977 by Leicester University Press
Distributed in North America by Humanities Press Inc., New Jersey

Copyright © Leicester University Press 1977

All rights reserved. No part of this publication may be reproduced, stored in a retrieval system, or transmitted, in any form or by any means, electronic, mechanical, photocopying, recording or otherwise, without the prior permission of the Leicester University Press.

Designed by Arthur Lockwood
Set in IBM Press Roman by Charnwood Typesetting Ltd
Printed in Great Britain by Unwin Brothers Limited,
The Gresham Press, Old Woking, Surrey
ISBN 0 7185 1136 0

CONTENTS

List of figures   page 7
List of tables   page 9
List of abbreviations   page 10

Preface
J.V.S. MEGAW
Professor of Archaeology, University of Leicester   page 11

Note on radiocarbon dating   page 12
Bibliography   page 13
Acknowledgments   page 13

1 Human population history, from Afro-Asia to   page 15
the New World, and its possible relationship
to economic change
DON BROTHWELL
Senior Lecturer, Department of Environmental Archaeology,
Institute of Archaeology, University of London

2 The 'frontier' concept in prehistory: the end   page 25
of the moving frontier
JOHN ALEXANDER
University Lecturer in Archaeology, Faculty of Archaeology
and Anthropology, University of Cambridge

3 The advantages of agriculture   page 41
BRYONY ORME
Lecturer in Prehistory, Department of History,
University of Exeter

4 The origins of agriculture in the Near East   page 51
A.J. LEGGE
Staff Lecturer in Archaeology, Department of Extra-Mural
Studies, University of London

5 Hunters, gatherers and first farmers in West Africa   page 69
THURSTAN SHAW
lately Professor of Archaeology, University of Ibadan, and
currently Visiting Research Professor, Ahmadu Bello
University, Nigeria

6 Hunters, pastoralists and early agriculturalists   page 127
in South Asia
BRIDGET ALLCHIN
Fellow and Tutor of Wolfson College, University of Cambridge

0823685 124901

7 The Hoabinhian: hunter-gatherers or early
  agriculturalists in South-East Asia?   page 145
I.C. GLOVER
Lecturer in Prehistoric Archaeology, Institute of
Archaeology, University of London

8 The hunting Neolithic: adaptations to the food   page 167
  quest in prehistoric Papua New Guinea
JIM ALLEN
Fellow, Department of Prehistory, Research School
of Pacific Studies, Australian National University

9 Man and environment in Polynesia   page 189
PETER GATHERCOLE
Curator, University Museum of Archaeology and
Ethnology, Cambridge

10 The earliest hunters, gatherers and farmers of   page 199
   North America
JOAN J. TAYLOR
Rankin Lecturer in Prehistoric Archaeology,
University of Liverpool

11 From foraging to farming in early Mexico   page 225
WARWICK BRAY
Senior Lecturer in Latin American Archaeology, Institute
of Archaeology, University of London

Index   page 251

FIGURES

1. The emergence of major biologically distinctive populations of the late Pleistocene and early Holocene.   page 17
2. Variations in modern human populations.   18-19
3. Estimates of the sequence of population increase.   21
4. Possibilities of exploiting an environment (relationships of hunter-gatherers to farmers).   26-7
5. a. Hadza family hut; b. The gallery of an Iban longhouse.   44
6. Eskimo woman carrying her child.   45
7. Children at home, in a woman's house of the Bomagai-Angoiang.   45
8. Zulu warriors.   47
9. Slaughter patterns in gazelle from two levels at Nahal Oren.   55
10. Proportions of major food animals at Nahal Oren and Tell Abu Hureyra.   57
11. Air masses and precipitation in Africa in January and July.   70
12. Types of West African landscape.   72-3
13. Acheulian and Sangoan stone tools.   75
14. Nigeria: 'Middle Stone Age' tools.   76
15. Nigeria: microliths from Mejiro Cave, Old Oyo.   78
16. Nigeria: microliths from Rop rock shelter.   79
17. Mali: stone industry from Kourounkorokale rock shelter.   80-1
18. Sierra Leone: stone industry from Yengema cave.   82
19. Sierra Leone: stone industry from Yengema cave.   84
20. Ghana: stone arrowheads from Ntereso.   84
21. Mali: stone and iron implements from Kourounkorokale rock shelter.   85
22. Mali: pottery from Kourounkorokale rock shelter.   86-7
23. Ghana: stone industry from 'Bosumpra' cave, Abetifi.   88
24. Ghana: pottery from the Rop and Abetifi caves.   89
25. Guinea: tools, picks and axes from Blande rock shelter.   90-1
26. Ghana: stone artifacts and pottery of the Kintampo industry.   92
27. Nigeria: necked and lugged axes.   92
28. The Late Stone Age of West Africa in relation to vegetation zones.   94-5
29. Jebel Qeili: representation of Guinea corn on a Meroitic rock engraving.   98
30. West Africa: food plants.   100-1
31. West Africa: distribution of 'yam zone'.   104
32. *Ensete,* the African or 'false' banana, showing edible parts. 105
33. Isochronic diagram of the spread of cattle in Africa.   108
34. Southern Sahara: types of Stone Age harpoons and points.   112
35. Areas of domestication of principal African cereals.   113
36. The Indian sub-continent, showing rainfall and principal archaeological sites mentioned in the text.   129
37. Bardwal, Gujarat: nomadic pastoralists.   130
38. Adamgarh cave: Mesolithic tools.   132
39. Langhnaj: Mesolithic tools.   132
40. Harappa: pottery types.   134
41. Vedda bowmen, Sri Lanka.   137
42. Nevasa and Chandoli: Chalcolithic stone-blade industry.   140
43. Harappan stone-blade industry.   140
44. Stone-blade industries from Neolithic and Chalcolithic settlements, showing percentages of artifact types from each site. 141
45. Principal Hoabinhian sites.   146
46. Sukajadi Kec.,Northern Sumatra: north-west face of Hoabinhian shell midden.   147
47. Hoabinhian stone implement types.   150-1
48. Laang Spean, Cambodia: cave site with Hoabinhian occupation.   152

49. Philippines: the Tasaday tribe. page 154
50. South-east Asia, showing the extent of the Sunda and Sahul Shelves. 159
51. Present-day distribution of ever-wet, and occasionally seasonally dry,
   vegetation. 161
52. Highland Papua New Guinea: paddle-shaped spade. 170
53. Papua New Guinea agricultural systems. 172
54. Papua New Guinea: distribution of archaeological sites. 176
55. Part of the Kuk swamp site. 177
56. A typical prehistoric ditch visible in the section of a modern drain. 178
57. Kuk, New Guinea Highlands: stone hoe blade. 180
58. Flaked and polished waisted blades from New Britain and excavated
   examples from Yuku. 182
59. Map of the Pacific area. 190
60. Distribution of pre-projectile point and Palaeo-Indian complexes. 201
61. Northern Eurasia showing existing and former glaciers. 203
62. Suggested Old World sources of the four earliest prehistoric traditions
   in the New World. 206
63. Distribution in the New World of the Core Tool, Flake and Bone
   and Blade, Burin and Leaf-Point traditions. 208
64. Clovis projectile points. 210
65. Folsom point embedded in bison rib. 210
66. Stone and bone implements from Sandia Cave, New Mexico. 212
67. Folsom point. 212
68. Stone and bone implements from the Lindenmeier site. 212
69. Pattern of Palaeo-Indian hunters' stalking of grazing bison. 214
70. Olsen-Chubbuck kill-site, Colorado. 214-15
71. Lanceolate projectile point types. 216
72. Old Cordilleran tradition: cascade points. 216
73. North and Mesoamerica: main culture areas. 217
74. Paiute woman of northern Utah. 219
75. North America: early cultures, phases and traditions. 220-1
76. Plant and animal domestication in the Tehuacan valley. 226
77. The importance of agriculture compared with hunting and plant-
   collecting in the diet of three areas of Mexico. 228
78. The annual subsistence cycle in the Tehuacan basin of highland
   Mexico between 6800 and 5000 B.C. 230
79. The relationship between maize-yield, land use and population
   size in the Valley of Oaxaca. 237
80. The relationship of population size and carrying capacity under various
   systems of food procurement. 245

TABLES

1. The moving frontier.   page   29
2. The end of the moving frontier.   30
3. Moving frontiers between farmers and hunter-gatherers
  (excluding Europe).   34-6
4. Land-use potential at ten sites in Palestine.   60

ABBREVIATIONS

Note Places of publication are given only for works published outside the United Kingdom.

Bull.Inst.Franc.Afr. noire	*Bulletin de l'Institut Français d'Afrique noire*
Curr.Anthrop.	*Current Anthropology*
Geogr.J.	*Geographical Journal*
J.Afr.Hist.	*Journal of African History*
J.Archaeol.Sci.	*Journal of Archaeological Science*
J.Hist.Soc.Nigeria	*Journal of the Historical Society of Nigeria*
Proc.Prehist.Soc.	*Proceedings of the Prehistoric Society*
W.Afr.Archaeol.Newsl.	*West African Archaeology Newsletter*
W.Afr.J.Archaeol.	*West African Journal of Archaeology*

PREFACE

The 11 essays which follow represent a number of personal statements on one of
the most interesting and literally vital aspects of economic and cultural change in the
history of man within his natural environment. I hope therefore I may be forgiven if
I introduce these essays on an equally personal note of explanation as to why an
English Midlands University should have become the venue for a symposium on not
only non-British but largely non-European prehistory.

In March 1974 when a residential conference was held at Leicester under the title
of the present volume, its purpose was in fact simple - one might almost say
simplistic. This was a time when the theoretical bases of archaeology seemed still to
be growing in complexity, challenged by more and more sophisticated model
building. Notwithstanding, I felt that, despite a growing public awareness of the
existence of archaeology beyond Europe, much new and exciting work in other parts
of the world remained largely unnoticed, perhaps as a result of the mounting
pressures in Britain of rescue (or if one prefers the prior American term, salvage)
archaeology, and the resultant demand for strictly British field archaeologists. Since
I myself had trained predominantly in later European prehistory, but had spent
more than a decade in Australasia, I was concerned to take the opportunity of
presenting to as wide and varied an audience as most Adult Education week-ends
assemble, such new facts and theories as might reasonably be packed into 48 hours.

It still seems to me a matter for surprise not that Grahame Clark's *World
Prehistory* (1969) should be justifiably so widely read, but rather that it not be read
more widely still. Certainly it is true that there are an increasing number of titles
which attempt as wide an introduction as possible to early culture history (Fagan
1974; Pfeiffer 1972) and, no less important in the present context, relate such matters
to man as part of the total environment (Lee and DeVore 1968; Ucko and Dimbleby
1969) - I have cited a few additional references below. In the interim between
symposium and publication, a number of significant additions to the literature have
appeared. Barbara Bender's review (1975) of farming in prehistory is an invaluable
summary, particularly of the varied theories concerning the transition to food-
production; her chosen case-study areas, South-West Asia, Mesoamerica and Peru,
overlap only in part with the present selected topics. Naturally there are points of
contact, as for example in the accumulating evidence from a number of widely
separated localities for a much more gradual and widespread series of events than was
once envisaged in the term 'the Neolithic revolution', first really given form by Vere
Gordon Childe in the late 1920s and finding their full orthodox treatment in his *Man
makes himself* (1936) or, in hardly less popular treatment, the various editions of
Sonia Cole's *Neolithic Revolution.* Of much significance in recent years has been the
work of the British Academy Major Research Project in the Early History of
Agriculture (Higgs 1972; 1975) which may be said to have grown not only out of
Grahame Clark's pioneering work in 'economic prehistory' but also out of a concern
to develop a comparative view of the possible rules governing the occupation and
exploitation of certain closely defined territories. In their differing ways the essays
in this volume by Don Brothwell, John Alexander and Anthony Legge are equally
concerned with defining not only geographical but cultural frontiers. Certainly these
and other contributions have by no means offered an answer or even postulated a
hypothesis for every aspect of the changes from a basically hunting or gathering
economy to semi-sedentary agriculturalism. For instance, in the context of
Australia, one of a minority of areas where the environmental conditions for such a
change did not result in 'farming' as the word is generally understood until the period
of white settlement, one may cite Bryony Orme's contribution concerned, as several
scholars are more and more, with the *relevant* application of ethnographic and
indeed ethological data to archaeological material. Ms Orme shows clearly that the
boundary between, say, food collection and food production is indeed a blurred one,
at least with regard to the 'why' if not the 'how', the explanation of culture change
not just the possible effects of that change. These are topics conveniently discussed in a

number of brief summaries (Chang 1972; Netting 1971; Smith 1972; Spooner 1973). The complex relationship between population and resources in Mesoamerica, here outlined by Don Brothwell, is also examined by Warwick Bray in a final and suitably wide-ranging review of theoretical possibilities and archaeological and ethno-historical observations. My own view is that this is where the truly novel results of investigations into the prehistory of agricultural systems in South and South-East Asia and Melanesia have, and will continue to have, much to tell us, as indicated in these pages by Bridget Allchin, Ian Glover and Jim Allen.

The mechanisms of colonization and cultural adaptation to differing environments considered from a historical basis by John Alexander are more explicitly discussed in the ever-intriguing context of Polynesia by Peter Gathercole, and in a very different context by Thurstan Shaw for West Africa. I have made passing reference to Gordon Childe and, as has been observed elsewhere, it is perhaps not surprising that he, very much the expatriate Australian, should never have been happy with the use of ethnographic data as a method of testing archaeological hypotheses. I hope that both the regional and the general studies in the present survey will focus attention on the not only legitimate but necessary application of a number of differing disciplinary approaches, of which the ethnographic approach is only one.

This is not a text-book for a limited audience of impressed students and specialist scholars; rather I would regard it as a tract for the times. Indeed, if there is a general message to be gleaned from what should be regarded as an interim survey of still developing views and continuously reworked data, it is just that; as the development of agriculture needs to be studied as a widely varying and continuously evolving process, so too (to quote, and not for the first time, an Old World specialist in the examination of that very process of agriculturalism) we must realize that 'every observation we make is conditioned by the ideas of our own time'.

Leicester, 1 March 1976.

NOTE

While this volume was in proof the joint symposium of the Royal Society and British Academy on the beginnings of agriculture held in London 9-11 April 1975 was published (Hutchinson, Sir Joseph, Clark, J.G.D., Jope, E.M. and Riley, R., *The Early History of Agriculture,* 1977). This symposium was significant particularly for contributions from biologists concerned with the evolution of domesticated plants and animals.

NOTE ON RADIOCARBON DATING

Following current convention, uncorrected (i.e. non-calibrated) radiocarbon dates are indicated with lower case letters thus: 5735 bc. BP designates 'before the present' or before A.D. 1950.

BIBLIOGRAPHY

Allchin, Bridget, 1966. *The Stone-tipped Arrow: Late Stone Age Hunters of the Tropical Old World.*
Bender, Barbara, 1975. *Farming in Prehistory: from hunter-gatherer to food-producer.*
Chang, K.C., 1972. *Settlement Patterns in Archaeology (Addison-Wesley Module in Anthropology 24).*
Childe, V. Gordon, 1928. *The most ancient East.*
Childe, V. Gordon, 1936. *Man makes himself* (4th, posthumous edition with preface by Glyn Daniel 1965).
Clark, J.G.D., 1952. *Prehistoric Europe: the economic basis* (reprinted 1974).
Clark, J.G.D., 1969. *World Prehistory: a new outline.*
Clark, J.G.D. 1971. *The Stone Age Hunters.*
Cole, Sonia, 1970. *The Neolithic Revolution* (5th edn and later reprints).
Coon, Carleton S., 1972. *The Hunting Peoples.*
Fagan, B.M., 1974. *Men of the Earth: an introduction to world prehistory* (Boston).
Forde, C.D., 1963. *Habitat, Economy and Society.*
Higgs, E.S. (ed.), 1972. *Papers in Economic Prehistory.*
Higgs, E.S. (ed.), 1975. *Palaeoeconomy.*
Lee, Richard B. and DeVore, Irven (eds), 1968. *Man the Hunter* (Chicago).
Netting, Robert McC., 1971. *The Ecological Approach in Cultural Study (Addison-Wesley Module in Anthropology 6).*
Pfeiffer, John E., 1972. *The Emergence of Man* (New York, 2nd edn).
Sahlins, Marshall D., 1972. *Stone Age Economics* (Chicago).
Service, Elman, 1966. *The Hunters* (Englewood Cliffs, N.J.).
Severin, T., 1973. *Vanishing Primitive Man.*
Smith, Philip E., 1972. *The Consequences of Food Production (Addison-Wesley Module in Anthropology 31).*
Spooner, Brian, 1973. *The Cultural Ecology of Pastoral Nomads (Addison-Wesley Module in Anthropology 45).*
Streuver, Stuart (ed.), 1971. *Prehistoric Agriculture* (Garden City, N.Y.).
Ucko, P.J. and Dimbleby, G.W. (eds), 1969. *The Domestication and Exploitation of Plants and Animals.*
Wolf, Eric R., 1966. *Peasants* (Englewood Cliffs, N.J.).

ACKNOWLEDGMENTS

Although individual contributors have made their own acknowledgments elsewhere, I must here offer my thanks collectively to them all and also to John B. Campbell, Colin Flight, R.R. Inskeep and William J. Watson, who also delivered papers at the symposium but who could not for a variety of reasons prepare them for publication. Equally I am most grateful to Thurstan Shaw and Joan Taylor for filling gaps in our regional coverage which would have otherwise been all too apparent. My thanks are due also to Brian Threlfall of the Department of Adult Education at the University of Leicester and my secretary at the time, Dorothy Walker, without whom there simply would have been no conference. A.G. McCormick redrew the majority of the illustrations in this book and my thanks are due to the Secretary and Assistant Secretary to the Press, Peter Boulton and Susan Martin, who have been as patient with me as editors as my colleagues have been as contributors; without them there simply would have been no book, and that would have been a pity.

DON BROTHWELL

1 Human population history, from Afro-Asia to the New World, and its possible relationship to economic change

What I want to achieve here is a rather brief digest of human population history beyond Europe which, to me at least, seems relevant to a fuller understanding of the emergence of the variation we see in more recent peoples, with some comments on economic differences which have evolved since Pleistocene times. I also want to show that population history, density, and movements have some relevance in the understanding of economic change, and for that matter of various other cultural traits. Man is a biosocial species, and there are intimate links between his biology and his culture which deserve more exploration than they have received in the past in the field of archaeology.

The history of advanced hominids of the kind represented by living man could well be linked with critical evolutionary diversification in late Middle or early Upper Pleistocene times. By the late Pleistocene, we have osteological evidence from sites in Europe, from Mapa in China, and perhaps (though far less certainly) from Omo and Kanjera sites in East Africa, of noticeable physical change beyond the *Homo erectus* level. In the Upper Pleistocene, contemporary with the gradual evolution of the European Neanderthalers over some 50,000 years, were less specialized 'residual' populations, perhaps widely spread below the Sahara and Sudan (Eyasi, Rhodesian, Saldaha), and with at least pockets of 'residual' stocks still living in South East Asia (Solo people of Java). It is also accepted now that somewhere, and perhaps extending over much of Southern Asia, in particular, was emerging a far more progressive form, exemplified by the Skhul and Jebel Kafzeh people in the west, and by the 40,000-year-old Niah find in Borneo. Another representative of this advanced Australasian group may well be the 30,000-year-old Lake Mungo individual from Australia (Macintosh 1972; Thorne 1971). As yet, there is no good evidence to show how much the less progressive people contributed genetically to the emergence of later advanced groups. However, it is certain that by about 30,000 years ago, only advanced populations remained. Moreover, this transformation in the Old World seems to have been relatively so rapid that local evolution from non-progressive and more primitive groups seems far less likely than that of progressive communities, with perhaps population-density problems encouraging their continual expoitation of 'foreign' land areas, moving continuously out as a part of the process of survivorship. This colonialism was nothing new; the very early hominids, the australopithecins, may have moved from Africa as far as South-East Asia, and *Homo erectus* had also pushed north into perhaps less favourable climates in northern Europe. Thus, contrary to Loring Braes's (1971) interpretation of advanced hominid expansion, and in spite of the silence of most palaeontologists on this problem, I think one can, even on this very scrappy evidence, see Asia as a major focal point of later population history.

Regarding possible correlations in artifact and biological change, one fact to be faced in prehistoric studies is that stone tool typology cannot easily be equated with human biological change and variation. Thus, late Middle Pleistocene axe/chopper divisions in Asia do not seem to fit in with apparent population history, and in the same way, both the Neanderthalers and the non-Neanderthal 'progressives' of South-East Asia used Mousterian tool forms (Brothwell 1961). This is not to say, of course, that some cultural traits may not have been equated with biological differences, but these may have been linguistic or tribal rather than an aspect of *material* culture.

By late Pleistocene to early Holocene times, say from 25,000 to 10,000 years ago, there is some evidence for the crystallization out of the major racial groups that we see today (fig. 1). With the advanced material culture of the Upper Palaeolithic and later culture phases, leading to some degree of population increase and further dispersal, founder effect, and other evolutionary factors, may have resulted in minor physical change. This is why there is such a wealth of small-scale variation to be seen in groups today. Some of this variation, such as height, robustness, degree of pigmentation, and resistance to particular disease, may well have assisted in the adaption of people and their cultures to particular environments.

The variation which has evolved just within Eastern Asia, is well illustrated by reference to, say, a 'classic' mongoloid group from Japan (fig. 2b), the non-mongoloid Ainu, Australian Aborigines and Fijians (figs. 2a, f). These are groups adapted to different environments and cultures, but probably with some part of the variation accountable to one or other of the evolving Upper Pleistocene stocks in Asia and Australasia. This problem of the differentiation of modern varieties from earlier and perhaps less distinctive Pleistocene stocks is also seen in the emergence of Negro/Khoisan forms in Africa (fig. 2e) and the Negritos of Southern India (fig. 2c), the Andaman Islands and parts of South-East Asia. William Howells (1960; 1973) believes these African and Asian groups to be 'intimately related', but asks, 'How do we get Negritos into the Pacific from Africa, or vice-versa?' To me, this does not seem such a formidable problem if we see the emergence of these groups from a string of Upper Pleistocene populations mating and evolving over 30,000 years or so in a tropical belt mainly in Asia but perhaps extending through into East Africa.

Yet a further question of this kind is the region or regions of origin of the

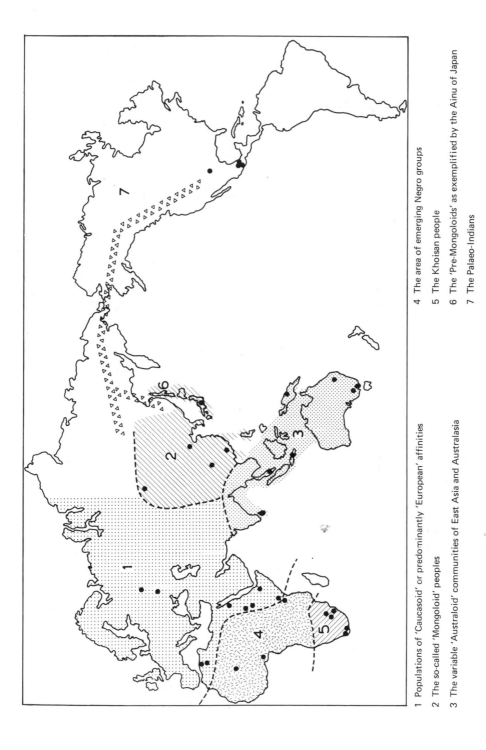

1 Populations of 'Caucasoid' or predominantly 'European' affinities

2 The so-called 'Mongoloid' peoples

3 The variable 'Australoid' communities of East Asia and Australasia

4 The area of emerging Negro groups

5 The Khoisan people

6 The 'Pre-Mongoloids' as exemplified by the Ainu of Japan

7 The Palaeo-Indians

Figure 1. The emergence of biologically distinctive populations of the late Pleistocene and early Holocene. Black circles indicate key sites.

a

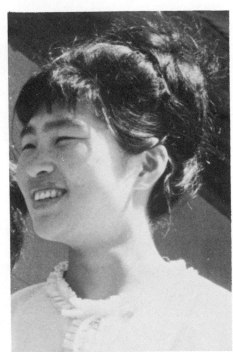

b

c

d

e   f

Figure 2. Variation in modern human populations.
a. Ainu, Northern Japan *(photograph: R. Harvey)*.
b. Mongoloid individual, Japan *(photograph: R. Harvey)*.
c. Toda woman, Sri Lanka *(photograph: R. C. Bosanquet)*.
d. Papuan man *(photograph: R.J. Lampert)*.
e. Negro of Swazi tribe.
f. Australian Aboriginal.

Palaeo-Indians of the New World. They probably trickled across the Bering Straits, and in genetic totality they were probably a fairly heterogenous assemblage. Physically, and especially facially, they are not like 'classic' mongoloids. Blood group data also emphasizes their biological distinctiveness. These prehistoric Amerindians seem most likely, therefore, to have evolved from predominantly non-mongoloid groups. The Ainu of Japan (fig. 2a) may also represent a population derived from similar ancestral groups, and the living Kets of Siberia may be another indication of the evolution and importance of non-mongoloid Upper Palaeolithic people in more north-eastern parts of Asia. It is a pity that we still have so little early Amerindian skeletal material for study. The few possible early cases are mainly from Mexico, and show robustness and noticeable variation, suggesting that there were plenty of genetic differences in these earlier peoples from which to derive modern regional differences (Romano 1970).

So far, I have tried to present a case for the importance of Asia and South-East Asia in the emergence of populations which were eventually to spread widely in Asia, the Pacific, the New World, and perhaps even Africa. If we consider the very tentative estimates of population numbers since the end of the Pleistocene, it is interesting to see that Asia seems to have been ahead of other major regions when it comes to numbers of people. Such estimates are based on various information, historical estimates, extrapolation back from more recent statistics and so on. In fig. 3 we see some present-day estimates compared with tentative figures for 2,000 years ago, and *highly* tentative numbers for 10,000 years ago. Asia stands out as an area of considerable population increase, perhaps especially of the mongoloid peoples. For China alone, crude historical evidence suggests an erratic move upwards between 500 B.C. and 1000 A.D. from 20 million to about 125 million. Population pressure is therefore no new phenomenon, and I think is still greatly underestimated as an important factor in explaining the centrifugal movement of peoples in antiquity, or of the recurring impetus this gave to populations to pass the threshold from the hunting and collecting level through to partial agricultural economics (Brothwell 1971).

Of course, such population estimates are extremely crude, and may be challenged, but it must be remembered that one thing is certain, and that is that humans have probably always been talented at increasing their numbers. Also, that some time in the past, and the later Pleistocene is quite a possibility, variables such as social organization - including increasing emphasis on territory limits, improved hunting technology, and increased plant knowledge - enabled communities to consider survivorship in other ways than the alternatives of starvation or migration. This other alternative is the active curtailment of a population within a region by intensifying food-producing efforts. If one questions the importance of population pressures and of the reaction of societies to such stresses, then look at our own. Here, as so often elsewhere and in the past, the efforts to produce sufficient food and habitations, and decisions regarding migration, are ultimately relatable to population numbers.

The significance of the possible relationship between population history and the emergence of agricultural economics seems to have been rather missed, or at least neglected. If a number of populations have a common ancestry, then culture trait similarities are surely as likely to reflect this common origin as independent trait evolution. In other words, that man is a biosocial species, and with the dispersion of

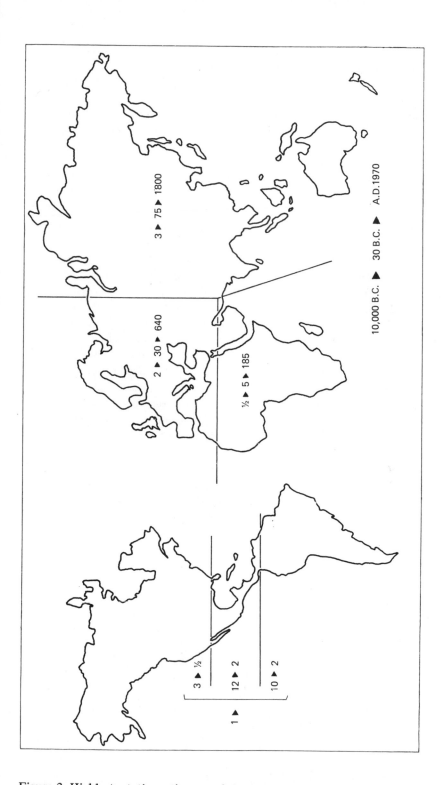

Figure 3. Highly tentative estimates of the sequence of population increase in major segments of the world expressed in units of 10^6.

124001

human groups, not only genes move about but also basic know-how and ideas critical to the emergence of new cultural phases. Let me illustrate this point. Artificial cranial deformation, a somewhat exotic human practice, has been fairly widespread in some recent populations in both Old and New World groups. There is some limited evidence of it in earlier populations, and it seems likely that there are cases in late Pleistocene or early Holocene skulls from China and Australia. Thus, if we can establish a Pleistocene antiquity for the trait in a broad area of Australasia, might not this occurrence in more recent groups be traceable to a common area in the past? There is certainly a limit to the probability that unusual culture traits all have separate origins, and I think deformation is an example of when to resist separate origins and give due regard to population history.

We might similarly argue that some Upper Pleistocene groups were probably already aware of the value of animal control, and their complex plant-lore and knowledge when necessary provided a good basis from which to adapt quickly to agricultural practices. Indeed, can we really resist any longer the fact that animal 'domestication' in its initial stages was indeed a Pleistocene phenomenon? (Higgs and Jarman 1972). I use the term animal 'domestication' to mean simply man-animal relationships which are likely to restrict breeding potential and thus possibly lead to eventual changes in gene pool composition. In the case of the dog, the centre of domestication is still thought of as the European and South-West Asian Mesolithic, although other evidence rather challenges this. The objection to this scheme is that man/dog relationships were possibly well-established when the Palaeo-Indians moved into the New World. Similarly the dingo may have arrived in Australia by 8000 B.C. at least, and if so, it would be pushing dog movements to the limits to derive these early dingos from the Near Eastern stocks within a thousand or so years.

One can also question whether, if 'domestic' forms appear at various Mesolithic sites, the basic determinants of change must be found centuries or millennia before the positive osteological evidence. It is unlikely that the early stages of domestication amounted to intensive, planned, micro-evolutionary transformation, but rather a faltering attempt on the part of man to dominate over one or other plant or animal species. I remain unconvinced that these early phases of domestication will have left more than very minor changes - still well within the range of variation for a wild population.

So, what are the main points I have been trying to make? First, let me say that I am not supporting a simple Elliot Smithian culture - jumping diffusionism! Economic change, and especially the emergence of agriculture, must have always been bound up with a number of factors - cultural needs, biological environment, and so on. What I have tried to demonstrate is that I think some aspects of population dynamics and population history are still rather neglected in the study of ancient peoples and their economics. To me, it seems worth questioning the origins of the communities in which we see some form of agriculture developing, and at the same time looking back into the late Pleistocene for early links between them. Eventual emergence of economic change may not so much indicate independent creativity in relation to food needs, as the passing of a threshold - related to population factors - which necessitates the exploitation of long-known alternatives.

REFERENCES

Brace, C.L., Nelson, H. and Korn, H., 1971. *Atlas of Fossil Man* (New York).
Brothwell, D.R., 1961. 'The people of Mount Carmel. A reconstruction of their position in human evolution', *Proc. Prehist. Soc., 27,* 155-9
Brothwell, D.R., 1971. 'Palaeodemography', in W. Brass (ed.), *Biological Aspects of Demography.*
Higgs, E.S. and Jarman, M.R., 1972. 'The origins of animal and plant husbandry', in E.S. Higgs (ed.), *Papers in Economic Prehistory.*
Howells, W., 1960. *Mankind in the Making. The Story of Human Evolution.*
Howells, W., 1973. *The Evolution of the Genus Homo* (Reading, Mass.).
Macintosh, N.W.G., 1972. 'Radiocarbon dating as a pointer in time to the arrival and history of Man in Australia and islands to the north west', *Proc. 8th International Conference on Radiocarbon Dating* (Wellington, New Zealand), XLIV-LVI.
Romano, Arturo, 1970. 'Preceramic human remains', pp. 22-34 in T.D. Stewart (ed.), *Handbook of Middle American Indians, 9, Physical Anthropology* (Austin, Texas).
Thorne, A.G., 1971. 'Mungo and Kow Swamp: morphological variation in Pleistocene Australians', *Mankind 9,* 85-9.

JOHN ALEXANDER

2 The 'frontier' concept in prehistory: the end of the moving frontier

The Leicester symposium was one of the first attempts by archaeologists in the British Isles to consider the problems of 'frontier studies' which have preoccupied modern historians in North America for a century, and more recently have been developed in Australia, Northern Asia and South America, in prehistoric contexts (Bohannan and Plog 1967; Sharp 1955). It is appropriate, for the last 70 years have seen the end of frontiers of North American type and anthropologists have been able to study their more immediate effects (Lewes and McGann 1970). It is possible to bring to the study of earlier 'frontiers' more sensitivity and understanding of the problems of adaptation than before and therefore to identify and understand more clearly the archaeological evidence left.

The archaeological study must begin from the intensive study of the North American 'frontier' defined originally by Frederick Jackson Turner in 1893 as 'the temporary boundary of an expanding society at the edge of substantially free lands' (Turner, 1962). In North America this was at the expense of both farming and hunter-gatherer groups. The definition is valid for a variety of regions through the world during the last eight millennia, and so too are the general conclusions of American historians since that time that; 1. The 'free' land available to them further west, its continuous recession and the advancement of settlement westwards, greatly affected the East Coast, parent societies; 2. During the advance westwards, individuals and communities shed much 'cultural baggage', for the societies they planted required fewer social, political and economic controls; 3. The effects on the indigenous population was catastrophic, but a number of different responses can be observed.

In a recent study Billington (1967) has provided a number of ideas of particular

0823685

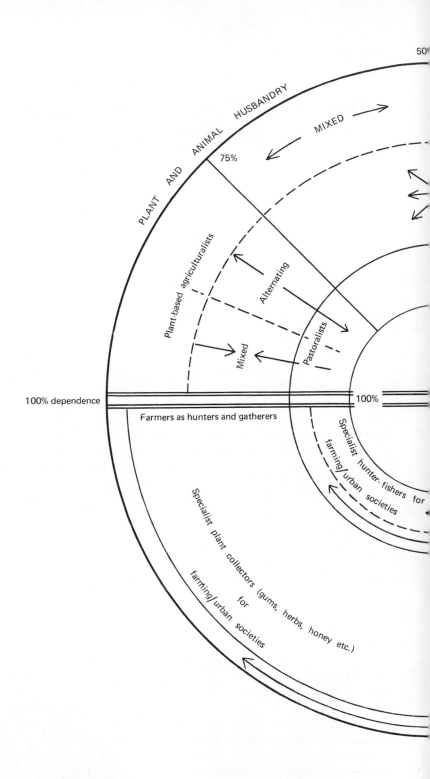

Figure 4. Possibilities of exploiting an environment (relationships of hunter-gatherers to farmers).

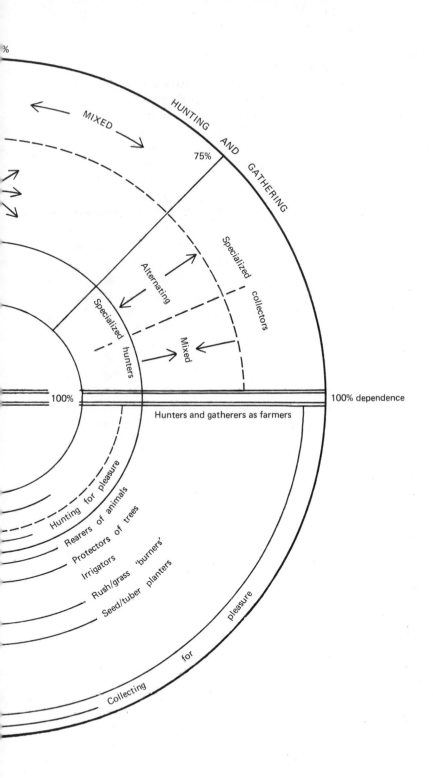

%

MIXED

HUNTING AND GATHERING

75%

Specialized collectors

Alternating

Specialized hunters

Mixed

100%

100% dependence

Hunters and gatherers as farmers

Hunting for pleasure

Rearers of animals

Protectors of trees

Irrigators

Rush/grass 'burners'

Seed/tuber planters

Collecting for pleasure

interest to those studying earlier periods. He distinguishes a frontier as both a geographical area - a migratory zone of varying width - and as a social process. He also distinguishes between those pioneers (intrusive elements) who used nature, that is depended on natural resources, but discovered routes, advertised favourable areas and lessened indigenous self-sufficiency, and those who subdued nature, and in the process, the indigenes. There has also been a growing interest in the effect of these developments upon the indigenes, and the work of Elkin (1951), Lindgren (1938) and Redfield et al. (1936) provides insights relevant to archaeologists.

Earlier frontiers between farmers and hunter-gatherers must have existed in the past in all parts of the world where farming, whether of plants or animals, was developed or introduced. This comprises all the main geographical regions excluding the islands of the Pacific Ocean and some arctic and mountain zones. Hunting-and-gathering societies have been identified as preceding farming in all regions. The relationship can be further refined by accepting the distinction of a 'moving frontier', which existed either until all currently usable land had been taken over, or until the natural boundaries of the region were reached, or until the limits of plant and animal climatic tolerance were reached. When this happened a 'static frontier' developed in which farmers and hunter-gatherers settled down into a more stable relationship. This can be expressed diagrammatically (see table 1).

Attention in this paper will be concentrated on ways of identifying that relatively short period of time between the end of a mobile and the development of a static frontier, since the recognition and understanding of it would add a great deal to the knowledge of any region. The end of the moving frontier must always have been a period of great sociological and economic importance and this is well shown in North America, where its effects continue to be studied. Farming-community problems could now no longer be solved by partial or total migration (except through warfare) within the region. Change and development must have come in new ways, for example by more careful husbandry, population control or social innovation (Wyman and Kroeber 1957).

A RECOGNITION OF MOVING FRONTIERS

It seems possible to identify at least 28 distinct plant and animal complexes in which 'frontier' conditions between farmers and hunter-gatherers have existed. For the purpose of this paper frontiers between farmers of different crops or technologies have been ignored. While the origins of these complexes are often still obscure, evidence of later development is often greater and the end of the mobile frontier can sometimes be recognized or suggested (see table 2).

Australia. The Australian continent provides the clearest sequence, the simplest situation and the best-documented series of events. It seems particularly relevant for the study of farming complexes immigrant into a region.

Before the eighteenth century A.D., almost the whole of the continent was inhabited by hunter-gatherers, who over many millennia had exploited its subtropical and tropical environments. Between 1780 and 1975 a mobile frontier existed between immigrant temperate and tropical farming complexes (defined here by associated plants and animals), and the indigenes, resulting in much destruction and absorption.

TABLE 1   THE MOVING FRONTIER

Farmers		Hunter-Gatherers (H-Gs)
A.	Pioneers using nature (often using H-G techniques)	Accepted by H-Gs	Little change but reduction in self-sufficiency
			Archaeologically detectable
B.	Pioneers subduing nature		Increasing interference ending in static frontier
		Steadily less acceptable to H-Gs	
	Land acquisition by negotiation or conquest until:		Archaeologically detectable
	1. Limit of currently usable land reached		Destruction
	2. Geographical boundaries of land reached		Absorption by farmers
	3. Limit of (currently domestic) plant and animal tolerance reached		Symbiotic relationships established
			Retreat into isolation
			All archaeologically detectable

TABLE 2   THE END OF THE MOVING FRONTIER

Farmers		Hunter-Gatherers
A.	Partial migration to new region if new domestic plant and animals available	Isolation or development of static frontier
B.	Land seized from neighbours by warfare	
C.	Develop new farming technologies either for intensive use of existing, or for previously disregarded, land	Further destruction or absorption
D.	Increased and specialized exploitation of wild resources	Symbiotic relationships possibly established
E.	Voluntary restriction of population	
F.	Development of sociological devices for absorbing time and energy	Isolation or development of static frontier

All archaeologically detectable?

A static frontier situation now seems to be developing. The archaeological evidence for this frontier will lie in cemeteries showing racial types side by side and individuals with mixed characteristics; in farming and hunter-gatherer settlements showing changes in settlement types and in the development of new ones; in raw materials used and in artifact types.

The speed of change here allowed little time for hunter-gatherers' adaptation and no indigenous communities have yet developed their own version of the immigrant farming complexes.

North America. Here two separate frontier situations must be considered: the more recent and better-known temperate crop-and-animal complex from Europe, and the earlier tropical maize-squash complex from Meso-America; both were immigrant.

The European complex (its main components being wheat, barley and the associated cow, horse, sheep) imposed itself, in eastern North America, upon other farmers and it is only in the north and west where it came into contact with hunter-gatherers that it concerns us here. The position may be summarized as follows. The whole temperate zone beyond the limit of maize-growing and much of the arctic zone was exploited by hunter-gatherers before the arrival of Europeans. A mobile frontier existed between them and hunter-gatherers between 1600 and 1900 A.D. in the north and west. The longer period of contact (than in Australia) resulted in some acculturization (e.g. horse-riding and gun-using hunters), but there was destruction and absorption. A static frontier has been developing during the last century (Burt 1940; Webb 1952). A great deal is known archaeologically of its material effects and they can be linked, most effectively, with literary and ethnographic evidence. The model is a most useful one.

The maize-squash complex spread earlier from the south and the crops and/or farmers must have established themselves among hunter-gatherers. This took place before the arrival of the Europeans and details can only be established through archaeology.

It has been established that the whole sub-tropical zone was exploited by hunter-gatherers before the arrival of farming and that the period c. 500 B.C. - A.D. 500 saw the main spread. It was a slow one and a considerable degree of adaptation by and acculturalization of hunter-gatherers took place. Since the spread was from the highly sophisticated Meso-America region, the processes may in some ways have resembled the later ones in the temperate zone (Willey 1966:79).

Meso-America. The maize-squash complex of this region is the best-defined of the indigenous American agricultures and something of its progress can be traced over five millennia. Since it arose among hunter-gatherers its initial spread presents two series of problems: those of an 'internal' frontier when farming was spreading as a way of life *within* otherwise hunting-and-gathering communities; and those when it was spread by folk movements. The spread of maize cultivation into North and South America seems to partake of both (Meggers and Evans 1964).

South America. Here at least three indigenous agricultural complexes and three immigrant ones can be recognized, five of them having had, or still having, relationships with hunter-gatherers. The three indigenous ones were restricted to the tropical/subtropical forests and the mountain valleys (the cassava-manioc complex of the eastern lowlands, the beans-squash complex of the north-west, and the tuber complex of the central mountain valleys). They may be presumed to have developed and spread among hunter-gatherers and to have passed the mobile frontier stage before the end of the first millennium B.C. There is little evidence yet of the degree of acculturalization of the hunter-gatherers in the regions into which farming spread (Stewart and Farron 1959).

A fourth, and immigrant, tropical complex began in the Amazonian lowlands in the seventeenth century A.D. and is still in its mobile frontier phase; it has replaced a static frontier between indigenous groups. It has resulted in much destruction of hunter-gatherers and, presumably because of the speed of events and the technological and social difference between the immigrants and indigenes, in little adaptation.

The fifth, the immigrant temperate (wheat-horse-cattle-sheep) complex of the south-east, ended its mobile frontier phase in the nineteenth century A.D. and resulted in the destruction or absorption of most of the hunter-gatherer communities it encountered.

Africa. Here long-established hunter-gatherer populations existed before the development of farming, so that mobile frontiers must have existed between them and the six distinct farming complexes which can be recognized. The temperate wheat-barley complex of the Mediterranean coastlands and Ethiopia was established, relatively slowly it would appear, between the fifth and first millennium B.C. The slowness may well have allowed much adaptation by local hunter-gatherers or symbiotic relationships between them and farmers to have developed. On the southern flanks of this region in the Saharan borderlands two stages of specialized pastoralism can be recognized; the first before the second millennium B.C. with cattle, caprids and equids, the second, early in the first millennium A.D., with camels. The central Australian models of the last century may have some relevance for the first of these (McBurney 1967:312).

In sub-Saharan Africa indigenous complexes of seed (sorghum) and tuber/ rhyzome (yam etc.) farming can be identified and mobile frontiers may be postulated for both of them. In West Africa the spread of ideas may well have been slow and much adaptation and symbiosis may have taken place (Shaw 1972). In east and central Africa the same two complexes can be recognized. The mobile frontier connected with seed agriculture seems visible archaeologically in the first and early second millennium A.D. and is partly linked with the spread of 'bantu' languages and negroid peoples. It was sufficiently slow for adaptation and symbiosis to develop in many regions although the full range of alternatives found in the North American model are not present. In central and west central Africa excellent evidence of symbiotic relationships has survived (Clark 1967). In the extreme south a specialized pastoral economy based on cattle existed at the arrival of the Europeans and apparently represents a form of indigenous hunter-gatherer adaptation (Fagan 1965).

Asia. This, the largest continent, has also the longest known history of indigenous farming. In temperate Asia three main complexes can be identified. In western and southern Asia the cereal (wheat/barley)-caprid/bovid complex developed among hunter-gatherers, and mobile frontiers of the two kinds suggested for Meso-America must have existed between the eighth and fourth millennia B.C. Their slow development must presumably have allowed for adaptation and for symbiosis to develop (Flannery 1969; Bender 1975; 107).

In eastern Asia another cereal (millet) complex appears to have had a similar history of development. In central Asia a specialized pastoral complex developed in the second millennium B.C., partly at least in regions previously populated by hunter-gatherers (Chang 1970; Watson 1969).

In tropical Asia three complexes can also be recognized. In peninsular India one cereal complex developed by the second millennium B.C. and in northern India, south China and South-East Asia another (rice) had developed by the first millennium B.C. In both areas mobile frontiers must have existed during this time. (Allchin B. and F.R. 1968:261).

The general position is summarized in table 3.

THE STUDY OF THE MOVING FRONTIER

The study of the known moving frontiers suggests the following: 1. That it ends either when the physical boundaries of the region (mountains, deserts or seas), or when the climatic tolerance of the crops or animals, are reached. 2. That in advance of pioneer farmers, a penetration of the wilderness is made by 'temporary hunter-gatherers', members of farming societies who choose to specialize in the exploitation of 'bush' foods or skins, or by prospecting or trading. These, sometimes inadvertently, prepare the way for others by reporting paths and especially favoured areas, and by reducing the self-sufficiency of the indigenes. 3. That inside each farming complex differing dynamics, both social and technological, affect the rate of spread. There would not appear to be any 'steady spread' phenomena applicable throughout the world (Edmonson 1961).

Three generalized models already suggest themselves:
1. *Steady horizontal spread* of the kind suggested by Ammerman and Cavalli-Sforza (1972: 674): 'Wave Front' theory as it has been called, following the work of Wishart *et al.* (1969). The work on European evidence is of considerable relevance elsewhere.
2. *Selective horizontal spread.* This involves some kind of 'hopping', whether for water, particular soils, or some other reason (Ammerman and Cavalli-Sforza 1973).
3. *Selective vertical spreads.* These might be described as variations of transhumance (Higgs *et al.* 1964, 1966).

Each of these may involve, on modern evidence, 1. Initial negotiated land-occupation whilst farming numbers remain too small to affect hunting and gathering patterns; 2. Fighting when indigenous economies are disrupted. There is evidence of fighting on all second millennium A.D. frontiers.

The moving frontier, except in some areas of tropical forest, notably the Amazon Basin, between farmers and hunter-gatherers has now ended in all parts of the world and comparative studies can be undertaken. Although they ended at widely different times in the 26 areas listed here, many of the physical and psychological problems connected with their end may be assumed to be similar and the study of recent ones may prove useful in understanding earlier ones (Bohannan and Plog 1967, part 4).

The effect of the end of the frontier on farmers can be seen to be traumatic and widespread, involving groups far from the actual frontiers of the region. On the

TABLE 3   MOVING FRONTIERS BETWEEN FARMERS AND HUNTER-
GATHERERS (excluding Europe)

E.E.M.F. = Estimated end of moving frontier

Hunter-gatherers are known to have existed previous to the development of farming
in all except the one zone of the Pacific Islands.

Tropical Zones

Africa

1.   *Tropical seed-growing complex*
     E.E.M.F: 2M B.C.   a) Western savannas

     E.E.M.F: 1M A.D.   b) Eastern and southern savannas

2.   *Yam-oil palm complex*
     E.E.M.F: 1M A.D.   West and central forests

3.   *Camel (pastoral) complex*
     E.E.M.F: 1M A.D.   West semi-desert

4.   *Cattle (pastoral) complex*
     E.E.M.F: West: 3M B.C.   a) West savannas
                East: 1M A.D.   b) East savannas

Asia

5.   *Tropical seed-growing complex*
     E.E.M.F: 1M B.C.   Central and South India

6.   *Yam-banana complex*
     E.E.M.F: 2M B.C.?   Malay Peninsula and some islands

7.   *Rice complex*
     E.E.M.F: 2M B.C.   North India, Southern China, Japan
                                              and South-East Asia (including some
                                              islands)

Philippines-Indonesia-New Guinea

8.   *Yam complex*
     E.E.M.F: 2M B.C.?   Forests

9.   *Taro complex*
     E.E.M.F: 1M B.C.?   Forests

Americas

10. *Cassava-manioc complex*   South and Central America
     E.E.M.F: 1M B.C.?   lowland forests

11. *Maize-squash complex*
    E.E.M.F: Central and South: 2M B.C.   North, Central and South America:
    E.E.M.F: North: 1M B.C.   forests and semi-deserts

Australia
12. *Maize-sugar complex*   North: forests

13. *Cattle (pastoralism) complex*   Savannas and semi-deserts

    Known end of mobile frontier: c. A.D. 1900

There is no evidence of a 'mobile' frontier (in the sense used here) in the Pacific Islands.

Temperate Zones

Asia

1. *Wheat/barley complex*
   E.E.M.F: 5M B.C.   West and central forests

2. *Temperate millets complex*
   E.E.M.F: 4M B.C.   East. ?Centre.

3. *Horse (pastoralism) complex*
   E.E.M.F: 1M B.C.   Centre steppes

4. *Camel (pastoralism) complex*
   E.E.M.F: 2M B.C.   South-West semi-deserts

5. *Wheat/barley/oats/rye*   North and eastern forests/steppes
   Known end of mobile frontier: c. A.D. 1910

Africa
6. *Wheat/barley complex*
   E.E.M.F: 3M B.C.   a) Mediterranean coast and Ethiopia
   Known E.M.F: c. A.D. 1900   b) Extreme south: subtropical zone

7. *Cattle/sheep (pastorialism) complex*
   E.E.M.F: 3M B.C.?   a) Central and southern Saharan fringes

   E.E.M.F: 1M A.D.   b) Extreme south: subtropical zone

North America
8. *Wheat/barley complex*
   Known E.M.F: c. A.D. 1900   North-eastern and north-western
                                           forests and plains

South America

9.   *Tuber complex*
     E.E.M.F: 1M B.C.?   Central mountain valleys

10. *Beans-Squash*
     E.E.M.F: 2M B.C.?   Northern mountain valleys

11. *Wheat/sheep/cattle/horse*
     Known E.M.F: c. A.D. 1700   South-east plains

Australia

12. *Wheat/sheep complex*
     Known E.M.F: c. A.D. 1900   South-east, south-west, south plains

frontier, population increased, often selectively, by the arrival of ambitious, fugitive or restless individuals or groups, as Case (1969) has demonstrated. When these can no longer take new land and when the boundaries of a region are reached, quite new decisions must be taken by them and by their parent communities. Four obvious alternatives exist.

1. A move can be made into new climatic regions if suitable new plants and animals are domesticated or obtained from elsewhere. The development of rye and oats cultivation in Europe is an example of this.
2. Mobility can be maintained within the old region by seizing land by force from weaker (agricultural) neighbours; a reflex movement of this kind might have widespread repercussions within the region. South Africa seems to offer an example of this (Fagan 1965: fig. 50).
3. By abandoning mobility, population size can be restricted to the optimum for the land and technology available.
4. If mobility is reduced existing land can be used more intensively. This may include the use of empty land by a change in the balance of crops or animals, improved technology or the use of less productive land (Gourou 1966: 106).

The sociological and psychological effects of this are also marked, for communities must now absorb restless spirits, sexual surpluses etc. New social mechanisms may include: (i) More elaborate social hierarchies, since prestige-seeking can absorb much time and energy (presumably a variant of Parkinson's Law). This may be peaceful or warlike, (ii) Increased specialization in exploiting wild resources - fish, fowl etc. This may be in conjunction, or in competition, with hunter-gatherers, (iii) Increased specialization in craft-work. It seems possible that aspects of Childe's 'Neolithic Revolution' might in fact be linked with frontier 'backwash' (Hallowell 1967).

The effect of the end of the mobile frontier on hunter-gatherers presumably varies with proximity to farming communities. Those living in lands unexploitable by farmers may be released from the pressure of other, displaced, hunter-gatherer groups competing for their territories. Deliberate retreat into, or a maintenance of, complete isolation is another solution (Woodburn 1968), but for those near enough to develop specialized relationships, semi-permanent symbiotic relationships based on the supply of 'bush' meat, honey etc. are likely. Clientship seems a natural development from this last situation (Turnbull 1961).

The closer the proximity of hunter-gatherer groups to farming zones, the more intimate the relationship and the greater the pressure, not only for land but perhaps for labour. As herdsmen or other workers, hunter-gatherers have in recent times faced absorption, whether slave or free. Their best hope of survival has lain in acquiring specialized craft skills. This may well have happened in earlier times. As a result of all these factors, static frontier relationships develop. This may vary from 'intelligent parasitism' to 'stabilized pluralism' or 'reactive adaptation' (Broom and Kitsuse 1955:44).

SUMMARY

At least 28 times in human history mobile frontiers between farmers and hunter-gatherers have existed. Depending on the size of the geographical region in which the domesticated plant and animal complex was at home and the expertise of the farmers, the moving frontier lasted from one hundred to several thousand years. The study of recent moving frontiers and especially of their end provides insights which should aid in the study of earlier frontiers, especially since many of the developments which can be isolated leave material remains.

REFERENCES

Alexander, F., 1947. *Moving Frontiers: an American theme and its application to Australian history* (Melbourne).

Allchin, B. and Allchin, F.R., 1968. *The Birth of Indian Civilization.*

Ammerman, A.J. and Cavalli-Sforza, L.L., 1972. 'Measuring the rate of spread of early farming in Europe', *Man, 6,* 674.

Ammerman, A.J. and Cavalli-Sforza, L.L., 1973. 'A population model for the diffusion of early farming in Europe', in *The Explanation of Cultural Change,* ed. C. Renfrew.

Bender, B., 1975. *Farming in Prehistory: from hunter-gatherer to food-producer.*

Billington, R.A., 1967. 'The American Frontier', in Bohannan and Plog 1967.

Bohannan, P. and Plog, F. (eds), 1967. *Beyond the Frontier* (New York).

Broom, L. and Kitsuse, J., 1955. 'The validation of acculturation', *American Anthropologist, 57,* 44.

Burt, A., 1940. 'The frontier in the history of New France', *Canadian Historical Association Report, 93.*

Case, H., 1969. 'Neolithic explanations', *Antiquity, 42, 76.*

Chang, K.C., 1970. 'The beginnings of agriculture in the Far East', *Antiquity, 44,* 175.

Clark, J.D., 1967. 'The problem of neolithic culture in sub-Saharan Africa', in *Background to Evolution in Africa,* ed. W. Bishop and J.D. Clark (Chicago).

Edmonson, M.S., 1961. 'Neolithic diffusion rates', *Current Anthropology, 2,* 71.

Elkin, A.P., 1951. 'Reaction and interaction: a food gathering people and European settlement', *American Anthropologist, 53,* 164.

Fagan, B., 1965. *Southern Africa.*

Flannery, K.W., 1969. 'Origins and ecological effects of early domestication in Iran and the Near East', in *The Domestication and Exploitation of Plants and Animals,* ed. P.J. Ucko and G.W. Dimbleby, 1969.

Gourou, P., 1966. *The Tropical World.*

Hallowell, A.I., 1967. 'The backwash of the frontier: the impact of the Indian on American Culture', in Bohannan and Plog 1967.

Higgs, E.S. *et al.,* 1964, 1966. 'The climate, environment and industries of Stone Age Greece: Pts. I-II', *Proc.Prehist.Soc., 30,* 199 and *32,* 1.

Lewes, A. and McGann, T. (eds), 1970. *The New World looks at its History* (Austin, Texas).

Lindgren, E.J., 1938. 'An example of culture contact without conflict: reindeer Tungus and Cossacks of N.W. Manchuria', *American Anthropology, 40,* 605.

McBurney, C., 1967. *The Haua Fteah.*

Meggers, B. and Evans, J. (eds), 1964. 'Aboriginal cultural development in Latin America', *Smithsonian Misc. Collections, 146.*

Murdock, G.P., 1968. 'The current state of the world's hunting and gathering peoples', in *Man the Hunter,* ed. R. Lee and I. DeVore (Chicago, 1968).

Redfield, R. *et al,* 1936. 'Memorandum on the study of acculturation', *American Anthropologist, 381,* 149.

Sharp, P., 1955. 'Three frontiers: Canadian, Australian and American', *Pacific Historical Review, 24,* 369.

Shaw, Thurstan, 1972. 'Early agriculture in Africa', *J. Hist. Soc. Nigeria, 6* no.21, 143.

Stewart, J. and Farron, L., 1959. *The Native Peoples of South America* (New York).

Turnbull, C.M., 1961. *The Forest People* (New York).

Turner, F. Jackson, 1962. *The Frontier in American History* (reprinted with foreword by Ray Allen Billington, New York).

Watson, W., 1969. 'Early animal domestication and cereal cultivation in China', in *The Domestication and Exploitation of Plants and Animals,* ed. P. Ucko and G. Dimbleby, 1969.

Webb, W., 1952. *The Great Frontier* (Boston).

Willey, G., 1966. *An Introduction to American Archaeology,* vol. I (New York).

Wishart, D.J. *et al.,* 1969. 'An attempted definition of a frontier using a wave analogy', quoted in Ammerman and Cavalli-Sforza 1973.

Woodburn, J., 1968. 'An introduction to Hadza ecology', in *Man the Hunter,* ed. R. Lee and I. DeVore (Chicago).

Wyman, W.D. and Kroeber, C.B., 1957. *The Frontier in Perspective* (Madison, Wisc.).

BRYONY ORME

3 The advantages of agriculture

One of the more interesting problems of prehistory is set by the question 'Why did man begin to farm?' It was first posed in the nineteenth century, during the early Victorian upsurge of archaeology and anthropology. It has been argued elsewhere (Orme 1973) that all archaeological interpretation may be based on the concious or unconcious use of ethnography, and certainly that the first centuries of investigation into prehistory depended heavily on ethnography. In the mid-nineteenth century, culminating in the 1860s, archaeology and anthropology were so much a part of each other, and both developing so rapidly, that it was natural for the questions raised by the one to be answered by the other. Thus the prehistorian found the answer to his question, 'why farm?', clearly displayed in the reports of the ethnographer: the farmer's food was on his doorstep, in field or byre, whilst that of the hunter all too often ran away. In the first half of this century, exponents of the Neolithic Revolution have usually taken the same view of farming, as a progression from the hardship of the hunter's lonely, nomadic and hungry life to one of security and sociability. Latterly, the question altered, to enquire not why but how farming began. This new enquiry has generated page upon page of speculation, a good deal of thorough archaeological research, some new methods and new philosophies, and a recent synthesis of the work to date (Bender 1975). But there is remarkably little by way of an answer. In fact, as other papers in this volume suggest, the problem to be tackled is still the original one: why farm? The Victorian's answer has been shown to be inadequate, but nothing has yet replaced it and it is unlikely that we shall know *how* until we know *why* farming developed.

The original question of the nineteenth century in fact came to life again with the Hunters' Revolution of the late 1960s. The appearance of *Man the Hunter* (Lee and

DeVore 1968), accompanied by the first publication of Lee's work on the !Kung Bushmen (Lee 1969), and followed by Sahlins' 'The original affluent society' in *Stone Age Economics* (1972), demonstrated that most modern hunter-gatherers had an easy life most of the time, with plenty of food and plenty of leisure. This was surprising in itself, and all the more so when one realized that the people studied lived generally in harsh environments, whether semi-desert or sub-arctic. Farming in the primitive societies appeared far more arduous in terms of the labour needed to secure food, and in terms of the responsibilities involved, both for animals and for the land. One could no longer assume that early man domesticated plants and animals to avoid drudgery and starvation. If anything, the contrary appeared true, and the advent of farming saw the end to innocence.

As it was ethnography that raised the question anew and in a new form: 'why bother to farm?', perhaps ethnography may help to provide an answer. Had the founding fathers of prehistory and their successors looked a little more closely at contemporary primitive man, they might have noticed a few of the advantages of agriculture which this paper will suggest were conducive to the adoption of farming instead of hunting and gathering as a means of subsistence. Some of the suggestions that follow are more serious in intent than others, yet any, all or none may have appealed to prehistoric man, and we have no notion of his priorities.

The first advantage which primitive farmers enjoy when compared with hunter-gatherers is suggested by a combination of archaeological evidence and ethnography, and it concerns Man the Gatherer. The cultivation of plants developed independently in various regions of the world, at much the same point of time, in the millennia following the end of the last Ice Age. Why? The answer may lie in the new combination of factors which arose with the retreat of the ice-sheets: modern man, *Homo sapiens sapiens,* came into direct and prolonged competition with other animals for his food. To simplify grossly, during the Upper Palaeolithic much of the evidence suggests that man lived off a mixed diet with a fairly high meat content, eating the reindeer which ate the moss. In the post-glacial period, both man and deer ate the moss's replacements: wild cereals and leafy vegetation. The frustration of hunter-gatherers finding their best stands of wild emmer denuded by their competitors may have prompted some members of this supposedly more intelligent species to guard and protect their wild foods. This could be done by enclosing them within a fence, by living within sight of the food, and by killing or controlling the animals.

The first cultivated plants that we know of were cereals and legumes, and the first domesticated animals were the herbivores that lived off such plants. Thus Man the Gatherer may have become a farmer in part to outwit his competitors, and perhaps the Mesolithic populations of Europe outwitted the red deer without going to the lengths adopted in the Near East.

The farmer's second advantage relates to man as a gregarious animal. Many studies of modern hunter-gatherers reveal that whilst they normally live in small scattered family groups for most of the year, people do come together in large numbers on occasion, most probably yearly, though sometimes less often. Thus the !Kung Bushmen gather at waterholes in the dry season, the Netsilik Eskimo congregate during the winter months and the Tiwi meet at funerals (Lee 1968, Balikci 1970, Hart and Pilling 1960). Throughout the world these public gatherings may take place when there is a glut of food, or at times of scarcity, or during 'normal' conditions. They cannot therefore be seen solely as a response to temporary abundance, when the very presence of food would serve as sufficient explanation for the gathering.

Searching through the ethnographic accounts of these periodic gatherings, certain themes recur, amongst them the frequency with which ceremonies and festivities act as a focal point, and the oft-stated desire of hunter-gatherers for the meetings to be prolonged (for examples, see Sahlins 1972, chapter 1, and Lee 1972). The meetings are aptly named the public phase of the hunter-gatherers' life, for it is then that events such as initiation, marriages, funerals, and the settling of disputes takes place, all of which require a number of participants and witnesses. Those present have to eat, and the longer they stay the harder it becomes to find food nearby. They also have to maintain friendly relations with each other and this too becomes harder as time passes and the initial excitement of meeting wears off. Inevitably, although the people say that ideally they would like to stay together, they run out of food, and out of patience with each other, and so they split up to go their separate ways to peace and plenty. It is interesting to note here Lee's comment that !Kung who can find an outsider to settle their quarrels for them are able to prolong their public gatherings, suggesting that lack of food is not the major factor causing dispersal, at least in this instance (Lee 1972). One should also note that those traditional exceptions to the hunter-gatherer norm, the Indians of the North-West Coast of America, have a well-developed social system that provides a framework for large groups to live together (Drucker 1963). In this respect they are like the majority of farmers, whose culture provides a social framework for more-or-less permanent gregarious living, as well as the means to cope with those who are anti-social. Given a social system that enables people to stay together as a group, they may stay long enough to *produce* food, a process which normally takes several months. This in turn enables them to prolong their stay, and so they can indulge their gregarious tendencies to a greater extent than most hunter-gatherers. The work involved in food production may seem worth while when it enables more people to live together more of the time than before. It would be interesting to know if this factor is of any relevance to the development of cultivation in Meso-America where domesticated crops precede permanent settlement by several millennia, according to the present archaeological evidence.

The third advantage that farmers enjoy suggests, like the above, that settlement is one of the most important factors influencing man to abandon hunting and gathering. Settled man can acquire possessions. He can build himself heavy wooden houses, and fill them with heavy and fragile objects, especially clay pots. He can, to put it at its simplest, acquire material wealth. Nomadic hunter-gatherers are only hampered by such things, and fig. 5 illustrates the contrast in the possessions of nomadic and settled man better than any verbal description. Staying put, which enables man to accumulate goods in this way, and to be better sheltered than most hunter-gatherers, requires law and order and, in the long run, staying put also requires the existence of a regular and assured food supply. Since few areas of the world are as well-endowed with wild foods as the Pacific Coast of America, the production of food by man seems an inevitable consequence for those groups that hankered after the accumulation of material wealth.

The fourth advantage is undoubtedly appreciated more by women than by men. Nomadic women have to carry their babies and young children with them

Figure 5a. Hadza family hut, containing most of the family's possessions. The Hadza are nomadic hunter-gatherers of the Kalahari desert *(reproduced from James Woodburn,* Hunters and Gatherers: the material culture of the nomadic Hadza, 1970, *by courtesy of the author and the Trustees of the British Museum).*

Figure 5b. The gallery of an Iban longhouse, showing a part of the family's possessions. The Iban are farmers, growing dry rice by shifting cultivation *(reproduced from Derek Freeman,* Report on the Iban, *London School of Economics monograph on social anthropology no.41, Athlone Press, 1970).*

Figure 6. Eskimo woman carrying her child in the hood of her outer coat. The Eskimo are highly mobile hunter-fishers of the northern regions of America *(photograph: National Film Board of Canada).*

Figure 7. Children at home, in a woman's house of the Bomagai-Angoiang, farmers in the New Guinea mountains *(reproduced from W. C. Clarke,* Places and People: an ecology of a New Guinean Community, *copyright ©1971 by The Regents of the University of California; reprinted by permission of the University of California Press).*

everywhere, along with their equipment and all the food they collect (fig. 6). Settled women have no such burden, for they can leave their offspring at home in the care of another woman or an older child (fig. 7). This in itself is surely an advantage, and it has moreover an interesting consequence. Because farming women do not have to carry their children, and perhaps because farming yields more suitable baby food than hunting and gathering, especially where milk animals are kept, the families of farmers tend to be larger than those of hunter-gatherers, where women try to avoid having more than one child to carry. As a result, in the long run more children are brought up to be farmers than to be hunter-gatherers, resulting in the expansion of the one means of subsistence in relation to the other. This is the sort of factor which can help to explain the spread of farming into new lands, for example the movement into Europe discussed by Clark (1965) and Ammerman and Cavalli-Sforza (1972).

Women are the focal point of another of the benefits of farming, a benefit not to be dismissed lightly. The hunter's wife spends a considerable amount of time collecting food away from camp and probably away from the supervision of her husband. She may be accompanied by another woman as she wanders through the bush but, judging by some ethnographic reports, her husband is very likely to suspect her of taking time off for the occasional love affair with an equally nomadic hunter, in between digging up roots and catching a few insects for supper (e.g. Hart and Pilling 1960). The farmer, on the other hand, has craftily tied down his females to hearth and home, with more babies, more cooking and more housework than ever their nomadic sisters have to face. Even the women's contribution to food-producing is probably carried out close at hand, in fields overlooked by all the village gossips. Many women in farming societies rarely travel more than a few miles from home, unlike their husbands and in marked contrast to all members of nomadic societies (Murphy and Murphy 1974). Quite how the farmer's greater control over his women contributed to the adoption of farming as a means of subsistence one cannot tell, but it was probably soon appreciated as an advantage that helped to compensate for the responsibilities of food production.

Most differences between hunters and farmers are a matter of degree, and there is no sharp dividing line between the two means of subsistence. However, the last advantage to be considered here occurs so regularly amongst people who farm, and so rarely amongst those who live by hunting and gathering, that it could almost be used as a subsistence indicator. Yet its significance in this context has not really been explored, either by ethnographers or by prehistorians. The advantage in question is warfare: farmers fight whilst hunters do not. Hunter-gatherers rarely have sufficient people in one place for long enough to achieve organized warfare, even if they sometimes manage a battle or a raid, whereas farmers are constantly on the warpath or in the war-canoe. From the point of view of most readers, warfare will hardly seem to be an advantage but, judging by numerous ethnographies (e.g. Gardner and Heider 1969, Best 1924), farmers relish their battles as strongly as a football match and in much the same spirit. Here again, the North American Indian provide an exception to prove the rule. The settled Indians of the Pacific Coast indulged in intervillage and inter-tribal warfare (Drucker 1963) and the Plains Indians escalated from occasional to endemic raiding with the introduction of the domestic horse (Hoebel 1960). The hunter's challenge comes normally in stalking and catching his prey. Warfare both replaces and improves upon this, with its

Figure 8. Zulu warriors in the full display of their regimental uniforms (African farmers and cattle herders) *(reproduced from George French Angas's* The Kafirs Illustrated, 1849, *by kind permission of the Killie Campbell Africana Library).*

accompanying display, ceremonial and prestige (fig. 8).

These, then, are some of the advantages which farming provides. Whilst far from being a comprehensive list, they do suggest that man may have developed into a food-producer for several, rather varied reasons. Chief amongst them were the desire to live a more sociable life, accompanied by the development of a framework of law and order that made permanent settlement possible, and a desire to outwit competitors, both animal and human. Food production, as an end in itself, may have been relatively unimportant. Perhaps the prospect of an afternoon sitting in the sun outside the men's clubhouse, swapping war stories, within sight of a well-fenced field with wild animals safely outside and women safely within, hard at work weeding or hoeing, to produce next year's feast, makes the effort of clearing that field seem worth while after all.

REFERENCES

Ammerman, A.J. and Cavalli-Sforza, L.L., 1972, 'Measuring the rate of spread of early farming in Europe', *Man, 6,* 674-88.

Balikci, A., 1970. *The Netsilik Eskimo* (New York).

Bender, B., 1975. *Farming in Prehistory: from hunter-gatherer to food-producer.*

Best, E., 1924. 'The Pa Maori', *Dominick Museum Bulletin, 6* (Wellington).

Clark, J.G.D., 1965. 'Radiocarbon dating and the expansion of farming cultures from the Near East over Europe', *Proc.Prehist.Soc., 31,* 58-73.

Drucker, P., 1963. *Indians of the Northwest Coast* (reprint, Garden City, N.Y.).

Gardner, R. and Heider, K.G., 1969. *Gardens of War: life and death in the New Guinea Stone Age.*

Hart, C.W.M. and Pilling, A.R., 1960. *The Tiwi of North Australia* (New York).

Hoebel, E.A., 1960. *The Cheyennes: Indians of the Great Plains* (New York).

Lee, R.B., 1968. 'What hunters do for a living', in Lee and DeVore 1968.

Lee, R.B., 1969. '!Kung Bushman subsistence', in Vayda 1969.

Lee, R.B., 1972. 'Work effort, group structure and land use in contemporary hunter gatherers', in Ucko, Tringham and Dimbleby 1972.

Lee, R.B. and DeVore, I. (eds), 1968. *Man the Hunter* (Chicago).

Murphy, Y. and Murphy, R., 1974. *Women of the Forest* (New York).

Orme, B.J., 1973. 'Archaeology and ethnography', in Renfrew 1973.

Renfrew, C. (ed.), 1973. *The Explanation of Culture Change.*

Sahlins, M.D., 1972. *Stone Age Economics* (Chicago).

Ucko, P.J., Tringham, R. and Dimbleby, G. (eds), 1972. *Man, Settlement and Urbanism.*

Vayda, A.P.(ed.), 1969. *Environment and Cultural Behavior* (New York).

A. J. LEGGE

4 The origins of agriculture in the Near East

Much of the work concerned with early agriculture and domestication has been directed towards establishing the earliest dates at which plant and animal domestication may be recognized, and has often been based on the use of rather subjective criteria for identification. This problem has been the subject of detailed comment elsewhere (Higgs and Jarman 1969; Legge 1972; Jarman and Wilkinson 1972) and does not require further discussion here. However, it is argued that if agriculture and animal domestication are to be seen as innovations or discoveries at a certain time, then this must depend upon the observation of new attributes within the economy, and, in turn, such attributes can only be demonstrably 'new' by comparison with earlier economic systems.

Consequently any such discussion must involve the comparison of economies by the observation of change through time: 'hunter-gatherer' communities, and those of early food producers, must be studied by the same methods of analysis, and based upon data recovered by the same techniques. In European terms this economic change is usually represented by the transition from a Mesolithic to a Neolithic technology, though in the Near East these boundaries are less clear-cut, and the terms in consequence have a lesser meaning. Even within the European setting it is by no means axiomatic that economy is wholly culture-linked; Jarman (1972) has shown the extent to which 'Mesolithic' traits, such as red deer economies, may continue into a Neolithic culture. Recent experiments have shown the comparative ease with which red deer may be domesticated (Blaxter *et al.* 1974) and there seems little reason to postulate a change in the relationship between man and red deer because of the appearance of pottery and one or two other 'Neolithic' attributes.

The results obtained in recent excavations in the Near East, and the use of different approaches to the analysis of the data obtained, have combined to modify the understanding of agricultural origins and the nature of early domestication. It is no longer possible to see an absolute separation between 'food producers' and 'hunter-gatherers' in the archaeological record, and even these broad generalizations about the economic systems of prehistory have arisen as a result of the classification of animals into early 'domesticated' species (applied to those surviving in that relationship until now) and those exploited only by hunting. Indeed, Higgs and Jarman (1969) have suggested that close relationships between man and animals may be a long-term adaptation through the Pleistocene period. It is argued here that the 'new' economic system that has been identified as early plant and animal domestication represents no more than a change of *emphasis* within the system, and that this is reflected by a change in the relative importance of plant and animal foods in the economy, and in the species selected for exploitation.

In much of the Near East where early agriculture has been identified, a perspective given by comparison with earlier economic systems has been lacking. In Anatolia, Iraq and Iran much is now known of the early Neolithic settlements, but little, as yet, of the economy at earlier Mesolithic or late Palaeolithic sites. This means that our knowledge of the early Neolithic in these areas, detailed as it is, lacks this necessary perspective and confers the appearance of a higher degree of innovation within the economy than is perhaps justified.

The literature of recent years has also placed a heavy emphasis upon the slow nature of the domestication process, and with a consequently gradual progression towards agriculture, or 'food production' as opposed to 'food collecting'. This has resulted in a virtual taxonomy of stages in this economic evolution, moving from 'terminal food gatherers' to 'proto' and 'incipient' agriculturalists, and finally an emergence onto the threshold of 'effective village farming' (Braidwood and Howe 1960). In recent publications Braidwood (1971, 1972) has observed that the postulated stages of incipience in the development of cultivation are elusive in the results of field archaeology, and he draws attention to the claimed 'hunters' villages' as being relevant to this problem, and goes on to question the meaning of a distinction between 'a level of incipient cultivation and domestication and a highly intensified village-dwelling level of specialised collecting and hunting'. This raises a question concerning the nature of these hunters' villages, and the type of economy that was practised. It has often been stated that the existence of stone-built houses does not imply year-round occupation, and that such structures are the result of the exploitation of areas in which natural caves are absent, but probably still on a seasonal basis. Yet the possibility of seasonal occupation at these 'hunters' villages' has seldom been examined, nor has the relationship between man and animals been explored. The designation of 'hunters' rests largely on the presence of animals such as the gazelle. At the Anatolian site of Suberde (Perkins and Daly 1968) the fauna of all levels is mainly sheep and goat, and it is suggested that exploitation was based on 'co-operative drives, slaughtering whole flocks at a time'. However, the sheep and goat bones show no animals of *less* than three months of age, nor older than three years. It might be argued that such a pattern is evidence for a high degree of selection, rather than the random killing suggested in herd slaughter. Perkins and Daly base their claim for 'hunting' at Suberde on a comparison of the percentages of juvenile sheep and goat in the bone assemblage with the figures for a British Iron Age site, and a wild sheep population. The figures obtained show a high percentage of juveniles killed at the British Iron Age site, 45 per cent, with 35 per cent at Suberde and 33 per cent in recent wild sheep. Jarman and Wilkinson (1972) have discussed the problem of using the population age-structure of wild herds for such comparisons in archaeology and it is evident that all age classes can only be reflected in the killing of whole herds, or by fully random predation, neither of which is evident in the age distribution in the sheep and goat at Suberde. A further problem exists in the Suberde juvenile/adult proportions by the use of an age of 15 months by tooth eruption or bone fusion to represent the juvenile/adult threshold. This figure is significantly lower than that used by Higgs and White (1963), who take a figure of 24 months as maturity in sheep, and Silver (1969) suggests ages of 36 - 48 months for 'unimproved' breeds, an age that corresponds with recent estimates by Payne (1973) for recent domesticated sheep in Turkey.

It is clear that the use of so low an estimate as 15 months for maturity in sheep and goat will distort the juvenile/adult proportions in the site fauna, and under-represent young animals. The criteria used by Perkins and Daly are not clear in their account of the Suberde work, and it is possible that the problem outlined above has produced a low figure for juvenile animals. Even without this possibility, the pattern of exploitation proposed, of 'whole herd' slaughter, would represent a profligate waste of resources, and is unlikely to represent a situation of long-term economic stability. Alternatively, even the preliminary data offered by Perkins and Daly can be more convincingly interpreted as the result of an economy which includes the husbandry of sheep and goat, a possibility also argued by Clason (1972).

At this point it is worthwhile to remember that all discussion of the origins of domestication and agriculture is essentially a discussion of *change*, whether this be an observed change in the morphology of plants or animals, a change in the species exploited, in site location, or in the relative importance of animals and plants in the food supply. As shown above, the observation of economic change in the study of early agriculture has usually lacked the depth of a perspective through time. In Palestine, a greater perspective is possible in the study of economic change, due to the detailed information about the late and Epi-Palaeolithic cultures. The Natufian culture has attracted much interest in the past in providing an appropriate chronological and cultural setting into which the 'incipient' stage of agricultural development could be placed. Much of this attribution remains speculative as very little detailed information has been available about the patterns of exploitation and economy practised at that time, and no information at all had been recovered concerning the economic importance, or even availability, of plant foods. The recent excavations at Nahal Oren were designed as an attempt to recover some data relevant to this problem (Legge 1973). It was fortunate indeed that this site has substantial deposits not only of the Natufian culture, but also an equal thickness of the earlier (late Palaeolithic) Kebaran culture below this, and with both A and B phases of Kenyon's 'Pre-Pottery Neolithic' at the top of the sequence. This represents an apparently continuous occupation of the site from c. 18,000 B.C. to c. 6,000 B.C. and spans the period in which the early stages of agricultural innovation and domestication are postulated. The methods used in excavation are described elsewhere (Legge 1972, 1973) and included the use of froth flotation and water sieving of all excavated deposits. The use of these techniques makes possible the full recovery not only of artifacts, but also of carbonized seeds and animal bones, so that the economy practised at the site can be followed in considerable detail through some 12,000 years of occupation.

In the analysis of this material a number of original observations have emerged, and it has been possible to confirm others which have been the subject of speculative comment. The importance of the gazelle in the economy emerges clearly, with this animal showing at least three times the abundance of all other mammalian species, and reaching its highest frequency in the Aceramic Neolithic. This in itself is an observation of some interest, in showing a remarkable continuity of exploitation from the Upper Palaeolithic to the late Aceramic Neolithic. In view of the fact that gazelle were so abundant, and continued in importance to a surprisingly late time, the nature of their relationship with man was examined by the same methods which have been used to demonstrate early domestication in the sheep and goat (Legge 1972). This work is based on the analysis of killing pattern by age in relation to a particular species, and, on this basis, it is impossible to separate this pattern in the gazelle at Nahal Oren from that observed with sheep and goat at Ali Kosh (Flannery 1969), Beidha (Perkins 1966), and Shanidar (Perkins 1964). The results of a more recent analysis of the Nahal Oren data is shown in fig. 9, where the 'slaughter curve' for the gazelle is compared with that of sheep/goat populations from the 'Bus Mordeh' levels of Ali Kosh and from Tepe Guran (Flannery 1969), and it may be argued that this close similarity in slaughter pattern is indicative that herding of the gazelle was established. The publication of these data has led to suggestions that 'selective hunting' may be involved, which presumably is intended to imply a less close, or less advanced, relationship to that of domestication. Perhaps the most important point is that, on this criterion, the pattern of exploitation is no *less* effective in extracting the *maximum* output of food from the gazelle herd than is the case with the sheep and goat. In attempting to explain this observation, and the later replacement of the gazelle by sheep and goat, we must turn to other factors in the economy.

By the use of flotation, carbonized seeds were recovered from all the deposits excavated at Nahal Oren, representing some 12 species identified, and a smaller number of as yet uncertain species (Legge and Dennell 1973). The total sample is only 133 seeds, and most of these represent potential foods; indeed, the majority are from plants that are domesticated at the present day. What is evident from these plant remains is that most species which later provided the economic basis of fully agricultural societies were available, and presumably utilized, as food from the earliest Kebaran levels at c. 18,000 years B.C. Equally, the quantity of seeds recovered is very small, and averages only 4-6 seeds recovered from each cubic metre of soil that was processed by flotation. From these figures alone it would be possible to argue a case that the relative abundance of animal bones in relation to the small quantities of plant foods is indicative of the actual importance that each had in the economy. It has been stated elsewhere (Legge 1972) that these figures contrast sharply with those recovered from sites where a fully agricultural basis for the economy is in little doubt, and results obtained from the same process of excavation and soil flotation at Tell Gezer (Legge 1972) show the relative proportions of plant and animal remains completely reversed. Figures resting on only two sites are, of course, open to criticism in that many factors could be involved to account for this disparity, such as functional differences within the site, and problems of the rate of sediment deposition and its nature. However, a wide experience of the use of

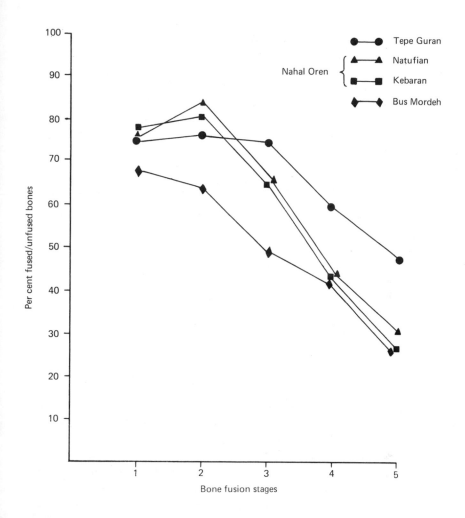

Figure 9. Slaughter patterns in gazelle from two levels at Nahal Oren (Legge 1973) compared with domesticated sheep and goat from Tepe Guran, and the Bus Mordeh levels of Ali Kosh (Hole, Flannery and Neely 1969). The curves show the proportions of animals killed at certain stages of growth, represented by the fusion of the growing points in specific bones to the shafts, which occurs in a known sequence. Each growth stage represents the proportion of 'unfused' and 'fused' bones at different stages towards full skeletal maturity. In the Kebaran sample from Nahal Oren, about 22 per cent of the bones are 'unfused' at stage 1, and 78 per cent of the animals survived beyond this age. By stage 4, 54 per cent of these bones are 'unfused', so that over half of the animals were killed by this age. The similarity of the four curves suggests close husbandry of each animal population. The stages are based upon: 1, scapula, distal humerus; 2, 1st phalange; 3, distal tibia; 4, distal metapodial; 5, distal radius and proximal tibia.

flotation in the recovery of seeds in various countries has shown that, in relation to the likely human population, the quantity of animal bones is usually small where carbonized seeds are abundant, but sparse where animal remains are common. At the Natufian site of Ain Mallaha in Upper Galilee (Perrot 1960) a number of samples were recently processed by flotation, and although emmer wheat and other species were found, the quantities recovered in relation to processed soil are very small. The same holds true even for sites analysed by these methods in Britain; at Neolithic, Bronze Age and Iron Age sites seed remains are relatively abundant, yet in the soils from two Mesolithic sites processed by the writer, Morton (Coles 1973) and Brafield (unpublished), the quantity of seeds is again small in relation to other indications of fairly dense settlement.

To summarize this suggestion (and it remains only that), the attempt to express the classes of material recovered according to the quantities of soil processed shows that at sites such as Nahal Oren and Ain Mallaha the human population was small (perhaps 30-50 persons), the amount of plant remains recovered are few, yet animal remains are abundant. On the other hand, at the fully agricultural sites of Tell Gezer, and Ayios Epikitos on Cyprus (Peltenberg 1972), carbonized seeds are found in abundance, but animal remains are relatively few. One further observation is relevant in this argument. At the cave sites such as Nahal Oren, the area of occupation is small and can have housed only a limited human population. This, and most of the other long-occupied caves, are classed by Vita-Finzi and Higgs (1970) as 'home bases' or 'preferred' sites, and whether they were seasonally or permanently occupied, the animal population within the site territory must have exceeded the human population in number by many times. Conversely, at agricultural sites where the human population may be numbered in many hundreds or even thousands (for example, Tell Gezer: Webley 1972), it is in most cases doubtful if the animal population even equalled that of the people.

It is useful now to consider other more recent data, and to look again at the later part of the Nahal Oren sequence. One of the key excavations from this area for our future understanding of early food-producing economies is the recent work at Tell Abu Hureyra (Moore 1975). This site has yielded substantial deposits of Mesolithic, Aceramic Neolithic, and Ceramic Neolithic. The full use of sieving and flotation has given complete samples of fauna and carbonized seeds, and preliminary results are now available. The faunal assemblage, analysed by the writer (Legge 1975) can be divided into four assemblages which correspond to broad chronological divisions within the site (fig. 10). This work is based on fauna recovered during the 1971 season, which has a limited exposure of the Mesolithic levels; at the time of writing, the later material recovered in 1972 is now being analysed. Consequently, only preliminary conclusions can be drawn, as the published figures are based upon only a small part of the available samples, particularly in the case of the Mesolithic layers. It can be seen from fig. 10 that the Mesolithic assemblage indicated a high proportion of gazelle, with some quantity of equid and sheep or goat. In the first stage of the Aceramic Neolithic, the faunal assemblage observed is similar, with gazelle increasing to some 82 per cent at the expense of other animals, a frequency that is closely paralled in the similar cultural setting at Nahal Oren. The later Aceramic Neolithic shows a complete reversal of this trend, with a faunal assemblage that is dominated by sheep and goat, and the gazelle falling sharply to little more than 18 per cent. The Ceramic Neolithic period shows a closely similar faunal assemblage. The

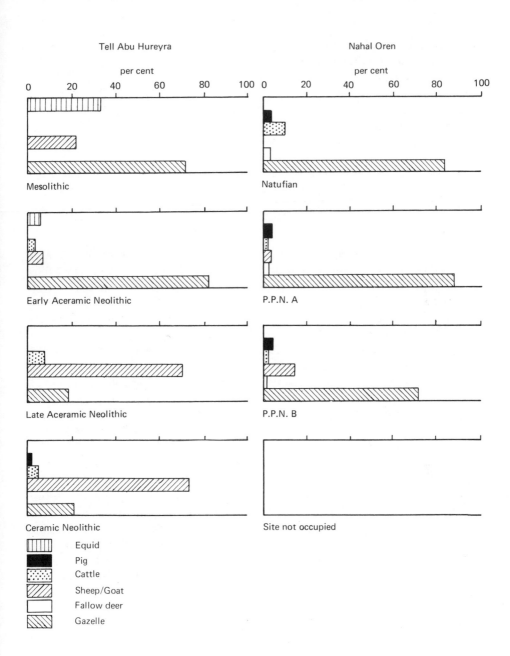

Figure 10. Proportions of major food animals at Nahal Oren (Legge 1973) and Tell Abu Hureyra (Legge 1975). Note the emphasis on gazelle in the Aceramic Neolithic (pre-Pottery Neolithic) at both sites, with an equally heavy emphasis on sheep and goat in the later Aceramic Neolithic and Ceramic Neolithic at Tell Abu Hureyra. The diagram is not intended to imply that wholly contemporary phases are represented from each site, but rather to provide a comparison of economic stages in similar cultural settings.

changes observed within the sequence are closely paralleled at Nahal Oren and Jericho. At this latter site, gazelle predominated in the earlier phases of the Aceramic Neolithic (PPN A) and is replaced in the later Aceramic Neolithic (PPN B) by an equally high percentage of sheep and goat (Clutton Brock 1971). Clutton Brock (1974) has identified sheep in both phases of the Aceramic Neolithic at Jericho though in small quantities. Sheep are also present in the early Aceramic Neolithic at Tell Abu Hureyra, and in the larger assemblage from the later Aceramic Neolithic at this site sheep appear to out number goat by almost three to one on the basis of the metapodial measurements. The animal remains from Nahal Oren show a similar high frequency of gazelle in the early Aceramic Neolithic (PPN A), the time at which this animal appears in its greatest abundance at this site. In the later Aceramic Neolithic (PPN B) there is evidence of an increased frequency of goat bones, rising from about 5 per cent to 15 per cent of the assemblage. Although this is a smaller increase in frequency than that seen at other sites, it should be noted that neither sheep nor goat was present in any significant quantity before the PPN A levels, and is wholly absent from most of the earlier part of the sequence. Other Aceramic Neolithic sites are known in Syria and Palestine, but details of the faunal remains are either uncertain or not yet available, with the exception of the site of Munhatta (Ducos 1969). This site is wholly of the PPN B period, and in common with the other sites mentioned, ovicaprines are the most numerous group in the faunal remains at 51 per cent, although gazelle make up a further 42.8 per cent of the assemblage.

Data available concerning the plant foods utilized at this time is in many ways less satisfactory, either because collections were made at a time when adequate methods were not available, or that more recent work is not yet fully published. Consequently only the most general conclusions can be made, and based only on data from Nahal Oren (Legge and Dennell 1973), Jericho (Hopf 1969), Tell Abu Hureyra (Hillman 1975), and Tell Mureybit (Van Zeist and Camparie 1968). At Nahal Oren and Tell Abu Hureyra it is evident that a wider range of species are present in the Aceramic Neolithic than at earlier times, and, at Tell Abu Hureyra, the Aceramic Neolithic is marked by the appearance of morphologically 'domesticated' einkorn and emmer wheat, although these species are absent from the early Aceramic levels at the adjacent site of Tell Mureybit. This may argue that the preliminary grouping of the Abu Hureyra seeds under a single heading of 'Aceramic Neolithic' is masking changes taking place within that period, and it is clear that both Jericho and Nahal Oren show a greater increase in the number of species between the 'PPN A' and 'PPN B' than could be argued, on the present limited data, in the transition from the Natufian to 'PPN A'. On the basis of fauna, and a limited quantity of data concerning plant remains, it may be argued that the economy of the PPN A period can be most closely related to that of the earlier Natufian period, and is not marked by any degree of economic innovation that is usually associated with the term 'Neolithic'. As Kenyon (1969) regards the PPN A as evolving directly from the Natufian culture, it may well be that the observed changes in technology are not connected with any significant modification of the species exploited in the economy.

The three major Tell sites in this area, Jericho, Abu Hureyra, and Mureybit, are each associated with basal levels of 'Mesolithic' industries, which indicate an initial settlement of the sites before c. 7,000 B.C. In each case this is succeeded by an early Aceramic Neolithic which is marked by some technological changes, including more substantial house plans, but with remarkably little change evident in the economic base. Attempts have been made to regard these earlier levels as 'hunters' villages' or with an economic basis of 'intensive plant collection'. In each case, the extent and duration of the Mesolithic settlement is unknown, although the Aceramic Neolithic occupation is extensive, clearly demonstrated especially at Jericho and Tell Abu Hureyra.

Attempts to explain this situation with the presence in most cases of 'wild' forms of cereals, and animals which are not domesticated at the present time, have included suggestions that the cereals were collected from distant areas where the species concerned grow wild at the present day (Van Zeist 1968). On the other hand, Hillman (1975) considers alternative possibilities, including the local cultivation of a morphologically 'wild' form of einkorn, a suggestion made earlier by Jarman (1972). Certainly recent territorial studies in archaeology would not favour the view that substantial amounts of food would be collected so far from the occupation site. Equally, as Braidwood has recently suggested (1972), is it realistic to distinguish between 'intensive collection' and 'early agriculture' on this basis? Inevitably, such distinctions will be based upon a largely subjective judgment, influenced by the appearance of 'Neolithic' attributes in the toolkit, and on the use of morphological criteria applied to plants and animals for the identification of early domestication. Yet it remains inconceivable that the large populations of the early Aceramic Neolithic levels at Jericho, Mureybit, and Hureyra, could be supported over periods of one or two millennia with an economy based on plant collection and 'selective' hunting, especially if the scale of settlement is taken as indicative of year-round occupation.

Jarman (1972) for Tell Mureybit, Hillman (1975) for Tell Hureyra, and Helbaek (1966) with regard to Beidha, have all suggested that morphologically 'wild' einkorn might be cultivated. The same case may be argued in relation to the gazelle, which provided the economic basis for animal exploitation from the late Palaeolithic period, up to and including the Early Aceramic Neolithic. It is known that gazelle may be habituated to close human presence, and readily tamed. Indeed, recent experiments with other species raises the question of whether any herd animal cannot be controlled in this way. In recent years, the musk ox, the eland, the elk (Wilkinson 1972), and the red deer (Blaxter 1974) have all been successfully brought under close human control, and are fully 'domesticated'.

SITE TERRITORIES

In the study of early agriculture, too little emphasis has been laid on the potential that each site has for different patterns of exploitation. Indeed, suggestions of agricultural innovation have been made at sites that could be exploited only by grazing animals, and it has been shown (Vita-Finzi and Higgs 1970) that most of the known and densely occupied Natufian sites in Palestine are marked by a lack of arable land, though in ecologically varied settings and with good grazing resources.

Such territorial studies do, in fact, point to the main 'break' in the technological and economic succession that may be seen in the period under review. As shown above, most of the known Mesolithic sites in Palestine share the same location with earlier phases of the Palaeolithic, and often exhibit a long continuity of occupation (Nahal Oren, Kebarah, Hayonim, El Wad, Rakafet). Yet these same sites are marked

Site	Marsh (%)	Arable (%)	Dune (%)	Rough grazing (%)	Good grazing (%)
Nahal Oren	27	8	0	58	7
Shuqbah	0	18	0	82	0
Rakafet	0	47	0	45	8
El Wad	48	12	7	28	5
Kebarah	36	14	13	31	6
Hayonim	0	11	0	74	9
Quafsah	0	62	0	32	0
Ain Mallaha	44	15	0	29	12
Sheik 'Ali	0	78	0	12	10
Megiddo	12	62	0	26	0

Table 4. Land-use potential at ten sites in Palestine, based upon the data of Vita-Finzi and Higgs (1970). The site of Sheik 'Ali is late Aceramic Neolithic, and Megiddo is a large tell with long occupation. The other sites are caves (except the open site of Ain Mallaha) and all have Natufian and/or earlier occupations.

by an abrupt cessation of occupation after the Natufian, with this culture representing the last major period of habitation, though at Nahal Oren and Rakafet phases of the Aceramic Neolithic are known at the top of the succession.

Some of these sites were included in a territorial survey by Vita-Finzi and Higgs (1970), which shows the topographical and ecological diversity represented in the 'catchment' of each site. The method of 'site catchment analysis' used is based upon the fact that distances in hunter-gatherer and peasant farmer economies are measured in walking time rather than by a 'crow fly' linear distance. Only in very uniform landscapes will territories be circular, and in fact they become increasingly irregular in broken topography. The territorial limits are established by two hours of walking in each of several directions from the site (Anon. 1974), a time factor encountered in recent studies of hunter-gatherers (Lee 1968, 1969). For plant food collection or cultivation an even smaller area is likely to be systematically exploited and table 4 shows the porportions of the different soil types found within a 5 km radius of these sites. This distance represents the area which can be economically exploited with an agricultural economy and which might equally be expected to be fully exploited by 'plant collecting' in a pre-agricultural economy. In fact, it is demonstrable that peasant agriculturalists now seldom cultivate as far as 5 km from their homesteads, and, if they do, rapidly diminishing returns are met (Chisholm 1968). If the sites which have substantial occupations of the Natufian are considered (Nahal Oren, Rakafet, Shuqbah, Hayonim, Ain Mallaha, Kebarah) arable soils seldom exceed 20 per cent of the territory, and are usually less. Rakafet has a higher total at 47 per cent, and Quafsah, with 62 per cent arable land, was *not* settled in the Natufian or Aceramic Neolithic periods. This is a strong argument that arable soils were not a primary attraction at this time, and indeed, the absence of later occupation at Quafsah may indicate the reverse. Some support for this also comes from the cave of Shuqbah, also with only two soil types. Here there are extensive deposits of the Middle Palaeolithic, but no Upper Palaeolithic, and little Natufian compared with other sites. On the other hand, those sites with extensive Natufian and Upper Palaeolithic occupation, especially Nahal Oren, El Wad, and Kebarah, all have *five* soil types; Ain Mallaha has four, while Rakafet and Hayonim have three each (Vita-Finzi and Higgs 1970, on whose data table 4 below is based, describe only four soil types for Nahal Oren; however, their soil map of this site - fig. 4 in their article - clearly shows the presence of dune sands as a fifth soil type). One further characteristic of Shuqbah and Quafsah is the absence of wet soils or swamp from the catchment areas, a feature shared by the important cave sites on the west slopes of Mount Carmel.

This situation can be contrasted with the locations observed at some major tell sites in Palestine. The site of Jericho has roughly equal amounts of arable land and rough grazing within radii of 2 km and 5 km of the site, with the added advantage that much of the soil can be subject to irrigation. With such a regime applied to cultivation, the unique location of the site at 366 m below sea level gives a climate that provides a year-round growing season, and the possibility of double or treble cropping. The site of Sheik 'Ali (Vita-Finzi and Higgs 1970) with late Aceramic and Pottery Neolithic occupation also shows a complete reversal of the soil types selected in the location of the earlier settlements, with 78 per cent arable and a further 10 per cent potentially so. This trend continues into later times (Webley 1972) and the large tell of Meggido also shows a high concentration (62 per cent) on arable soils.

A detailed analysis of the soil types at Tell Abu Hureyra and Tell Mureybit is not yet available, though it is possible to affirm that settlements on this scale, as with Jericho, must be related to soils of a high arable potential.

SUMMARY

The observed situation in Palestine and Syria shows continuity of occupation in caves and at later tells, each group of which is related to a different pattern of adjacent soil resources. This change in the pattern of occupation is also associated with a marked economic re-adaptation. Cave sites, especially those located in areas of topographical and ecological diversity, were favoured for long occupation extending back to the Middle Palaeolithic or even beyond. It is possible to follow the economic basis at these sites in some detail, where long-term changes, probably related to climatic and other environmental factors, can be seen to influence the faunal assemblage. From Nahal Oren plant foods were also recovered from a long archaeological sequence, but showed comparatively little change in quantity or in the range of species observed during that time. This economic continuity extends down to the early Aceramic Neolithic, at which time the sites of Jericho, Hureyra, and Mureybit show quite closely similar assemblages of species. However, while the economic pattern in terms of species exploitation shows comparatively little change, there is evidence of some initial changes in site location. At some time during the Mesolithic the three tell sites mentioned above show their first occupation levels, which, at Hureyra at least, are extensive. Equally, at the other sites, such as Nahal Oren and Rakafet, there is continuity of occupation into the Aceramic Neolithic, though with a closely similar economic basis to that observed in the early levels of the tell sites. However, despite an apparent similarity in economy, it is clear that a profound difference exists concerning the scale of these settlements, and in the economic potential of the areas within which these two classes of site are situated. It may be argued that, as well as an apparent difference in scale, a profound difference in economic emphasis may also be anticipated, reflecting the very different pattern of soil resources that are available.

At the group of cave sites the evidence indicates an economic system that is relatively stable in the long term. The existence of a range of known plant food species in the Kebaran indicates the utilization of these foods from an early time at the site. Equally, the management of the animal economy through this long period remains virtually unchanged, *including the 'Pre-Pottery Neolithic A'*, a time at which animal domestication is widely accepted, though seldom in relation to species such as the gazelle. It is arguable that the precise form of relationship between man and the gazelle is less important than its outcome, and the result was an efficient pattern of exploitation difficult to separate from 'domestication' were the animals in question sheep or goat. Either way, it would seem probable that some degree of manipulation, control, or deliberate selection is involved, and, if this is acceptable in the case of animals, it may be thought equally possible that plants could be encouraged to grow in a manner advantageous to the human population. Added support for such a view comes from recent suggestions that in Britain the Mesolithic population modified the vegetation to the extent of increasing economically useful species (Simmons 1969, Simmons and Dimbleby 1974) and similar practices are known among 'hunter-gatherer' peoples in both in New World and Australia. It is suggested that the economy practised at the cave and other sites in question would include the careful management of both plant and animal resources, in locations with a high degree of ecological diversity, *but with a very limited potential for the development of cultivation.* At different times during the later part of these cave occupations, and demonstrably during the Mesolithic and Early Aceramic Neolithic, settlements begin in areas where the arable potential is high, and in particular at places which later became major city mounds. This, I would suggest, marks the point at which a major change in emphasis must be inferred in the economy, though with an essentially similar complement of plant and animal species. In the first situation, with settlement at caves and open sites such as Ain Mallaha, there are indications that the animal economy contributed the major part of the food income of the human group; plant collection, by its very nature in a diverse landscape, implies dispersed food resources and it has been argued elsewhere (Vita-Finzi and Higgs 1970; Saxon 1974) that some degree of mobility would be favoured in the animal economy. Most of the plant foods represented at the site are only seasonally available, or require storage and a sedentary life for their effective exploitation. No evidence, as yet, exists to demonstrate that either of these adaptations was practised at any of the cave sites in question, and the degree of sedentism required for plant food exploitation would conflict with the optimal management of animal resources. This is not to deny the possible, and indeed probable, importance of plant food resources on a seasonal basis; yet plant food *collection* appears to favour seasonality of occupation in the recent ethnographic record (Lee 1968, 1969; Thomson 1939). At the sites of Jericho, Hureyra, and Mureybit, the land resources are wholly different. These settlements are located in areas where cultivation would be preferred, and the potential for the exploitation of plant foods was very high. The PPN A levels at Jericho are estimated to have supported a population of two to three thousands (Kenyon 1969), while the similar levels at Abu Hureyra had 'an extraordinarily large population' (Moore 1974), yet this was achieved with essentially similar economic resources as those available in the Natufian levels at the same sites. As Kenyon has long suggested, it is difficult to conceive that this could be possible without an agricultural basis to the economy; to reject this on the basis that the cereals were morphologically 'wild', and that the animals were gazelle, would require a powerful alternative hypothesis.

This suggestion leads directly to a further interpretation. If it is accepted that the Early Aceramic Neolithic levels were supported by agriculture, even if with morphologically unchanged (i.e. 'wild') species, then the same may well be possible for the Natufian levels at the same sites. If the possibility of an 'agricultural' economy based upon morphologically 'wild' species of plants and animals is denied, then such an economy can hardly be suggested before the 'Pre-Pottery Neolithic B' period, with the sharp increase in frequency of sheep and goat and the appearance of 'domesticated' forms of cereals.

This leaves two possible hypotheses. Firstly, it may be argued that agriculture must be the economic basis of the PPN A, in order to support the large populations which are evident at the sites in question, and, if so, this was practised with the same complement of plant and animal species that were available in the Natufian. However, the scale of settlement and human population would demand an emphasis on the cultivation of plants and an inevitable reduction in the numbers of animals maintained at the site. The alternative to this view would seem to require that agriculture does not begin until the appearance of 'surviving' domesticated animals and morphologically changed plants, in which case only the later Aceramic Neolithic (PPN B) could have an agricultural basis.

CONCLUSIONS

During the Aceramic Neolithic, the sheep and goat replace the gazelle abruptly, and we see the virtual abandonment of this animal, a species that had been important in the economy for many millennia. A suggestion to explain the reasons for this change can be made by reference to the settlements in question, and the behaviour of the species concerned. The gazelle is an animal which has the advantage of being relatively indifferent to surface water supplies, while sheep and goat need to drink frequently. On the other hand, available data would suggest that the goat, and to a lesser extent, the sheep, will utilize a wider range of food plants than gazelle, and it is possible that the potential that these species possess for milking represents an added asset; the smaller body size of the gazelle would indicate that such utilization was improbable. These factors may be tentatively used to argue that the sheep and goat are more readily integrated into a sedentary, crop-producing economy, and that the 'failure' of the gazelle is related to its unsuitability for husbandry on a sedentary basis. Yet it has been observed that the success of the gazelle was such that it showed a steady increase from the Kebaran (c. 18,000 B.C.), and reached its highest frequency in the Early Aceramic Neolithic (PPN A). A reason for its 'failure' has been suggested; it remains a possibility that its steadily increasing success before this may be related to the *causes* which underlie the profound economic and locational shifts with which this paper is concerned.

The original calculations of the proportions of fallow deer *(Dama)* and gazelle *(Gazella)* in the Mount Carmel caves were calculated by Bate (Garrod and Bate 1937) and taken to indicate fluctuating climate, in that *Dama* would be dependent on surface water, while the *Gazella* is much less so, and that the fluctuations represent dry conditions (high *Gazella*) or moist conditions (high *Dama*). This suggestion has been heavily criticized, not least because many of Bate's samples from the earlier sequence were small. However, the work of Higgs (1961, 1967) has provided some support for Bate's hypothesis, in relating a site fauna to the adjacent environment, and it is of interest to note that the *Dama/Gazella* proportions from Nahal Oren (Legge 1972) match the *later* part of Bate's graph to a very high degree. Bate regarded the post-Pleistocene importance of gazelle as being indicative of greatly increased aridity, a factor which Childe (1954) regarded as a cause in the development of agriculture. Recently, Farrand (1971) has provided an extensive geological argument for a depression of 5-7°C in the mean annual temperature of the Near East during the Würm Glaciation, and 'a definite increase in effective moisture'. Nahal Oren (Legge 1972), El Wad (Garrod and Bate 1937), Rakafet (A. Garrard, pers.com.), and Quafsah (Bouchud 1969), all show an increase in gazelle, and a decline in fallow deer in the last stage of the Pleistocene, a trend which continues into the Holocene. It may be agreed from the similarity of this change at both coastal and inland sites that an environmental change was being reflected, not least of which would be a reduction in surface water to encourage the expansion of the less demanding species.

Childe's original statement concerning the nature and causes of the 'Neolithic Revolution' has been taken to imply a rapid shift in human society from the 'hunter-gatherer' economy to that of full agriculture, and in the face of stress caused by increasing dryness. In the archaeological record of the Levant it is possible to observe a time of rapid adaptation represented by the abandonment of caves and the beginning of settlement at the tell sites. This locational shift follows a time in which the species most tolerant of dry conditions shows a substantial increase, which might represent the stress conditions that Childe envisaged. It is argued here that the management of food resources was an adaptation characteristic of the late Pleistocene in this area. Following from this, it is postulated that the locational shift reflects a change in emphasis from an animal-based to a plant-based economy, shortly followed by the adoption of new animal species. The absence of apparent stages of 'incipient' or 'proto' agriculture from this sequence (and elsewhere?) suggests that a reconsideration of Childe's view is indicated.

Acknowledgments
I am indebted to Dr Jean Perrot for his invitation to examine the deposits at Ain Mallaha by flotation. Michael Jarman, Department of Archaeology, University of Cambridge, provided helpful comments on the manuscript of this article.

REFERENCES

Anon., 1974. 'Site catchment analysis: a concise guide to field methods', in *Palaeoeconomy,* ed. E.S.Higgs, 223-4.

Blaxter, K.L., Kay, R.N.B., Sharman, G.A.M., Cunningham, J.M.M. and Hamilton, W.J., 1974. *Farming the Red Deer.*

Bouchud, J., 1969. 'Etude paléotologique de la faune du Djebel Quafseh, Israel', International Quaternary Association 8th Congress, *Resumes* (Paris).

Braidwood, R.J., 1972. 'Prehistoric investigations in Southwest Asia', *Proceedings of the American Philosophical Society, 116* no. 4.

Braidwood, R.J. and Howe, B., 1960. 'Prehistoric investigations in Iraqi Kurdistan', *Studies in Ancient Oriental Civilisation, 31* (Chicago).

Braidwood, R.J., Cambal, H., Redman, C.L. and Watson, P.J., 1971. 'Beginnings of village farming communities in Southeastern Turkey', *Proceedings of the National Academy of Sciences of the U.S.A., 68* no.6, 1236-40.

Chisholm, M., 1968. *Rural Settlement and Land Use.*

Childe, V.G., 1952. *New Light on the Most Ancient East* (4th edn).

Clason, A.T., 1972. 'Some remarks on the use and presentation of archaeozoological data', *Helenium, 12,* 139-53.

Clutton-Brock, J., 1971. 'The primary food animals from the Jericho Tell from the Proto-Neolithic to the Byzantine period', *Levant, 3,* 41-55.

Clutton-Brock, J. and Uerpmann, H. -P., 1974. 'The sheep of early Jericho', *J.Archaeol. Sci.,* 1, 261-74.

Coles, J.M., 1971. 'The early settlement of Scotland: excavations at Morton, Fife', *Proc.Prehist.Soc., 37,* pt II, 284-366.

Ducos, P., 1968. *Origine des Animaux Domestiques en Palestine* (Publications de l'Institut Préhistoire, University of Bordeaux, 6).

Farrand, W.R., 1971. 'Late Quaternary palaeo-climates of the Eastern Mediterranean area', in *The Late Cenozoic Glacial Ages,* ed. K.K.Turekian (Yale).

Flannery, K., 1969. 'The fauna', in Hole, Flannery and Neely 1969.

Garrod, D.A.E. and Bate, D.M.A., 1937. *The Stone Age of Mount Carmel.*

Helbaek, H., 1966. 'Pre-Pottery Neolithic farming at Beidha', in 'Five seasons at the Pre-Pottery Neolithic village of Beidha in Jordan', by D.Kirkbride, *Palestine Exploration Quarterly, 98,* 61-7.

Higgs, E.S., 1961. 'Some Pleistocene faunas of the Mediterranean coastal areas', *Proc.Prehist.Soc., 27,* 144-54.

Higgs, E.S., 1967. 'Environment and chronology', in *The Haua Fteah (Cyrenaica),* ed. C.B.M.McBurney.

Hillman, G., 1975. 'Plant remains from Tell Abu Hureyra', in 'Excavations at Tell Abu Hureyra', by Andrew Moore, *Proc.Prehist.Soc., 41,* 70-3.

Hole, F., Flannery, K. and Neely, J.A., 1969. *Prehistory and Human Ecology of the Luran Plain* (Mem.Mus.Anth., University of Michigan I, Ann Arbor).

Hopf, M., 1969. 'Plant remains and early farming at Jericho', in *The Domestication and Exploitation of Plants and Animals,* ed. P.J.Ucko and G.W.Dimbleby, 355-60.

Jarman, H.N., 1972. 'The origins of wheat and barley cultivation', in *Papers in Economic Prehistory,* ed. E.S.Higgs, 1972.

Jarman, M.R., 1972. 'European deer economies and the advent of the Neolithic', in *Papers in Economic Prehistory,* ed E.S.Higgs, 1972.

Jarman, M.R. and Wilkinson, P., 1972. 'Criteria of animal domestication', in *Papers in Economic Prehistory,* ed. E.S.Higgs, 1972.

Kenyon, K.M., 1969. 'The Origins of the Neolithic', *Advancement of Science,* 26. 144-60.

Lee, R.B., 1968. 'What hunters do for a living, or how to make out on scarce resources', in *Man the Hunter,* ed. R.B.Lee and I.DeVore (Chicago, 1968), 30-48.

Lee, R.B., 1969. '!Kung bushmen subsistence: an input-output analysis', in *Environment and Cultural Behavior,* ed. A.P.Vayda (New York, 1969), 47-79.

Legge, A.J., 1972. 'Prehistoric exploitation of the Gazelle in Palestine', in *Papers in Economic Prehistory*, ed. E.S.Higgs, 1972.

Legge, A.J., 1973. 'The fauna', in 'Recent excavations at Nahal Oren, Israel', by T. Noy, A.J. Legge and E.S. Higgs, *Proc. Prehist.Soc., 39*, 75-99.

Legge, A.J., 1975. 'The fauna of Tell Abu Hureyra', in 'Excavations at Tell Abu Hureyra', by Andrew Moore, *Proc.Prehist.Soc., 41*, 74-6.

Legge, A.J. and Dennell, R.W., 1973. 'The plant remains', in 'Recent excavations at Nahal Oren, Israel', by T.Noy, A.J.Legge and E.S.Higgs, *Proc.Prehist.Soc., 39*, 75-99.

Moore, A.M.T., 1974. 'Preliminary report on the excavations at Tell Abu Hureyra' (privately published MS., see also Moore, A.M.T., 1975).

Moore, A.M.T., 1975. 'Excavations at Tell Abu Hureyra', *Proc.Prehist.Soc., 41*, 50-69.

Payne, S., 1973. 'The kill-off pattern in sheep and goats: the mandibles from Asvan Kale', *Anatolian Studies, 22*, 281-303.

Peltenberg, E., 1972. 'Interim report on the excavations at Ayios Epiktitos Vrysi, 1969 and 1971', *Report of the Department of Antiquities, Cyprus*.

Perkins, D., 1964. 'Prehistoric fauna from Shanidar, Iraq', *Science*, N.Y., *144*, 1565-6.

Perkins, D., 1966. 'The fauna from Magdamah and Beidha, a preliminary report', in 'Five seasons at the Pre-Pottery Neolithic site at Beidha, Jordan', by D.Kirkbride, *Palestine Explorations Quartery 98*, 66-77.

Perkins, D. and Daly, P., 1968. 'A hunters' village in Neolithic Turkey', *Scientific American, 219*, 97-106.

Perrot, J., 1960. 'Le gisement Natoufien de Mallaha (Eynan) Israel',, *L'Anthropologie* (Paris), *70*, 437-83.

Saxon, E., 1974. 'The mobile herding economy of Kebarah Cave, Mt. Carmel: an economic analysis of the faunal remains', *J. Archaeol.Sci., 1*, 27-45.

Silver, I., 1969. 'The ageing of domestic animals', in *Science in Archaeology*, ed. D. Brothwell and E.S. Higgs (2nd edn), 1969.

Simmons, I.G., 1969. 'Evidence for vegetational change associated with Mesolithic man in Britain', in *The Domestication and Exploitation of Plants and Animals*, ed. P.J.Ucko and G.W.Dimbleby (1969), 111-19.

Simmons, I.G., 1972. 'Towards an ecology of Mesolithic man in the uplands of Great Britain', *J. Archaeol.Sci., 2*, 1-16.

Simmons, I.G. and Dimbleby, G.W., 1974. 'The possible role of ivy (Hedera helix L.) in the Mesolithic economy of Western Europe, *J. Archaeol.Sci., 1*, 291-6.

Thomson, D.F., 1939. 'The seasonal factor in human culture', *Proc. Prehist. Soc.,10*, 162-232.

Webley, D., 1972. 'Soils and site location in prehistoric Palestine', in *Papers in Economic Prehistory*, ed. E.S. Higgs.

Wilkinson, P.F., 1972. 'Current experimental domestication and its relevance to prehistory', in *Papers in Economic Prehistory*, ed. E.S. Higgs.

van Zeist, W. and Casparie, W.A., 1968. 'Wild Einkorn and Barley from Tel Mureybit in Northern Syria', *Acta Botanica Neerlandica, 17*, 44-55.

Vita-Finzi, C. and Higgs, E.S., 1970. 'Prehistoric economy in the Mount Carmel region of Palestine', *Proc.Prehist.Soc., 36*, 1-37.

THURSTAN SHAW

5 Hunters, gatherers and first farmers in West Africa

Before the development of the large-scale transportation of food from one region of the world to another, the food that people ate depended upon the natural resources and the climate of the area they lived in. They either made use of the plants and animals natural to the region or of the plants and animals which the climate made it possible for them to rear. Therefore it is necessary to know something about the resources and climate of the relevant area.

West Africa lies in what is usually referred to as the 'summer rainfall' area - that is, the bulk of rainfall occurs from May to October (fig.11); although temperatures, being predominantly high, do not fluctuate seasonally as much as in Europe, the climate is much more markedly seasonal in rainfall, with a severe dry season from December to March. The rain is derived from the warm south-west winds blowing across the Atlantic; the coastal areas therefore receive most rain, with a decreasing gradient of rainfall as you go further north towards the Sahara desert, which receives practically none at all. Apart from differences caused by areas of high altitude (none very large or high in West Africa), the rainfall distribution results in a series of vegetation zones running east and west across West Africa, with tropical rain forest near the coast; to the north of this are the savannas: first the savanna/forest mosaic with patches of forest and patches of woodland; then the woodland savanna, and north of that the open or grassland savanna; this in turn gives way to the sahel zone, with sparse grass and a few acacia trees, merging into the Sahara desert proper.

It will be clear that the vegetation in the wet areas near the coast will be very different from that near the Sahara desert in the north, and that these different zones of vegetation will therefore produce different kinds of food. There is little natural grass in the rain forest areas, but trees provide edible nuts and fruits, and the roots

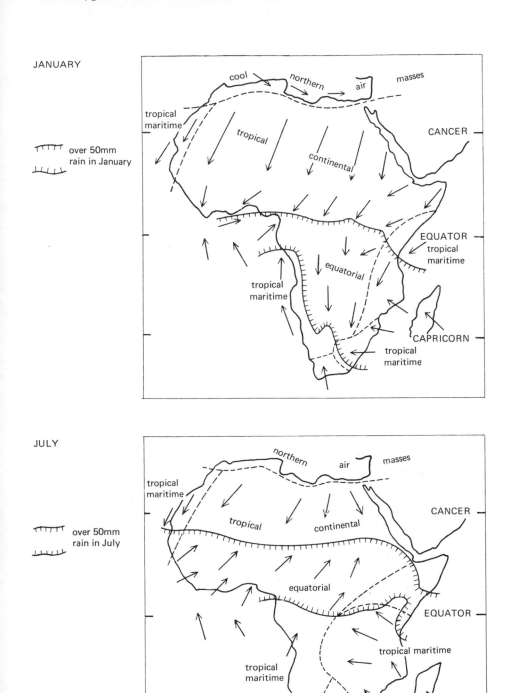

Figure 11. Air masses and precipitation in January and July *(after Grove).*

and tubers of vegetative plants and vines such as yams, although sometimes toxic, can be suitably treated to provide food fit for human consumption. The sahel and the savannas also have their own particular nut and fruit-bearing trees, but these are the areas above all of many kinds of different grasses, the seeds of which can provide grain for human food; in the course of time a number of these grasses were domesticated to provide cultivated cereals. Naturally the different vegetation zones carry different kinds of fauna, an important matter in considering animal sources of food for early hunters and trappers. The savannas carry much more game than the forests, chiefly because they provide more food for grazing animals, and these in turn attract predators. Thus whereas in the savannas there are such animals as giraffe, buffalo, bubal hartebeest, roan and many other antelopes, as well as baboon, patas and green monkeys, honey badger and hare, these do not occur in the forest and instead we have specialized forms of antelopes, particularly the small duikers, chimpanzee, colobus and other monkeys, potto, galago and pangolin. Correspondingly there is a much wider range of predators in the savannas, including lion, hyaena, jackal, wild dog, cheetah, serval and caracal, which do not occur in the forest, with only leopard, civet, genet and mongoose common to both. As soon as man became an effective hunter and trapper, he too can be regarded as a predator and the savannas would be a much more favourable environment for him than the forest, with a much greater weight of meat per square mile available (Bourlière 1964:51). The elephant and the aardvark belong to both savanna and forest. Some animals have forms specially adapted to savanna or forest conditions, such as tree-hyrax and bushpig in the forest, rock-hyrax and warthog in the savanna. The water animals, such as hippopotamus and otter, and, obviously, fish, are confined to rivers and lakes both in savanna and forest areas. Smaller animals, especially rodents such as squirrels, porcupines and various species of rats, particularly the cane-rat, distributed in both forest and savanna, are often prized sources of meat still today, and must have had an even greater importance as protein sources before the advent of stock-raising. The giant African snail, principally in the forest, is similarly important. Animal sources of food in the sahel and desertic regions are much scarcer than in the savannas, but there are a number of species adapted to waterless conditions, such as the addax and the dorcas and dama gazelles. Although the West African savannas carry much more game than the forest, they are still not as abundant as the grass savannas of East Africa, and a number of species common there, such as rhinoceros, zebra, wildebeest, eland and a number of other antelopes, are absent.

Such, then, in very brief outline, were the kinds of food resources potentially available to the earliest inhabitants of West Africa. The first people of whom we have certain knowledge have left behind their cutting, piercing and scraping tools of chipped stone (Acheulian) in river gravels on and around the Bauchi Plateau of Nigeria (fig.13a); there are also some signs of people making the same kind of stone tools in the Fouta Djallon area and along the Atakora and Togo range of hills down into southern Ghana. We do not know the precise date that the makers of these stone tools were gaining their livelihood in these areas, but it may have been in the period between 100,000 and 50,000 years ago. Large numbers of similar stone tools are known from the central and northern Sahara, and at this time it is likely that, coinciding with a southward advance of the polar ice-cap in northern Europe, climatic zones were compressed towards the equator, bringing cooler and moister

Figure 12. a. River Niger at Jebba: savanna landscape *(photograph: Aerofilms Ltd)*.

b. Southern rain forest: high forest on rocky coast below Cameroon
   Mountain *(photograph: Aerofilms Ltd)*.
c. Jos Plateau: high-level grasslands *(photograph: Aerofilms Ltd)*.

d. Sahel thorn shrub on loose, saline sandy soil with herds pasturing
   (photograph: Institut Français d'Afrique Noire).

e. Southern Senegal: riverside rice cultivation with oil palms behind
   (photograph: Agence Economique des Colonies, Paris).

conditions to the central and northern Sahara but more desertic conditions to the savannas of West Africa. Under these conditions the higher ground of the areas in the savanna belt where Acheulian tools are found may have been moister promontories into the arid zone from the better-watered areas to the north. In this situation game may well have moved back and forth seasonally from one area to another, and man may have followed them. In West Africa we have not yet found any occupation sites of the users of Acheulian tools or the sites where hunted animals were butchered, such as have been found in East Africa, but by analogy with those sites, by this time men had developed sufficiently sophisticated hunting techniques to tackle large animals. Doubtless smaller animals and a wide range of vegetable products gathered from the wild continued to form an important constituent of the diet.

The makers of Acheulian-type implements seem to have been succeeded by people who went on making some of the same kinds of tools but who also made numbers of heavy pointed tools, or 'Sangoan picks' (fig.13b). Their distribution is more riverine and woodland than the Acheulian and it has been suggested that they represent an adaptation to a more woodland way of life, the stone 'picks' being used either for grubbing up roots and tubers from the ground or for killing game in deadfall traps.

Later still, conditions on and near the Bauchi Plateau seem to have again become suitable for hunters and gatherers, perhaps like makers of Acheulian implements before them, following seasonal migration of game from further north; their stone tools, sometimes generically classified as 'African Middle Stone Age' (fig.14), are perhaps more correctly related to the 'Levalloiso-Mousterian' industries of northern Africa. Characteristic is a piece of stone in the shape of an elongated triangle, made by a special stone-chipping technique, which looks as if it must have been used as a dart or javelin point. Unfortunately we have no occupation sites either of makers of Sangoan or Levalloiso-Mousterian-type tools in West Africa, so we know nothing directly about their means of subsistence and the kinds of animals and plants they ate. At Tiémassas, on the coast of southern Senegal, bifacial projectile points were found to be stratified as an integral part of a 'Mousteroid' industry (Guillot and Descamps 1969).

It is when we come to the Late Stone Age of West Africa that our knowledge improves. We are speaking now of the period from something before 10,000 B.C. up to the beginning of the Christian era, and it is the period of time in which there was a considerable development of hunting and gathering techniques and adaptations to different environments within West Africa. It is in the later part of the period that a change-over was made from hunting and gathering to crop-growing and stock-raising. Over most of Africa the Late Stone Age is characterized by the development of very small stone tools, called for that reason 'microliths' (fig.15, 16). These are tiny pieces carefully trimmed to be slotted into arrowshafts to form points and barbs, and to make other kinds of composite implements. They demonstrate that their makers were possessors of the bow and that hunting with it formed an important part of the economy. Compared with the earlier parts of the Stone Age, the pace of cultural change was now quickening, although it remained very slow compared with modern times. There are more regional variants, as population increased and as increasing control over environment resulted in even more specific adaptations to different ecological niches.

Over the whole West African area there seems to be an earlier phase of the Late Stone Age, perhaps lasting nearly 10,000 years and ending around 3,000 B.C., in which the material culture did not include pottery. The majority of sites are in the

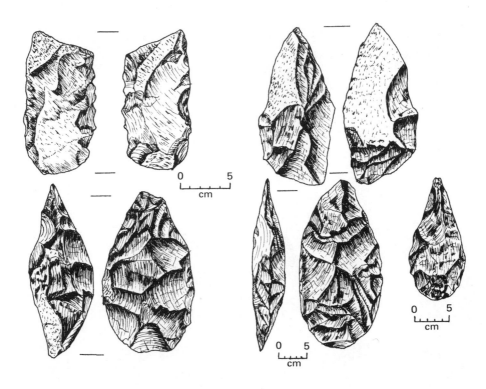

Figure 13. a. Nigeria. Acheulian stone tools; b. Sangoan tools *(after Soper)*.

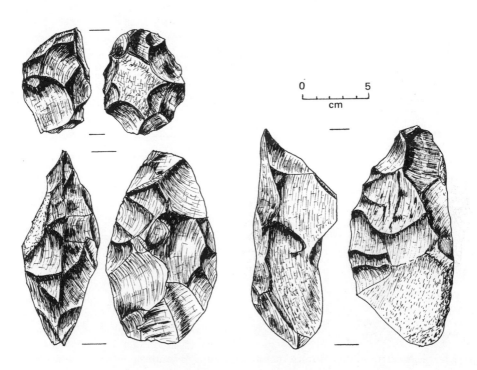

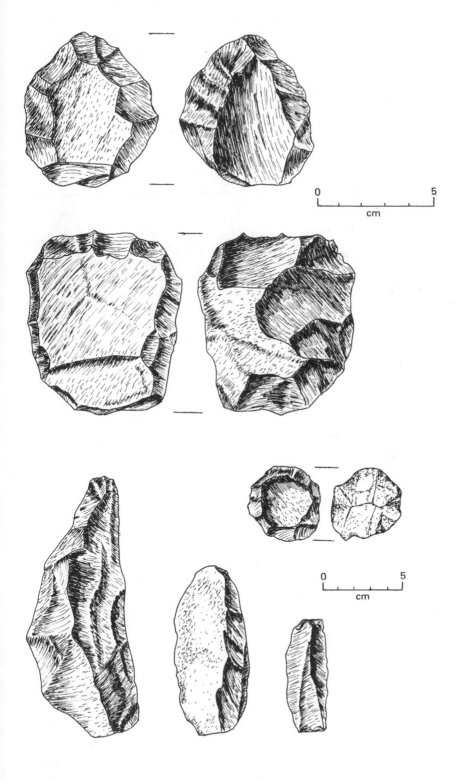

Figure 14. Nigeria. 'Middle Stone Age' stone tools *(after Soper)*.

savannas and the microliths probably indicate that hunting was an important activity and that meat from the game abundant in these zones was an important element in the diet. Representative sites are Adwuku (Davies O., 1964:171-3) in Ghana, Mejiro Cave at Old Oyo (Willett 1962) and the lower levels of Rop (Eyo 1972) and of Iwo Eleru (Shaw 1969, 1973) in Nigeria, of Kourounkorokale (Szumowski 1956) in Mali, of Rim (Wai-Ogosu 1973) in Upper Volta, and possibly of New Todzi in Ghana, although it is difficult to tell because of the way the site is described (Davies O.1968a). The sites of Koumi in Upper Volta (Creac'h 1951), of Keniaba in Mali (Corbeil 1951) and of Niamey Est in Niger (Mauny 1949:151-2) have also been claimed (Munson 1971:106) to belong to this pre-ceramic microlithic industry, but they are all surface collections and two included ground stone axes. It is similarly unproven whether the surface occurrence at Gangaber in Mali (Amblard-Rambert 1959) should be assigned to the pre-ceramic stage, since the exceptionally high proportion of 'segments' suggests that the occurrence represents some special activity, such as fishing or reaping, not involving pottery.

Unfortunately it tends to be only in the driest areas that bone is sufficiently well preserved for bone tools and weapons to survive and for it to be possible to make an analysis of bone refuse and derive information on diet from it; nor have we been fortunate enough to have conditions to preserve artifacts of wood (e.g. Fagan and Van Noten 1966) and other organic remains (e.g. Deacon and Deacon 1963; Parkington and Poggenpoel 1971) as in parts of southern Africa. Hunting would have been less important for the people who penetrated the forest, and gathering the products of the forest would have played a bigger part in providing their subsistence; this seems to be reflected in the tool-kit of the lower level of the Grotte de Kakimbon at Conakry (Hamy 1900) in the Republic of Guinea, and in the middle level at Yengema in Sierra Leone (Coon 1968), where microliths are replaced by pick and hoe-like implements, useful perhaps for grubbing up roots and tubers. What the forest people lost in hunting opportunities may have been compensated for by the shorter or virtually absent dry season, so that wild foods could be gathered at most times of year. Tubers are available in the ground throughout the year - if you can find them; perhaps an important activity during that part of the year when the vines were green and growing was to mark the spot for use at a later time in the year when the vine had died down and was less easy to find. Such a practice might be a first step towards cultivation.

From the sixth to the third millennium B.C. the highlands of the Sahara desert had a good deal more moisture than today; this sustained some Mediterranean-type flora and sufficient grassland pasturage and water resources to support both wild and domesticated animals. Around 5000 B.C. cattle pastoralists moved in, probably from the north, with an equipment of stone arrowheads which suggest that hunting of game was also important; the evidence that they grew domesticated cereals is slight (Camps 1969; Shaw 1972:147). Those moving into the Sahara from the north may have met negroid hunter-gatherers coming up from the savanna lands of West Africa to the south; the 'hunter-horizon' of rock art in the Sahara, believed to antedate 4000 B.C., shows dark-skinned people. At Dhar Tichitt, in south-eastern Mauretania, the Akreijit phase is regarded as representing such a group of 'southerners', retaining their microlithic tradition but acculturated to the ways of the northerners, with their bifacial tanged arrowheads, ground stone axes, stone bracelets and pottery. This would be around 2000 B.C. (Munson 1971:111).

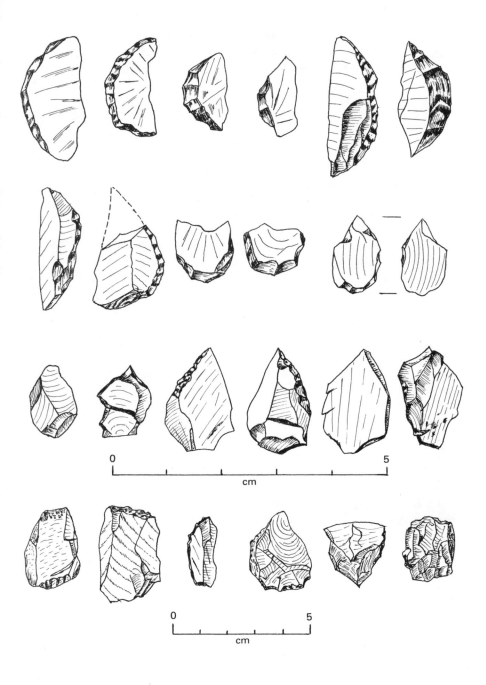

Figure 15. Nigeria. Mejiro Cave, Old Oyo: microliths *(after Willett)*.

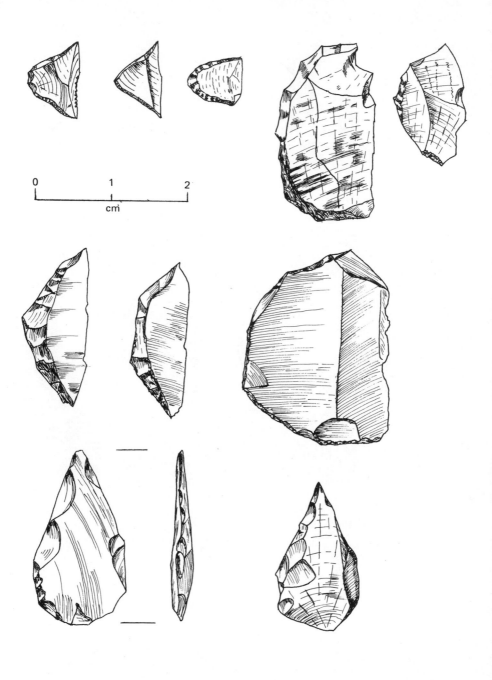

Figure 16. Nigeria. Rop rock shelter: microliths *(after Fagg B. 1944)*.

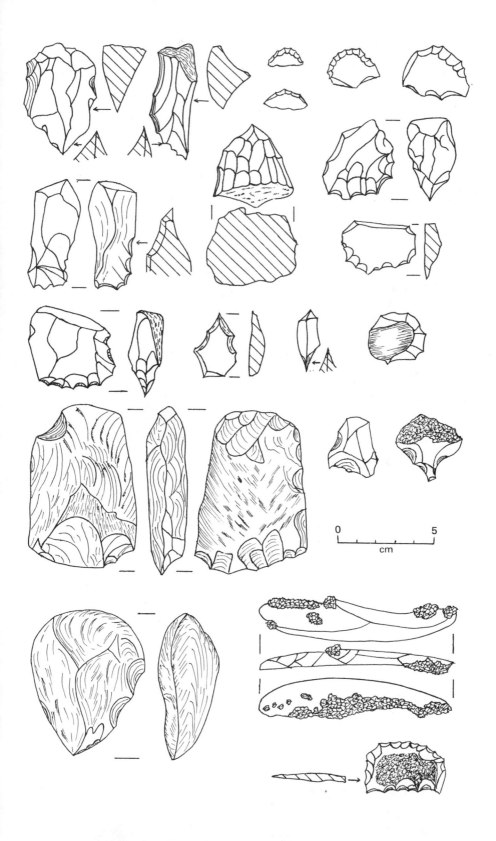

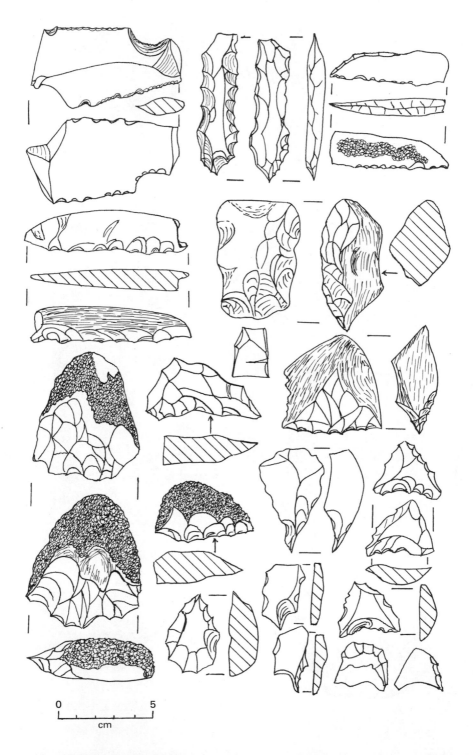

Figure 17. Mali. Kourounkorokale rock shelter: stone industry from the lower layer *(after Szumowski).*

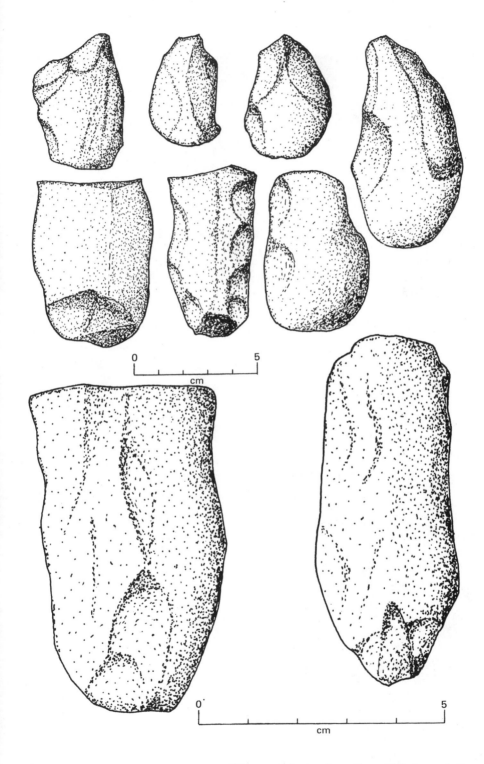

Figure 18. Sierra Leone. Yengema cave: stone industry from the middle layer *(after Coon).*

At this point we become bedevilled by the word 'Neolithic', and its ambiguity of meaning; originally used in Europe to signify the presence of the technological traits of ground stone axes, pottery and bifacially-flaked arrowheads, later, because agriculture and stock-keeping accompanied them in Europe, it was given the added connotation of 'agricultural', or 'food-producing'; and later still, this meaning alone. Ever since, the precise significance of the word, unless spelled out in each context, has remained confused. For this reason, although I suggested the term 'Guinea Neolithic' over 30 years ago to get rid of the portmanteau 'Tumbian' (Shaw 1944: 58), I now consider the term 'Neolithic' is better avoided in Africa wherever possible, certainly in sub-Saharan Africa (Bishop and Clark 1967:898; Shaw 1967:35; Munson 1968:11); but one has to take account of the persistence of this usage for francophone North Africa and the Sahara. Industries occur widely in the Sahara which have been termed 'Neolithic' because of their tool-kit, and in the central area date from the sixth millennium B.C. There is clear evidence for the advent of food producers in Cyrenaica by 4800 B.C. (McBurney 1967:298), but the 'Neolithic-of-Capsian-tradition', widespread in north-west Africa following preceding Epipalaeolithic cultures there, has now been shown to have no evidence of food production although it extends into the second millennium B.C. (Roubet 1971). At one time finds from Rufisque in Senegal were regarded as belonging to the Neolithic (Vaufrey 1946; Alimen 1957:229-33; Davies O., 1964:236) but they are probably best regarded as belonging to the general microlithic continuum of West Africa. In addition to this site near Dakar there are a number of sites in the savanna zone which maintain the microlithic tradition but add ground stone axes and pottery to it some time around 3000 B.C. Some occurrences are stratified above the aceramic stage, as at Rop (Fagg B.1944, 1972; Eyo 1972; Rosenfeld 1972; Fagg A.1972), Kourounkorokale (Szumowski 1956), Dutsen Kongba (York 1974) and Iwo Eleru, which is in the forest but not far from the savanna (Shaw 1969, 1973), but others occur independently, as at Nhampasseré in 'Portuguese' Guinea (Mateus 1952), in caves and rock shelters around Kindia (Delcroix and Vaufrey 1939) and Pita (Guebhard 1907; Hue 1912; Hubert 1922) in the Republic of Guinea, at Yagala and Kamabai in Sierra Leone (Atherton 1972), at Kokosu and Sopie in Liberia (Gabel 1974), at Abetifi (Shaw 1944, Smith A. 1975) and Kintampo (Flight 1968, 1970) in Ghana; Nsuta in western Ghana is in the forest but not far from the savanna (Nunoo 1948). There are admixtures of elements, such as bifacial arrowheads, characteristic of the 'Sahara Neolithic', at Oualia (Desplagnes 1907) in the Republic of Guinea and at Ntereso (Davies O., 1973) in Ghana.

In the sahel, fishing seems to have been an important economic activity to supplement the diet derived from cereal grains, wild or cultivated, and this pattern of subsistence is again reflected in the tool-kit with few or no microliths, as at Karkarichinkat (Smith A. 1974) in Mali, the lower levels of Daima in Bornu (Connah 1967, 1971, 1976), and in the Khimiya and subsequent phases at Tichitt (Munson 1971); the prevalence of bifacial arrowheads at the latter and at Karkarichinkat gives a strong flavour of the 'Sahara Neolithic'.

On the southern side of the savanna, in the forest, pottery and ground stone axes also seem to have been added to the preceding industry of pick and hoe-like tools, as in the 'Upper Yengeman' (Coon 1968), the upper levels of the Grotte de Kakimbon near Conakry (Hamy 1900), at the site of Blandè in the south-east corner of the Republic of Guinea (Holas 1950, 1952; Holas and Mauny 1953), at Afikpo in

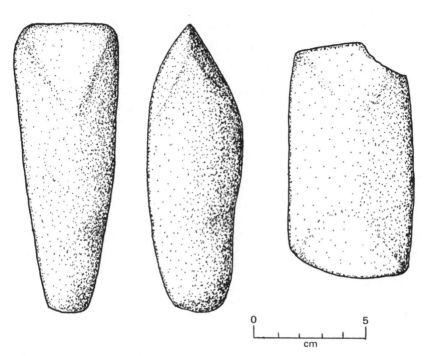

Figure 19. Sierra Leone. Yengema cave: stone industry from the upper layer *(after Coon).*

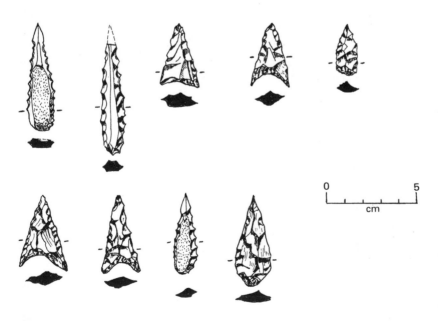

Figure 20. Ghana. Stone arrowheads of 'Sahara Neolithic' type from Ntereso *(after Davies 1966).*

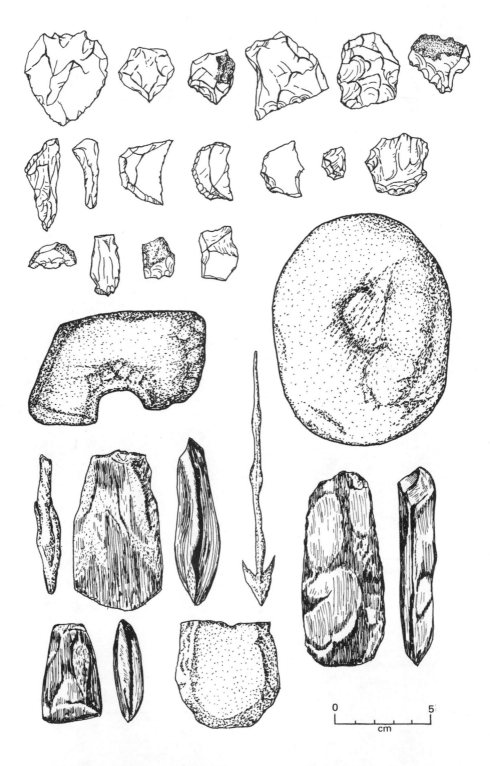

Figure 21. Mali. Kourounkorokale rock shelter: stone and iron implements from the upper layer *(after Szumowski)*.

Figure 22. Mali. Kourounkorokale rock shelter: pottery from the upper layer *(after Szumowski).*

0   5

cm

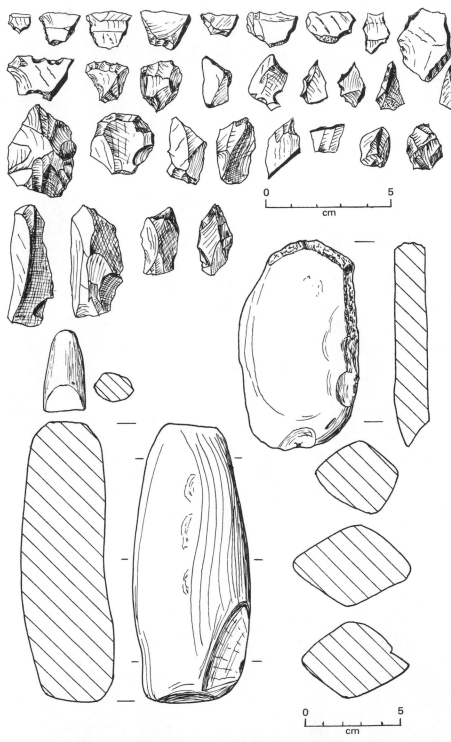

Figure 23. Ghana. 'Bosumpra' cave, Abetifi: stone industry *(after Shaw 1944)*. For the radiocarbon dates for this site see Smith 1975: the lowest level, yielding pottery and microliths, is dated to 3420± 100 bc.

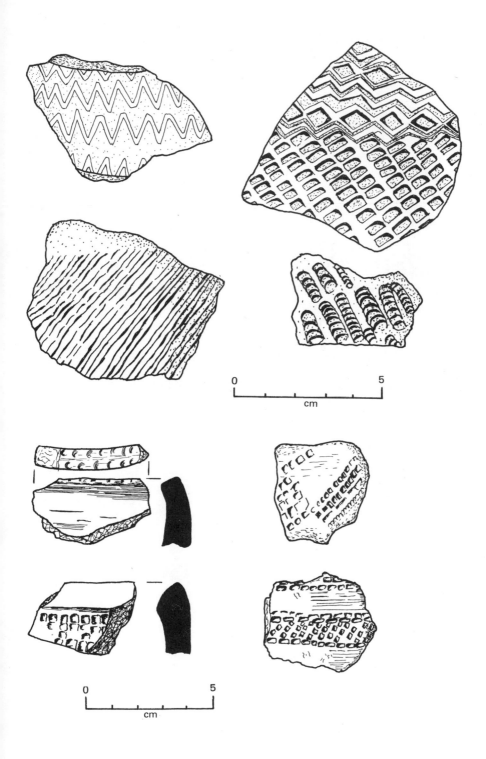

Figure 24. Pottery from the Rop (Nigeria) and Abetifi (Ghana) caves *(after Fagg, A. and Shaw 1944).*

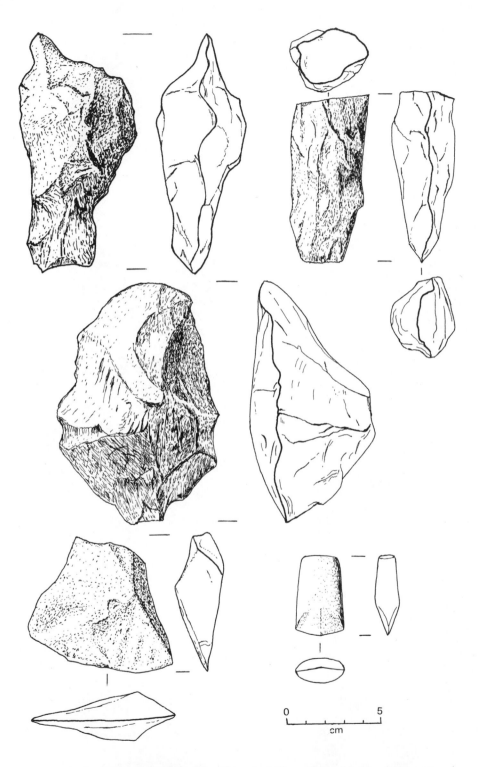

Figure 25. Republic of Guinea. Blandè rock shelter: bifacial tools, picks and axes *(after Holas and Mauny)*.

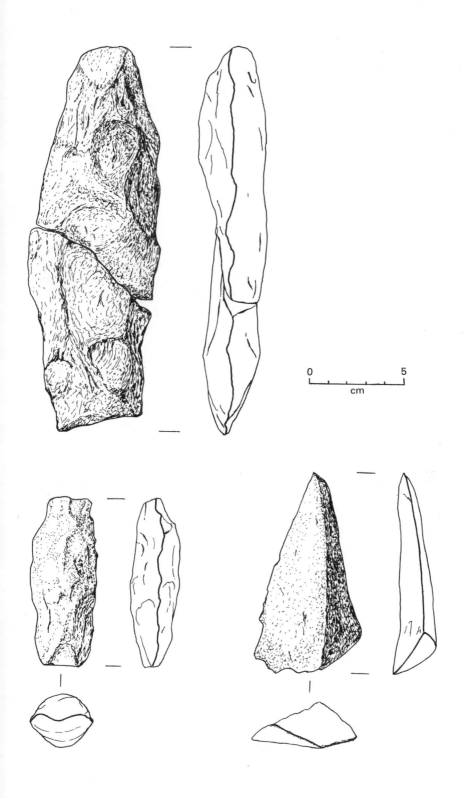

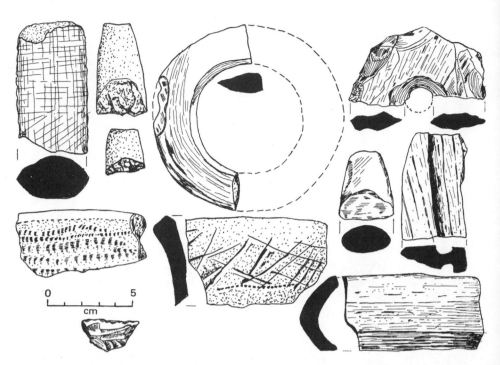

Figure 26. Ghana. Stone artifacts and pottery of the Kintampo industry *(after Davies)*.

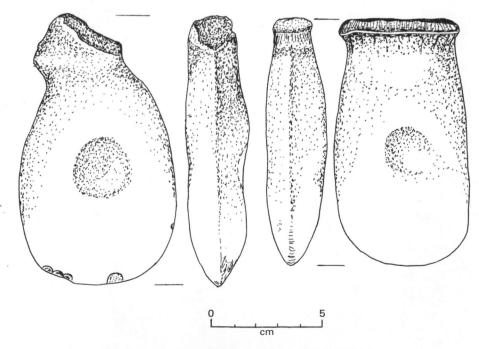

Figure 27. Nigeria. Necked and lugged stone axes *(after Kennedy)*.

south-eastern Nigeria (Hartle 1966, 1968) and in the island of Fernando Po (Martin de Molino 1965); the latter island seems to have been colonized fairly late in the Late Stone Age and to have pursued a fairly independent course of development while people on the mainland had benefited from the introduction of iron. The waisted form of ground stone axe shows affinities with similar ones from south-eastern Nigeria (Kennedy 1960), Camerouń and the Republic of Tchad (Clark, J.D. 1967: 618).

A specialized adaptation to completely different ecological circumstances occurred along the Atlantic coast of West Africa (fig. 28). Here, Late Stone Age peoples were exploiting the abundant shell-fish of the lagoons and estuaries, both for food and as bait for fishing, leaving behind huge mounds of shells. In the Ivory Coast such mounds have been shown to extend from 1600 B.C. up to the fourteenth century A.D. (Mauny 1973) and in Senegal one produced a ground stone axe made of bone (Joire 1947; Mauny 1957, 1961:156-62).

To summarize the Late Stone Age in West Africa, it can be divided into two phases; the first, beginning not later than 10,000 B.C., has two facies: one with microlithic stone industries associated with hunting in the savannas, the other with few or no microliths but picks and hoe-like tools in the forest. The second phase of the Late Stone Age, beginning some time around 3000 B.C. and having pottery and ground stone axes, may be considered to have four facies; the sahel has few or no microliths but a bone industry, which indicates that fishing was an important part of the economy; in the savanna the microlithic hunting tradition continues, occasionally with some suggestion of influences from the Sahara Neolithic, and similarly the pick and hoe tradition continues in the forest; on the coast a new ecological niche appears to have been exploited, utilizing the food resources of the lagoons and estuaries.

At the beginning of the Late Stone Age the subsistence base was undoubtedly various kinds and combinations of hunting, trapping and gathering. By the end of the Late Stone Age some of the peoples of West Africa were food producers as well as food gatherers. How and where did this transformation take place? The change from dependence on hunting, fishing and gathering the fruits of the wild, to crop-raising and stock-keeping, is the most important step which man has taken in the last 10,000 years. It was spread over a long period of time but it was nevertheless a revolutionary step, inasmuch as it fundamentally changed man's way of life and brought with it momentous consequences. It not only radically advanced man's capacity for controlling his environment, but it set up the conditions necessary for the emergence of what is usually called 'civilization'. It made sedentary life possible as never before, the storage of food, and the accumulation of wealth, and an increase in population; it led to division of labour, social stratification and new forms of social control. This revolution did not take place in a single location and spread to the rest of the world, but there were a limited number of 'foci' where such developments evolved. For Europe, western Asia and north-east Africa, the focus of importance was in the hill country of Anatolia, Iran and northern Iraq. Here were developed the cultivation of wheat and barley and the domestication of sheep, goats and cattle. Later, the techniques of food production were applied to the great river valleys of the Tigris/Euphrates, Nile and Indus, with the added techniques of drainage and irrigation (Clark, G. 1969:70ff; Ucko and Dimbleby 1969). By the fifth millennium B.C. there were domesticated sheep and cattle in Egypt and cereals were being grown (Caton-Thompson and Gardner 1934; Seddon 1968:490; Wendorf et al. 1970:1168). At present we have evidence for domesticated cattle

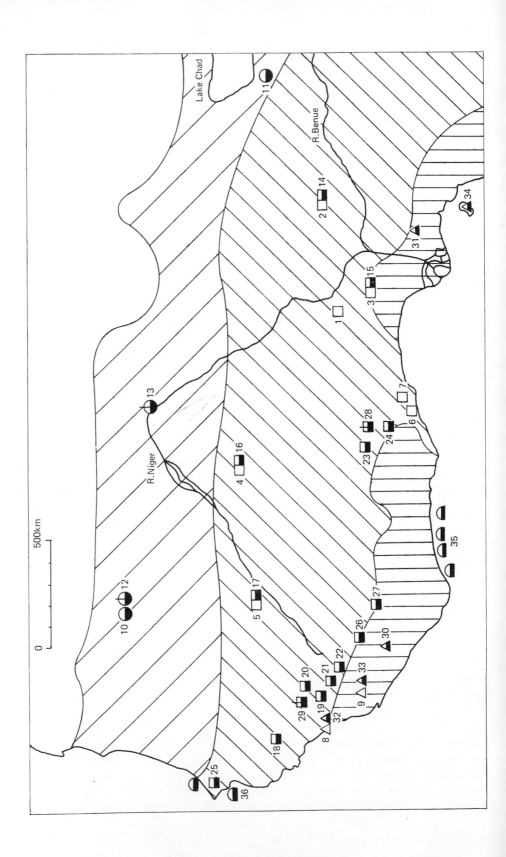

Figure 28. The Late Stone Age of West Africa in relation to vegetation zones.

earlier than this in the central Saharan highlands, and some evidence, though slender, for cereal growing (Mori 1965; Camps 1969).

It is not easy to find the evidence in the archaeological record for the beginnings of agriculture. The best evidence consists of the remains of identifiable crop remains in context, either in the form of charred seeds and nuts, or in the form of impressions accidentally made in pottery vessels by their happening to be set down on grain when soft in the course of their manufacture. Direct evidence of vegetative crops like yams is very hard to get. Indirect evidence comes from such things as hoe-like tools and grinding stones, but these have to be interpreted with caution as they can be used for purposes other than agriculture. Some evidence comes from ethnographic and linguistic studies but these usually lack any accuracy of time-depth. A great deal of the evidence concerning the origin of domesticated plants is botanical. It is the botanists who can tell us, as a result of their taxonomic and genetic studies, what are the likely wild ancestors of a domesticated plant, what is the distribution of the wild ancestor, what is the most likely locale of domestication, and whether a domesticated plant is indigenous to the area or whether it must have been imported. Vavilov did pioneer work in the inter-war period on the botanical evidence concerning centres of domestication for cultivated plants, and made Abyssinia one of his eight major centres in the world for the origin of domesticated plants. His conclusions were based on the principle that a proliferation of variant forms indicated a 'centre of origin' (Vavilov 1951) but as a result of more recent work 'there is little left of his original theory' (Baker 1971; Harlan 1971b; Harlan and De Wet 1973). It is now considered that wheat and barley cultivation and the use of the plough were introduced into Ethiopia by the ancient Cushitic inhabitants who were in a good position in northern Ethiopia to have contacts with countries at the northern end of the Red Sea (Simoons 1965), although some other crops were indigenously developed in Ethiopia. In spite of the erosion of Vavilov's particular theory, the evidence provided by botanists remains of paramount importance for the understanding of the history of agriculture in sub-Saharan Africa.

In 1959 Murdock propounded his theory that there was an ancient centre of plant domestication in his 'Nuclear Mande' area around the head-waters of the River Niger at the western end of the Sudan zone. Before Murdock, apart from the researches of a few pioneer botanists like Miège (1948), Chevalier (1938, 1949) and Portères (1951), and the speculations of Carl Sauer (1952), little systematic thought had been given to the origins of African agriculture: it had largely been something taken for granted among the negroid peoples of Africa, and there is an interesting twist to the now exploded 'Hamitic myth' in relation to agriculture. In the classical statement of that myth, crop-growing is seen as a lower way of life than pastoralism. Seligman (1930:100-1) stated his theory as follows: 'the incoming Hamites were pastoral "Europeans" - arriving wave after wave - better armed as well as quicker-witted than the dark agricultural Negros', and again, 'this process was repeated with minor modifications over a long period of time, the pastoralists always asserting their superiority over the agriculturists'. We can now see the Hamitic theory for the white supremacist myth that it was (Drake 1959; Armstrong 1964:3-7) and I will not waste more time on it, pointing out merely that in the references to the Negro agriculturists there was no appreciation at all of the magnitude of the adaptive shift involved in a change from food collection to food production under African conditions.

The great merit of Murdock's theory was that it shook people out of their diffusionist assumptions concerning the origins of African agriculture, and made them entertain the possibility of an independent domestication of African crops. This is a lasting gain, even if Murdock's theory as originally proposed can no longer be entertained. He based his argument primarily on linguistic distributions, but claimed 'modest support from archaeologists, on the basis of the admittedly fragmentary evidence from the very few relevant excavations reported to date, and from botanists who have identified the ranges of wild species from which the domesticated forms have presumably been ennobled.' Murdock does not cite to which archaeological excavations he is referring, and I know of none whose evidence supports him. His botanical evidence did not stand up well, either, to examination by a botanist. Baker (1962) examined the list of the plants which Murdock claimed were domesticated in the 'Nuclear Mande' area and on botanical grounds considered that roselle, sesame and cotton could equally well have been domesticated in Asia, and if they were domesticated in Africa, it need not have been in the Sudan zone. It is now believed that cotton was domesticated in Asia and introduced to Egypt in Meroitic times (Arkell 1971), although there was wild cotton in Africa of which the seeds were collected for stockfood in Egyptian Nubia by the middle of the third millennium B.C. (Chowdhury and Buth 1970). Similarly, Baker considered there was insufficient evidence to regard the following members of Murdock's list as only domesticated in the western Sudan: Guinea corn, bulrush millet, Kaffir potato, yam bean, water melon, calabash, tamarind, okra and one or two others. 'If the first domestication of these species in the Nuclear Mande area is, after all, unproven', said Baker, 'we are left with only a fraction of the original list.' Baker divided the remaining species into two groups. The first group is 'Sudanic' but virtually restricted to West Africa, and it was the existence of such 'endemics' that Murdock considered provided the strongest botanical evidence for a domestication centre in the Nuclear Mande area: the shea-butter tree, the fluted pumpkin, fonio and the African groundnut. Baker regarded the latter as Murdock's best bit of evidence, together with African rice, which Murdock added to his list as an afterthought; but its centre of origin is now believed to have been the inland delta of the Niger, not its headwaters area (Portères 1962:237). The second group in Murdock's list are savanna and woodland species, 'Guinean' rather than 'Sudanic' in distribution: Akee apple, kola, oil palm and yam. Baker denied that these Guinean species contributed any evidence in favour of the Nuclear Mande domestication centre; they occur wild as well as planted and there is as yet no certain knowledge about their antiquity as domesticates.

Let us consider what our evidence is for cereals. The important thing to remember about the cereals is that wheat and barley are temperate zone, 'winter rainfall', crops; these were the crops first domesticated in south-west Asia by dry-farming methods, and later their cultivation was adapted to the arid sub-tropics by means of irrigation in the valleys of the Tigris/Euphrates, Nile and Indus. It is virtually impossible to grow wheat and barley by dry-farming methods in the 'summer rainfall' areas of the tropics; no wild ancestors of wheat and barley grow there nor have they ever done so. Therefore for cereal agriculture to develop in sub-Saharan Africa, it had to be either by growing wheat and barley by means of irrigation, or as the result of the introduction of crops suitable for summer rainfall areas domesticated in the tropics outside Africa, or as the result of a process of domesticating wild African grasses. For the first of these alternatives - a diffused introduction of wheat and barley - there is

Figure 29. Jebel Qeili. Representation of Guinea corn on a Meroitic rock engraving, first century A.D. (after Shinnie).

no evidence outside the Republic of Sudan and Ethiopia. Wheat and barley may have been grown in the Nile valley nearly as far south as the latitude of Khartoum in the ancient kingdom of Meroe, for barley is specifically mentioned by a classical author (Strabo 17, II, 2), but he also mentions millet, and it is the Guinea corn type of millet, or sorghum, which appears to be represented on a Meroitic rock engraving dated to the first century A.D. (Shinnie 1967:96, 159) (fig. 29). The wheat and barley anciently introduced into Ethiopia adapted to the highland climate, and varieties proliferated in various ecological niches.

For the second alternative - the introduction of tropical-type cereal crops already domesticated outside Africa - only one candidate has been put forward for the time before Europeans introduced maize from America in the sixteenth century; that is finger millet, which was formerly thought to have an Indian origin (De Candolle 1886; Burkill 1935; Werth 1937; Portères 1951, 1972) but it is now considered to be of African origin (Harlan 1975). Until recently there was no archaeological evidence about finger millet in Africa before its occurrence at the Van Niekerk ruins in Rhodesia in a layer below and earlier than the ruins themselves and believed to belong to the eighth century A.D., but which could be as late as the fourteenth century (Summers 1958:92-4, 176, 318); however, it is now reported from Gobedra, near Axum, in northern Ethiopia, from before 850 b.c. (Phillipson 1976). Grains of it are reported from southern India dated to around 1800 B.C. (Allchin 1969:325). It was linguistic evidence which was suggestive of an introduction from India or Arabia, but on botanical grounds its origins is now placed in east Africa (Kennedy-O'Byrne 1957; Mehra 1962, 1963a and b; Purseglove 1972) and its transmission to India envisaged along the southern coast of Arabia (Anderson 1960).

This brings us to our third alternative for the development of African cereals - the domestication of wild African grasses. The most important of the African millets is Guinea corn, or sorghum, which we have already noted as grown in the kingdom of Meroe. In sub-Saharan Africa until recently we only had archaeological evidence for it in the second half of the first millennium A.D., from the Republic of Guinea (Filipowiak et al. 1968:617, 645), north-eastern Nigeria (Connah 1967:25), Tanzania (Sassoon 1967, 1971), Malawi (Robinson 1966:180), Zambia (Fagan 1967:62) and Rhodesia (Summers 1958:175-7), but now carbonized grains from Jebel Tomat, in the Republic of Sudan, have been identified as cultivated sorghum and dated to about A.D. 350 (Clark, J.D. 1973). The impression of a grain of sorghum on a pot from Adrar Bous in the Air region of the southern Sahara dated to the beginning of the second millennium B.C. (Clark, J.D. 1971a and b) was at first thought to represent cultivated sorgham, but the latest opinion is that it is wild (Clark, J.D. 1973). Archaeological evidence for sorghum in India in the mid-second millennium B.C. (Marshall 1931: pl.LXXXVII, photo 5; Vishnu-Mittre 1968) has now been questioned (Harlan 1975). The botanical evidence is unequivocal that sorghum is African in origin. For some time efforts have been made to sift the botanical evidence in order to identify the area of the origin of the crop (Dogget 1965, 1970; Hemardinquer et al. 1967), with the possibility that it was independently ennobled in more than one area of the continent (De Wet and Huckaby 1967:800). The most recent work favours the sahel strip from Lake Chad to the Nile (Harlan and Stemler 1972) and the process may have had more connection with the stimulus of Saharan desiccation after the middle of the third millennium B.C., rather than with cultural stimulus from the wheat and barley

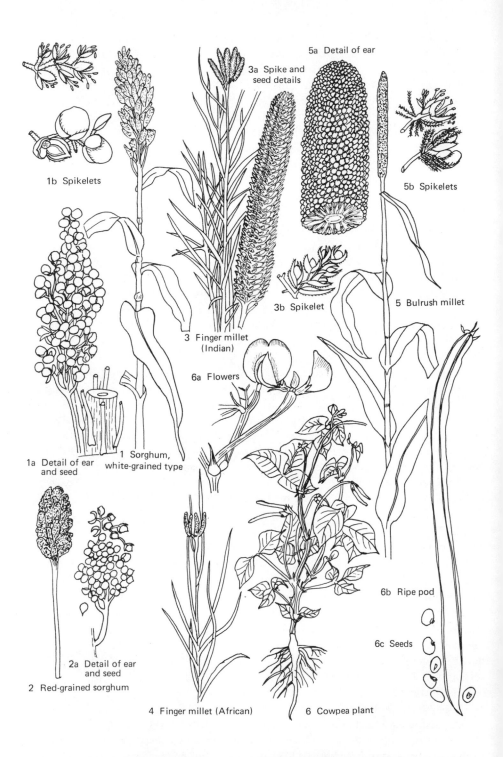

1b Spikelets

1a Detail of ear and seed

1 Sorghum, white-grained type

2a Detail of ear and seed

2 Red-grained sorghum

3a Spike and seed details

3b Spikelet

3 Finger millet (Indian)

4 Finger millet (African)

5a Detail of ear

5b Spikelets

5 Bulrush millet

6a Flowers

6b Ripe pod

6c Seeds

6 Cowpea plant

Figure 30. West African food plants *(after Nicholson)*. (Scales: 1, 2, 3, 4, 5, 6, 7b, 8a x 1/12; 1a, 2a, 3a, 5a, 6a, 6b, 6c, 7, 7a, 8, 9a, 9b, 10a x 2/3; 1b, 3b, 5b, x 2; 9, 10 x 4/9.

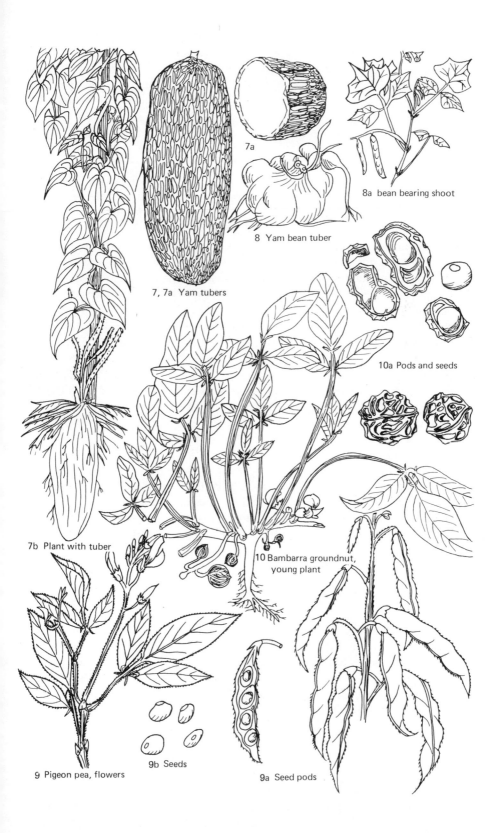

7a

8a bean bearing shoot

8 Yam bean tuber

7, 7a Yam tubers

10a Pods and seeds

7b Plant with tuber

10 Bambarra groundnut,
young plant

9b Seeds

9 Pigeon pea, flowers

9a Seed pods

growing areas of north-east Africa. We badly need to know what crops, if any, were being grown at the end of the fourth millennium B.C. by the inhabitants of such sites as Shaheinab, a few miles north of Khartoum, whose material equipment was of a kind usually associated with food production and where 2 per cent of the animal remains were of domesticated dwarf goat (Arkell 1953). There are now new techniques of excavation, using flotation, which give us confident hope that this evidence will be forthcoming.

Two grains of pollen from the Hoggar highlands of the Sahara, dated to the sixth millennium B.C., have been claimed to be derived from bulrush millet (or 'pearl' millet) (Camps 1969:188), but the next archaeological evidence for it that we have is more than four thousand years later at the Dhar Tichitt sites in southern Mauretania. Here there were settlements spanning from the mid-second to the mid-first millennium B.C., divided into seven phases. Impressions on pottery revealed the use of a number of different kinds of desert grasses: in the first three phases there were many seeds of bur grass, still collected to some extent as a famine food, and a single grain of bulrush millet, but it was impossible to tell whether it was wild or cultivated. In the fourth phase two other grass seeds appear and bulrush millet rises to 3 per cent of the total. In the fifth and sixth phases bulrush millet jumps to 60 per cent and 80 per cent respectively, rising to nearly 90 per cent in the seventh phase, and has all the characteristics of the cultivated grain. It looks, then, as if the Tichitt people were experimenting with wild grasses and hit upon bulrush millet as the best, or that it was introduced from outside to a community already practising cereal eating and among whom it rapidly gained popularity over the others (Munson 1968, 1970, 1971). Bulrush millet is known from sites in Malawi and Rhodesia dated to about the ninth century A.D. (Summers 1958: 176; Robinson 1966:180). The Kotoko living south of Lake Chad regard bulrush millet as their oldest kind of food grain (Lebeuf 1969). There are archaeological occurrences of bulrush millet in Rajasthan and Gujarat in north-west India during the second half of the second millennium B.C. (Vishnu-Mittre 1967). There is general agreement among botanists that bulrush millet was domesticated in Africa (Portères 1972), perhaps most likely in the western end of the sahel zone (Purseglove 1972) as well as in the sorghum domestication area (Harlan 1971b), perhaps also in Ethiopia (Doggett 1970:2,7).

There are three other types of millets which have been domesticated in Africa: two types of 'fonio' or 'hungry rice' *(Digitaria exilis, D. iburua)* and the grass whose botanical name is *Brachiaria deflexa*. A single grain of the latter, probably wild, dated to around 4000 B.C., occurred at Adrar Bous, in Air (Clark, J.D. 1971a, 1973), and it is known from the fourth phase of the Tichitt sequence but is considered to be wild; nowadays it is only cultivated in the Fouta Djallon area and the botanical view is that its domestication has no great antiquity, being so close to the wild varieties which are exploited in a number of parts of Africa (Portères 1972; Purseglove 1972). One type of fonio *(D. iburua)* belongs particularly to the Hausa area and probably originated there (Portères 1972); the cultivation of the other type of fonio is widespread in the savanna area of West Africa but its domestication may have taken place in the Middle Niger Delta region (Portères 1972), perhaps when the area was rather wetter than now, since at present this is the extreme northern edge of its distribution. No archaeological occurrences of fonio have been recorded.

The Middle Niger Delta is also considered to be the home of African rice domestication, perhaps with secondary centres in the lower Gambia River valley and the highlands of the Republic of Guinea (Portères 1972). Rice replaces yams as the staple in the western half of West Africa, but it is only since the Second World War that African rice has been recognized as a separate species and as indigenously domesticated. No archaeological occurrences of African rice have yet been recorded.

The last of the eight indigenously domesticated African cereals is teff, and its cultivation is confined to Ethiopia. It has been suggested that the Cushitic inhabitants who introduced emmer wheat to Ethiopia also domesticated local plants such as teff (Doggett 1965:59), but it has been argued, in the absence of any archaeological information on the subject, that teff must have been domesticated before the introduction of wheat and barley to Ethiopia or else it would not have been thought worth while to cultivate such a tiny grain. Although we have no archaeological evidence for teff in Ethiopia, it is known from a sherd impression in a South Arabian context dated to the first centuries B.C./A.D. (Beek 1969:400).

That concludes the list of indigenously domesticated African cereals, and we must now turn to root and tuber sources of food. Unfortunately the nature of these vegetative plants is such that as yet we have no archaeological information about their antiquity as cultigens and the hopes of getting it are slender. Whereas cereal grains may be preserved by being carbonized, their impressions be retained in pots, and their pollen be identified, tubers such as yams do not leave the same clues about themselves; they very often do not even produce pollen. It is therefore going to be very much more difficult to get direct archaeological information about these crops. This is most unfortunate, since yam cultivation was probably extremely important in the development of indigenous African agriculture, and it may have had a very considerable antiquity. What has tended to obscure the history of yam cultivation in Africa is that until recent years it was believed that the domestication of the indigenous African yams only resulted from the stimulus of the introduction of the Asian forms (Forde 1963:211; Gray 1962:183), although one of these is in fact quite a recent introduction (Miège 1948; Morgan 1962:236; Coursey 1972). Murdock speculated that the Asiatic food plants entered Africa via the Ethiopian lowlands and travelled westwards along what he erroneously called 'the yam belt'. Nowadays it is generally believed that the Asian food crops, including plantains, bananas, one type of cocoyam and the citrus fruits, reached Africa from Indonesia via Madagascar or the adjacent parts of the east coast in the first half of the first millennium A.D. (Gray 1962:182). There is some linguistic evidence that Asian yams reached India about the first century A.D. (Allchin 1974). It is believed that yam cultivation may be very ancient in the eastern half of West Africa, going back as much as four or five thousand years (Coursey 1967, 1972; Posnansky 1969:106). The prohibition in certain areas on the use of iron tools for the digging of yams in New Yam festivals, and the importance of such festivals, is suggestive that yam cultivation antedates the introduction of an iron technology (Coursey 1971) (fig. 31).

No other indigenous tuberous crop has the same importance as the yam, but the 'Hausa potato' is a cultivated crop, although the area of its domestication is uncertain (Dalziel 1955:459); both Ethiopia (Davies, O 1968b:481) and West Africa (Purseglove 1972:22) have been suggested. Just as it is likely that many tropical grasses were at one time grown for their grain, so it is likely that a number of African tubers, such as the Hausa potato (Busson 1965:405), were formerly much more widely cultivated than now and have come to be displaced by more successful ones, such as cassava, sweet potato, and the second type of cocoyam, all introduced from

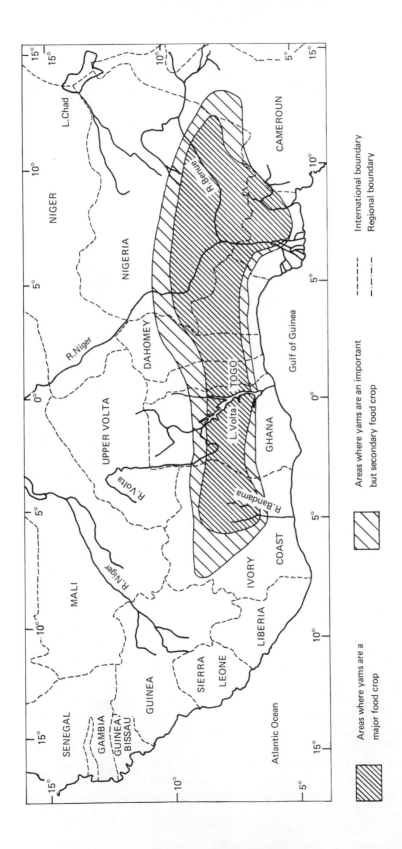

Areas where yams are a major food crop

Areas where yams are an important but secondary food crop

International boundary

Regional boundary

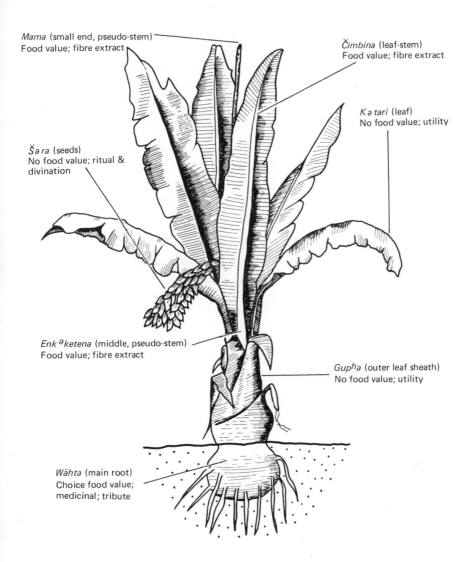

Mama (small end, pseudo-stem)
Food value; fibre extract

Čimbina (leaf-stem)
Food value; fibre extract

Kə tari (leaf)
No food value; utility

Šə ra (seeds)
No food value; ritual &
divination

Enk ə ketena (middle, pseudo-stem)
Food value; fibre extract

Gupha (outer leaf sheath)
No food value; utility

Wähta (main root)
Choice food value;
medicinal; tribute

Figure 32. *Ensete,* the African or 'false' banana, showing edible parts *(after Shack).*

Figure 31. West Africa. Distribution of 'yam zone' *(after Coursey 1967).*

America by Europeans. The yam bean is another African cultigen, but we have no information on its antiquity. Ensete, the 'false banana' or 'African banana', which bears no edible fruit but whose stem and root provide a staple diet in south-western Ethiopia (Shack 1966:1), must have been indigenously domesticated in that country, and, like teff, probably before the introduction there of wheat and barley (fig. 32).

Among indigenously domesticated pulses we can reckon two kinds of African groundnut, pigeon pea and cowpea (Purseglove 1972), the latter probably domesticated in Nigeria (Faris 1963). Although these may in some areas have long been an important item of the diet (Summers 1958:175-7; Flight 1970:72; Robinson 1970:171), they never seem to have formed a staple in the way that the millets and yams have. The same can be said about okra, roselle, gourd, melon, castor and sesame, all of which have an African origin - although we do not know as yet how ancient those origins are; however, we are beginning to get seeds preserved in archaeological contexts (Fouché 1937:31; Vogel 1969).

There remain the important tree crops - shea-butter, kola and above all, the oil palm. Remains of the latter were found at the site of Shaheinab in the Republic of Sudan dated to about 3300 B.C. (Arkell 1953), and at a Kintampo site in Ghana dated to before 1400 B.C. and associated with cowpea and domestic cattle (Flight 1970). The borderlines are very hazy between gathering the nuts of wild oil palms, giving protection to a wild tree, allowing trees to seed themselves in man-made clearings, and actual planting - but at some point along this line we are concerned with intentional food production rather than mere food collecting. The securing of a supply of palm oil as an ingredient in the diet may have had important consequences on population growth (Shaw 1972:159).

So much for the evidence concerning the domestication of indigenous crops in Africa. We must now turn to the question of domesticated animals. Evidence for the keeping of domesticated livestock comes from the bones of food refuse, but we are handicapped in many of the acid soils of the wetter parts of West Africa by the fact that bone is rarely preserved.

Whereas sub-Saharan Africa had to find its own local equivalent for wheat and barley, and in fact found other food crops for itself as well, the four animal domesticates introduced were able to become adapted to tropical conditions, and were sufficiently successful in doing so for there to be no point in looking for local substitutes or additions. Plenitude of game has also been adduced as a reason for there being little incentive towards domestication of indigenous animals (Clark, J.D. 1967:607), although this may have been more true of the savanna lands of Africa with their dense animal populations than of areas with different types of vegetation (Butzer 1971:150, table 9). The buffalo, the elephant, the zebra, the wart-hog, the bush-pig, the hartebeeste, the eland and certain other antelopes, the bush fowl, the cane rat and the giant African snail (Ajayi 1971) might have been domesticated but were not. The taming during Old Kingdom times in Egypt of gazelle, bubal and other antelopes, moufflon sheep, ibex and even hyaenas, was at one time considered to have been short-lived (Mauny 1967:587, 594 quoting Yoyotte in Posener et al. 1959:101 and Brentjes 1965), but it has recently been suggested (Clark, J. D. 1971b) that this was a practice going back to before Predynastic times; there was a cult element in it, and this may be equally ancient (Smith, H.S. 1969), but no domestication of any importance finally resulted. Therefore, when we come to animal sources of food south of the Sahara we are not involved in a search for evidence and dating concerning African domesticates as we were in the case of the millets and yams; we are simply concerned with the rate and pattern of a process of diffusion. At the moment we have reasonably certain information for the domestication in Africa of three animals only - the ass, the cat and the Guinea-fowl - and only the last of these as a food source.

There is direct evidence for domesticated cattle early in the fifth millennium B.C. in the Acacus, the north-easterly outlier of the Hoggar, and perhaps even earlier (Mori 1965; Camps 1969:207; 1974:223); in the Grotte Capeletti, in the Aurés mountains of Algeria, in the mid-fifth millennium B.C. (Roubet 1971; Carter 1972); in the Fayum in the second half of the fifth millennium B.C. (Caton-Thompson and Gardner 1934:89, where some uncertainty about the domestic status of the Fayum cattle was expressed; it has now been established that they were domesticated); at Adrar Bous, in Air, at the beginning of the fourth millennium (Clark, J.D. 1971a and b; Carter 1972); at sites in the Hoggar highlands in the second half of the fourth millennium (Hugot 1963), and at another site in Air (Smith, A 1973); in the southern Tilemsi valley at the end of the third millennium and into the second (Smith, A 1974); at Tichitt in Mauretania (Munson 1970) and at Kintampo in central Ghana by the mid-second millennium (Flight 1970; Carter and Flight 1972); and in north-eastern Nigeria by the mid-first millennium, where at Daima there were cattle thoughout the whole occupation from the sixth century B.C. to the eleventh century A.D., but where humped cattle only appeared at the end of the sequence (Connah 1967, 1976); cattle burials at Jebel Moya in the Sudan attest to the importance cattle had achieved here by Meroitic times (Addison 1949:56-9, 147-8).

Thus it is possible to construct an isochronic diagram (fig. 33) which, being an artifact of the present state of research, must be used with caution; nevertheless it suggests a generally southward movement of cattle-keeping from central North Africa which went on for a period of some three thousand years. To begin with, the movement was simply to take up grazing grounds in the central Saharan highlands which in the moister climate before 3000 B.C. were suitable for cattle; after about 2500 B.C. the southward movement would have been to escape the severe desiccation which then set in. Such a movement directly southwards out of the Sahara into West Africa seems more likely than the anti-clockwise coastal movement from North Africa, formerly proposed to account for the present distribution of the Ndama and West African Dwarf Shorthorn breeds (Curson and Thornton 1936; Payne 1964). Such a southward movement is different from the movement westwards out of the Nile valley which has been the picture traditionally painted (Balout 1965) and which assumed that domesticated cattle were first received in Egypt from south-west Asia. On this assumption two routes have been proposed for the spread of cattle westwards - one along the Mediterranean coast and penetrating into the Sahara over the higher, better-watered areas like Tassili and Hoggar; the other from Upper Egypt along the southern edge of the Sahara about latitude $20°N$ (Mauny 1967:583). Routes from Egypt via Kharga oasis to Tibesti, Wanyanga and Ennedi have also been suggested (Clark, J.D. 1967:603). An introduction of domesticated cattle from the Levant and a westward spread from Egypt may indeed represent what happened, but there are other possibilities which fit our radiocarbon dates better. Since cattle occur in Greece and Crete in the seventh millennium B.C. but not in Anatolia and south-west Asia until the sixth millennium, there is the possibility of 'cattle herdsmen emigrating along the northern shores and archipelagos of the Mediterranean, making landfall in

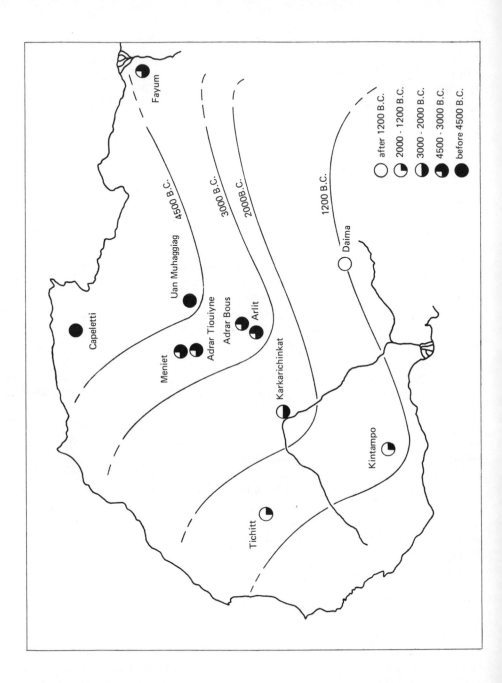

Figure 33. Isochronic diagram of the spread of cattle in Africa, based on information at December 1974. Scale: 1cm = c.350km.

Tunisia and spreading thence south and into the interior' (Higgs 1967a and b; Higgs and Jarman 1969). However, since there were wild cattle in North Africa and the Nile valley north of the tropic of Cancer during the Pleistocene and up to Roman times, the possibility of an indigenous domestication of cattle in North Africa must not be ruled out (Smith, A. 1973). This could have been the result of stimulus diffusion, with the idea of domesticated animals having been imported but not actual animals, or it could have been an entirely independent innovation; in this case we should expect to find a close man/cattle relationship in the form of specialized cattle hunting in the pre-domestication phase (Jarman 1969); we have no clear evidence about this yet.

The same widespread wetter conditions which allowed cattle-keeping in the Sahara may also have enabled tsetse flies to extend further north than they do today, and in this way a southern frontier for cattle was established around latitude 18°N. When the final desiccation of the Sahara set in around the third millennium B.C. this frontier shifted down to about 14°N; these two changes together exerted a strong stimulus to the cattle-keepers to move south and probably resulted in their being able to penetrate the tsetse-free area of East Africa (Mauny 1967:583-5, fig. 1).

We are at last beginning to get satisfactory instances of cattle bones associated with the 'Stone Bowl' folk of East Africa from about 1000 B.C. onwards (Sassoon 1968:22; Cohen 1970; Phillipson 1970a:4; Odner 1972; Bowyer 1973:99). These were a Late Stone Age people characterized by the stone bowls they made, and it is now clear that they were keepers of cattle and sheep-or-goats. In Zambia cattle appear along with the earliest Iron Age, from the fifth century A.D. onwards (Phillipson 1968; Vogel 1971). In south-western Rhodesia buried horn-cores appear in Phase III of the Leopard's Kopje Culture dated to the early part of the second millennium A.D. and may be associated with a cattle cult (Robinson 1966:25). Bone evidence shows that cattle and sheep/goats had reached Bambandyanalo on the Limpopo by the late eleventh century (Gardner 1963:29). The indirect evidence of cattle figurines confirms the general picture, and linguistic evidence has been adduced to show that cattle have been known in the more northerly parts of East Africa for as long as there have been speakers of Eastern and Central Sudanic languages in the area and probably also as long as speakers of Southern Cushitic as well (Ehret 1967).

The pattern which emerges from this evidence would seem to indicate a spread of cattle-keeping from the Sudan zone of Africa during the second millennium B.C. into East Africa. The southward spread continued, and we now (Phillipson 1976) have a greater knowledge of the routes and chronology of their spread than formerly (Fagan 1965:46). By the time Europeans arrived in South Africa in the late fifteenth century, the pastoral Khoikhoi (Hottentots) had large herds of long-horned cattle and fat-tailed sheep (Fagan 1965:31), yet only one Late Stone Age site (Parkington 1974) with cattle bones has been found, and it was thought they might have been introduced to the south-west Cape a comparatively short time before the Europeans arrived (Inskeep 1969:30). In the abundant rock art of southern Africa south of the Zambezi, paintings of sheep, although not numerous, occur in Rhodesia, South-West Africa, the south-west and the south-east Cape, while those of cattle are rare and occur only in the Drakensberg and the eastern Cape. This suggests that in southern Africa, sheep diffused differently from, and in many areas earlier than, cattle.

The earliest evidence for sheep or goats in Africa comes from the 'Neolithic' site of Haua Fteah in northern Cyrenaica, and is dated to the early fifth millennium B.C. (Higgs 1967a and b), but there were no associated cattle that were certainly domesticated. Sheep and/or goat occurred in conjunction with cattle in the Fayum in Egypt late in the fifth millennium B.C. (Caton-Thompson and Gardner 1934:89; Wendorf 1971), in the Predynastic cultures of the Nile valley and in the Hoggar in the fourth millennium. At Shaheinab in the Sudan domesticated goat was present around 3300 B.C. but there were no associated cattle (Bate, in Arkell 1953:15-18); the Shaheinab specimens were dwarf goats of the type developed in Africa (Hill 1974); sheep or goat were present, as well as cattle, in the mid-second millennium B.C. level at Kintampo in Ghana (Carter and Flight 1972) and during all the Tichitt phases in southern Mauretania except the first (Munson 1970). From the foregoing evidence it looks as if the domesticated goat spread out from the north-eastern corner of Africa ahead of cattle, since it reached Haua Fteah and Shaheinab ahead of them. If this is so and goats continued to spread into East Africa ahead of other domesticated animals, we have no evidence of this, and indeed until recently had little evidence for early goats at all. Now we have more sheep/goats than cattle from the Stone Bowl site of Narosura in Kenya (Odner 1972) in the first millennium B.C. In Zambia there is evidence from the ninth century A.D. (Fagan 1967; Phillipson 1970b:97, 113), and possibly from early in the first millennium A.D. from Rhodesia (Robinson 1961; Fagan 1966: 503). The latter is now made more credible by the recent reporting of well-preserved sheep bones in context from a site at the Cape dated to the early fifth century A.D. (Schweitzer and Scott 1973). There is now increasing evidence accumulating that pottery and sheep were spreading down the western side of southern Africa from Angola to the Cape by about 200 B.C. It is not clear yet whether this was a spread of cultural traits among an existing population or whether it represents a movement of people (Parkington 1974).

In common with other parts of the Old World, the archaeological record in Africa for the domesticated pig is much more scanty than for the other three domesticates. Pig is reported among the fifth-millennium bones from the Fayum (Caton-Thompson and Gardner 1934:89) and pigs may well have been known in Egypt before the Third Dynasty (Reed 1960:141). The wild pigs of Egypt may have been locally domesticated, rather than the domesticates having been introduced from south-west Asia (Reed 1960:139); in any case there is a possibility that pigs were domesticated in the Crimea before they were in Asia (Higgs and Jarman 1969:38). However that may be, the pig does not seem to have been an important food source in Africa, and this independently of Moslem prohibitions. Perhaps this is not so surprising, since the pig is a much less efficient converter of cellulose into a form of food digestible by man than the three ruminants; the pig, like the dog, competes directly with man for food, and thus 'only in a community where there is an excess of human food can pigs and dogs be tolerated as a part of the biosocial community' (Reed 1969:366).

I mentioned earlier that only the ass, the cat and the Guinea-fowl were domesticated in Africa, and as we are only concerned here with food animals, we need only consider the Guinea-fowl. In ancient times its distribution down the Nile valley is likely to have extended further north than at present and it seems to have been known in ancient Egypt from Predynastic times, although probably as a wild rather than as a domesticated bird (Keimer 1938; Davies, N.M. 1940). Formerly it appears to have been common in north Africa, whence it was taken across the

Mediterranean; there is literary reference to it in Greece by the fifth century B.C. The Romans knew it as a poultry bird but it seems to have become forgotten in Europe and was unknown there in mediaeval times. It was rediscovered by Portuguese explorers of the African coast at the end of the fifteenth century, hence the name (Zeuner 1963:457). There is as yet no archaeological or other evidence concerning the antiquity of the domestication of the Guinea-fowl in sub-Saharan Africa.

It is one thing to trace the course of a change from food collecting to food producing in sub-Saharan Africa, it is another to speculate on how and why the change took place. Gatherers of wild food are well aware that if you stick a seed in the ground it will grow into a plant - but what is the point of doing that if there are abundant supplies grown for you by nature? Why go to all the hard work and anxiety involved if you do not have to? In our agriculture-oriented economies we take it for granted that food production is 'a better thing' than food collecting because we have never experienced a life in which the wild resources of nature provide us with enough food and give us leisure to spare. What compulsion, then, made people undertake such a revolution in their way of life?

For a long time the commonly accepted mechanism was that of diffusion, which can either be in the form of an actual movement of people or in the form of one group learning a practice from a neighbouring one and in turn passing it on to their neighbours. The only possible source for a diffusion of agriculture into sub-Saharan Africa (before the introduction of Asian Crops from southern Asia less than two thousand years ago) is Egypt and the Nile valley, where wheat and barley were grown by means of irrigation, and whence they reached Ethiopia and the Kingdom of Meroe. But further south and west the practice of wheat and barley growing did not spread, chiefly for ecological reasons, since the 'summer rainfall' area is unsuitable for these crops. One possibility is that attempts were made to grow them, but they became supplanted by weeds - local grasses which were then domesticated (Darlington 1969:68-9); however, tropical weeds in fields of wheat and barley, which must be grown in the cool season, are regarded as unlikely (Harlan 1971a).

Since the domesticated animals did spread into sub-Saharan Africa by a process of diffusion, it is tempting to think that African cereal agriculture owes something to the same process. It may indeed, in the form of 'stimulus diffusion', but in the absence of evidence for the actual movement and spread of agriculturalists, it still requires some compelling reason to make people undertake the domestication of their own local grasses. The key to this may lie in a combination of a pre-agricultural way of life that was sedentary or semi-sedentary, and a change in climate. We are accustomed to thinking of the advent of agriculture putting an end to a nomadic existence and making sedentism possible - but in sub-Saharan Africa it may have been the other way round. We have seen how fishing was an important activity in the Late Stone Age in the southern Sahara and the sahel (p.83 above); this zone stretches across Africa from the Atlantic to Ethiopia and Uganda, and has recently been termed, perhaps rather grandiloquently, 'the Aquatic Civilization of Middle Africa' (Sutton 1974) (fig. 35). Now this is just the zone where the African cereals were domesticated. It may be that people in this zone had become accustomed to a sedentary or semi-sedentary way of life because of their need to stay by the waters where they fished and which provided them with a reliable diet, with abundant stands of wild grasses also within easy reach to provide them with grain. When

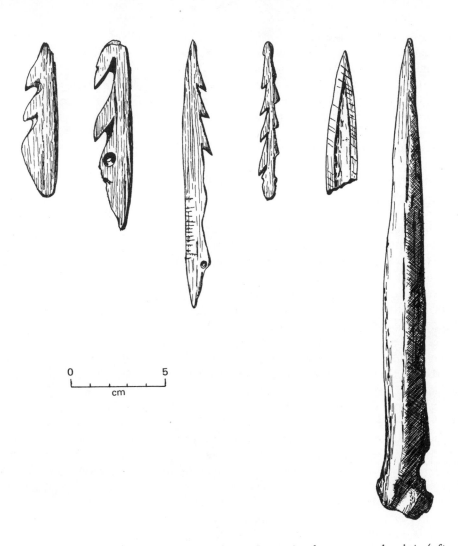

Figure 34. Southern Sahara. Types of Late Stone Age harpoons and points *(after Camps-Fabrer).*

Figure 35. Areas of domestication of principal African cereals in relation to the area of 'Middle African Aquatic Civilization'; distribution of bone harpoons and wavy-line pottery within broken line *(based on Harlan 1971b, fig. 5, and Sutton, map 1).*

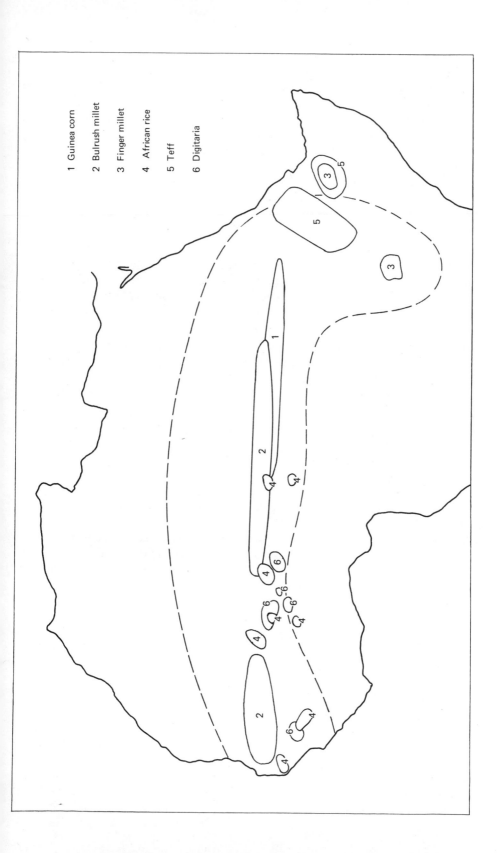

1 Guinea corn
2 Bulrush millet
3 Finger millet
4 African rice
5 Teff
6 Digitaria

aridification set in, it may have dried up some of the smaller lakes and concentrated fishing on the remainder and on permanent rivers; the resultant overfishing would further reduce the available fish supplies. This might tend to make the collecting of wild grains take a more important part in subsistence activities - but at the same time, aridification might have made the wild grasses scarcer and further to seek. The combination of these circumstances would be a strong stimulus to make these grasses grow artificially near at hand, close to the areas where fish were still available. With continuing desiccation, increasing reliance would be placed on grown sources of food.

What was the origin of the 'yam and oil palm agriculture' of the more southerly parts of the eastern half of West Africa? It has been suggested that it resulted from the stimulus of cereal cultivators to the north and only came about when 'the idea of agriculture' reached these southern areas (Morgan 1962:238; Alexander and Coursey 1969:421). However, it could have been an entirely independent development, perhaps even resulting in the domestication of some cereals as a result of their growing as weeds in yam patches. The natural habitat of both oil palms and yams is not in the rain forest but along forest margins, in forest/savannas mosaic, in gallery forests, beside streams and in forest clearings. The yam is a vine, adapted by its evolution to a severe dry season, but needing something to climb up; therefore it is suited neither to grassland savanna nor to high forest. Similarly the oil palm needs plenty of moisture at its roots but cannot propagate itself unless it receives adequate sunshine, which it would not do underneath a high rain forest canopy. One can then imagine that these foods were an important source of nourishment for our Late Stone Age hunters in the southern savannas, taking advantage of living in an ecozone where they would obtain food resources from both savanna and forest. Perhaps the pressure of population or competition for the available game resources of the savanna became such that some groups, accustomed to foraging into the forest anyway, were forced to penetrate it further and further south. We are probably wrong in thinking of the forest as completely unbroken, as elephants may have been responsible for causing clearings (Kortlandt 1972:18, 19). A process could have begun in which yams were not merely grubbed up on sight but marked down for future use, and it is a characteristic of the yam that it can regenerate after the removal of the tuber if too much damage is not done to the vine and roots; throwing away yam-heads at recurrently used camp sites could lead to intentional planting (Davies O. 1968b:479). Similarly the nuts of the oil palm would first have been collected when they fell to the foot of the tree, but these would be those left by wild animals; therefore perhaps trees were felled to obtain complete clusters of nuts, but a better solution was certainly found in the invention of the climbing rope. From such care and protection of trees it may be a short step to intentional planting, or the protection of young seedlings growing at the foot of mature trees.

The groups who were first forced to penetrate deeply and permanently into the forest, leaving the environment which was best suited to their previous way of life, subsequently found that yams and oil palms actually grew better in forest clearings in the wetter areas further south, once man had interfered with the natural vegetation to ensure their supply of sunlight; and the same kind of thing applied to oil palms. Perhaps it was the complementary diet thus provided, with protein from fish and bushmeat, especially the giant African snail so prolific in the forest, that helped to produce the high population densities in southern Nigeria.

In a number of areas of the world the adoption of agriculture resulted ultimately in a population build-up which in turn provided the circumstances for urbanization and state formation. This process occurred late south of the Sahara, because the already-domesticated winter rainfall crops of the temperate zone would not easily grow there and time was required for the domestication of suitable wild grasses accustomed to grow in the summer rainfall area, that is, south of the Inter-Tropical Convergence Zone. This Inter-Tropical Convergence is the 'front' between two weather systems, the hot, dry air mass over the Sahara and the equatorial air mass laden with moisture from the Atlantic; this front runs roughly east and west across Africa and moves north and south with the seasons of the year between the Sahara desert and the coast of West Africa. Because of the totally different regime to the south of it, with consequently different vegetation, the Inter-Tropical Convergence Zone is one of the most important geographical 'facts' of Africa and one which has powerfully affected her history in this very matter of the shift of food production. Since all the ancient 'civilisations' arose on the basis of a firmly established agricultural subsistence, the key to the lateness of such developments in sub-Saharan Africa lies not so much in the barrier constituted by the Sahara desert but far more in the barrier constituted by the Inter-Tropical Convergence Zone. The people of sub-Saharan Africa could not, like the fortunate people of Europe, take over the temperate zone crops of wheat and barley, the domestication of which had been pioneered for them by the peoples of south-western Asia. Before there could be the economic basis of food production necessary for the emergence of urban arts and ways of living, crops indigenous to the tropical zones had to be domesticated; and all the evidence from elsewhere indicates that the process of domesticating the potential indigenous crops of an area is a very slow one, to be measured in thousands rather than in hundreds of years. After all, the process took place in the Stone Age. Even after the establishment of a system of food production it may be a long time before population increase leads to the growth of towns and their associated skills. In south-west Asia it took some 5000 years from the beginning of agriculture to the emergence of 'civilization' and state formation; in the Indus valley and in Egypt it took less, but then they were largely or entirely indebted to south-west Asia for their agricultural knowledge and practice. In China there were some 5000 years of development and population increase from the beginnings of food production to the establishment of the Shang Dynasty. In Central America it took 6000 years from the beginning of domestication to the emergence of a single cultural complex (MacNeish 1965:93). South of the Sahara there was not the same length of time available as in south-west Asia or Mesoamerica before the area was overtaken by 'secondary' state formation, following upon the establishment of trading contacts with the Arab world.

In sub-Saharan Africa also there were probably factors of soil composition and human disease to slow down the population increase which usually follows the institution of food production. The most important of these was malaria, which seems to have enormously increased its hold and to have become endemic as a direct result of forest clearance for yam agriculture (Livingstone 1958; Wiesenfeld 1967; Coursey and Alexander 1968). Thus African agriculture provided its own negative feed-back, restraining massive population increase instead of fostering it. Our information about this is largely derived from our knowledge of sickle-cell anaemia, the distribution of which is intimately associated with the distribution of *falciparum* malaria. To give an over-simplified picture, the situation is as follows: if a person has received the sickle-cell gene from both parents he will suffer from anaemia and probably die without producing offspring; if a person has received the sickle-cell gene from one parent only, this will give him a considerable measure of protection against malaria; if a person has received the sickle-cell gene from neither parent, he is much more prone to sickness and death from malaria. Now there are high frequencies for the sickle-cell trait in African populations, the frequency tending to become higher as you go from north to south in West Africa, with the highest figure near the coast; there are also high frequencies in Uganda and in the coastal bulge of East Africa opposite Madagascar (Harrison et al. 1964:237-42). The gene has been able to build up to these high frequencies, in spite of its lethal effect on those receiving it from both parents, because of the added survival chances it gives to those receiving it from only one parent; all populations with a sickle-cell trait frequency greater than 15 per cent live in areas of high endemic malaria. Virgin equatorial forest provides poor breeding grounds for the mosquito *Anopheles gambiae,* the principal malaria vector, as the humus layer of decaying vegetation tends to absorb water and not make pools; such pools as do form are too shaded for *Anopheles gambiae* breeding. When agriculturists make clearings in the forest they inadvertently provide breeding pools for mosquitoes in their open water-holes and domestic rubbish, and the eaves and roofs of thatched huts make ideal dark lurking-places for them during the daytime. Furthermore, farmers provide bigger population groups assembled together, which are always needed to sustain any disease; small hunting bands probably suffered little from malaria. Thus the spread of agriculture was responsible for the spread of malaria. Estimates have been made of the length of time required for the accompanying increase of sickle-cell to build up to the present figures; for north-western Nigeria the figure is at least 1500 years; this is a minimum estimate and the figure could well be higher; the build-up is probably slower in the less humid areas (Wiesenfeld 1967).

The quest 'once undertaken by political philosophers for the origins of the state' may in the last analysis be 'fruitless' (Hopkins 1973:5) but there is a widespread belief that population increase following the food-producing revolution was one of the factors that had something to do with it. It has also been suggested that whether it was population pressure or not which encouraged the application of irrigation to crop-raising and to the development of agriculture in the lowlands and great river valleys, it seems that the big demographic pressures only occurred after this development (Tosi 1973). Now in many parts of Africa, disease may once again have prevented such a development, and the culprit in this case is river-blindness (Onchocerciasis). There have been cases in Africa where people with insufficient food resources have been tempted into fertile riverine areas, only to be decimated by the disease and the remainder forced to leave again after a few years (Hunter 1966). This may have happened many times in the past in Africa.

Trypanosomiasis, or sleeping-sickness, peculiar to sub-Saharan Africa, is another disease which has almost certainly held back the population build-up that might otherwise have resulted and exerted greater pressures towards various cultural developments. *Trypanosoma rhodesiense,* vectored by the savanna-dwelling fly *Glossina morsitans,* is likely to have had hosts in men and antelopes from prehistoric times, but *T.gambiense* is characterized by transmissions in permanent human settlements or at frequented river sites, as the strain needs constant contact between man and the forest-dwelling type of tsetse, *G. palpalis;* agricultural settlement and the exploitation of the forest environment for food are likely have have increased the incidence of the disease (Lambrecht 1964:79). As in the case of river-blindness, there are historically recorded cases of a population moving into a more riverain environment, thus bringing them into contact with *G. palpalis;* this resulted in an epidemic of sleeping-sickness which killed the majority and caused the survivors to flee (Lambrecht 1964:93, quoting Ford 1960).

Trypanosomiasis also affects animals, and animal disease is another factor to be taken into account as well as human disease, especially with regard to domestic animals. The area in Africa virtually devoid of cattle for this reason is 10½ million square kilometres. It has been estimated that if it were not for trypanosomiasis this area could support 125 million head of cattle - which is 11 million more than the 1962 estimate for the total cattle population of Africa. One result of this exclusion of cattle from such a large area of Africa is that the protein intake of the human population in Africa is mostly below 11 kg per head per annum compared with 40-90 kg in Europe (Dipeolu 1974).

Shortage of agricultural land has been put forward as another condition stimulating state formation. According to this view, there has to be a situation where there is no more land available on the borders of population increase to take up the pressure; this results in warfare and the formation of states (Steward 1949; Carneiro 1961; Webb 1968). In north-east Africa, the practice of agriculture was introduced from south-west Asia during the fifth millennium B.C. and its adoption in the fertile annually-inundated valley of the Nile resulted in a population explosion. But once a certain level of saturation was reached in the narrow valley, there was no more arable land available for expansion into the desert on either side. The result was warfare between the different farming communities of Upper and Lower Egypt, leading at the end of the fourth millennium B.C. to the formation of the state of the Pharaohs.

Food production techniques were not introduced to India from the Iranian Plateau until the end of the fourth millennium B.C., but their introduction into the Indus valley caused a population expansion similar to that in the Nile valley; and again the inability to expand into the surrounding deserts produced the Harappan civilization in the last quarter of the third millennium B.C. The same kind of thing happened in the Hwang-ho valley in China; here it is controversial whether the idea of agriculture was an import from south-western Asia (Clark, G. 1969:222), whether it was stimulated from south-east Asia (Chang 1970), or whether it was in an indigenous development (Ho 1969). In either case, it led to population pressures creating competition for agricultural land, to endemic warfare, and to state formation (Webb 1968:2, 4).

The practice of agriculture and stock-raising spread north-westwards across Europe from the area of Asia Minor a good deal earlier than it spread into India from the more easterly end of the nuclear area - but this did not result in any 'civilizations' comparable to the Harappan, because there was no land shortage. There were wide expanses of land suitable for farming which were able to take up the population increase following from the improved method of providing food, resulting in widespread peasant cultures, instead of narrowly confined 'civilizations'. The same kind of thing happened in sub-Saharan Africa, where the savannas, and forests too, provided vast areas of potential agricultural land.

In spite of these circumstances in sub-Saharan Africa - of human and animal disease on the one hand and of land abundance on the other - a sufficient agricultural basis had been established by the first millennium A.D. to support such ancient kingdoms as Ghana, Mali, Songhai, Kanem/Bornu, the Hausa States, Benin and Ife Oyo. Whereas in Africa south of the equator the San (Bushmen), the Hadza and the Pygmies have retained their hunting-gathering way of life up to today sometimes in conflict with pastoralists and agriculturists, sometimes in symbiosis with them, in West Africa the change to food production as the major basis of subsistence has become practically universal.

REFERENCES

Addison, Frank, 1949, *Jebel Moya.*
Ajayi, S.S., 1971. 'Wild life as a source of protein in Nigeria'. *Nigerian Field, 36(3),* 115-27.
Alexander, John and Coursey, D.G., 1969. 'The origins of yam cultivation', in Ucko and Dimbleby 1969, 405-25.
Alimen, H., 1957. *The prehistory of Africa* (trans. A.H. Broderick).
Allchin, F.R., 1969. 'Early cultivated plants in India and Pakistan', in Ucko and Dimbleby, 1969, 323-9.
Allchin, F.R., 1974. Personal communication.
Amblard-Rambert, A., 1959. 'Trouvaille de "quartiers d'orange" à Gangaber (Cercle de Gao, Soudan)', *Notes africaines* (Dakar), *811,* 1-2.
Anderson, E., 1960 'The evolution of domestication', in *Evolution after Darwin,* ed. Sol Tax (Chicago), 2,323-9.
Arkell, A.J., 1953. *Shaheinab.*
Arkell, A.J., 1971. Comment on G.A. Wright, 'Origins of food production in southwestern Asia: a survey of ideas', *Curr, Anthrop., 12,* 471-2.
Armstrong, Robert G., 1964. *The study of West African languages* (Ibadan).
Atherton, J.H., 1972. 'Excavations at Kamabai and Yagala Rock Shelters, Sierra Leone', *W.Afr.J.Archaeol., 2,* 39.74.
Baker, H.G., 1962. 'Comments on the thesis that there was a major centre of plant domestication near the headwaters of the River Niger', *J.Afr.Hist., 3(2),* 229-33.
Baker, H.G., 1971 Commentary on Section III of *Man across the sea,* ed. G.L. Riley, J.C. Kelly, C.W. Pennington and R.L. Rands (Austin and London), 428-44.
Balout, L., 1965 'Comment on Arkell and Ucko's "Review of predynastic development in the Nile valley" ', *Curr, Anthrop, 6(2),* 156.
Beek, Gus W. Van, 1969. *Hajir bin-Humeid* (Baltimore).
Bishop, W.W. and Clark J.D., 1967. *Background to evolution in Africa* (Chicago).
Bourlière, F., 1964. 'Observations on the ecology of some large African mammals', in *African ecology and human evolution,* ed. Clark Howell and François Bourlière, 43-54.
Bowyer, John R.F., 1973. 'Seronera: excavations at a Stone Bowl site in the Serengeti National Park, Tanzania', *Azania, 8,* 71-104.
Brentjes, B., 1965. *Die Laustierwerdung in Orient* (Wittenburg-Lutherstadt).
Burkill, I.H., 1935. *A dictionary of economic products of the Malay peninsula.*
Busson, F., 1965. *Plantes alimentaires de l'Ouest africain* (Marseilles).
Butzer, Karl W., 1965. 'Comment on "Review of predynastic development in the Nile Valley" ', *Curr, Anthrop., 6(2),* 157-8.
Butzer, Karl W., 1971. *Environment and archaeology* 2nd edn, (Chicago).
Camps, Gabriel, 1969. *Amekni. Néolithique ancien du Hoggar.* Mém C.R.A.P.E., 10 (Paris).
Camps, Gabriel, 1974. *Les civilisations préhistoriques de l'Afrique du Nord et du Sahara* (Paris).
Camps-Fabrer, H., 1967. 'Typologie de l'industrie osseuse en Afrique du Nord et au Sahara', Sixième Congrès Panafricain de Préhistoire (Paris), 179-83.
Carneiro, Robert L., 1961. 'Slash and burn cultivation among the Kuikuru and its implications for cultural development in the Amazon basin, in *The evolution of horticultural systems in native South America: causes and consequences,* ed. Johannes Wilbert (Caracas), 46-68.
Carter, P.L., 1972. 'African cattle: a case study'. Communication to the Linnaean Society, 16 November.
Carter, P.L. and Flight, Colin, 1972. 'A report on the fauna from the sites of Ntereso and Kintampo Rock Shelter 6 in Ghana: with evidence for the practice of animal husbandry during the second millennium B.C.', *Man, 7(2),* 277-82.
Caton-Thompson, Gertrude and Gardner, E.W., 1934. *The Desert Fayum,* 2 vols.
Chang, Kwang-Chin, 1970. 'The beginnings of agriculture in the Far East', *Antiquity 44,* 175-85.

Chevalier, A., 1938. 'Le Sahara, centre d'origine de plantes cultivées', *Mémoires de la Société de Biogéographie,* 6, 307-22.

Chevalier, A., 1949. 'L'origine des plantes cultivées dans l'Afrique du Nord et du Sahara, *Travaux botaniques didiés à René Maire* (Paris), 51-6.

Chowdhury, K.A. and Buth, G.M., 1970 '4500 year old seeds suggest that true cotton is indigenous to Nubia', *Nature,* 227, 85-6.

Clark, Grahame, 1969. *World Prehistory* (2nd edn).

Clark, J.D., 1967. 'The problem of Neolithic culture in sub-Saharan Africa', in *Background to Evolution in Africa,* ed. W.W. Bishop and J.D. Clark (Chicago), 601-27.

Clark, J.D., 1971a. 'An archaeological survey of Northern Air and Tenere', *Geogr.J., 137(4),* 445-7.

Clark, J.D., 1971b. 'Evidence for agricultural origins in the Nile valley', *Proc.Prehist. Soc.,* 37(2). 34-79;

Clark, J.D., 1973. Personal communication.

Cohen, Mark, 1970. 'A reassessment of the Stone Bowl culture of the Rift Valley, Kenya', *Azania,* 5, 27-38.

Connah, Graham, 1964-66. *Northern History Research Scheme - Second Interim Report,* Zaria.

Connah, Graham, 1967. Progress report on archaeological work in Bornu.

Connah, Graham, 1971. 'Recent contributions to Bornu chronology', *W.Afr.J. Archaeol, 1,* 55-60.

Connah, Graham, 1976. 'The Daima sequence and the prehistoric chronology of the Lake Chad region of Nigeria', *J.Afr.Hist.,* 17, 31.

Coon, Carleton S., 1968. *Yengema Cave Report* (Philadelphia).

Corbeil, R., 1951. 'L'industrie lithique et microlithique au Soudan français (Cercle de Bamako)', *Conference report, Première Conference Internationale d'Africanistes de l'Ouest (Dakar, 1945),* 2, 391-2.

Coursey, D.G., 1967. *Yams.*

Coursey, D.G., 1971. 'The new yam festivals of West Africa', *Anthropos, 66,* 44-84.

Coursey, D.G., 1972. 'The origins and domestication of yams in Africa'. Paper prepared for Burg Warterstein Symposium No.56 on the origin of African plant domesticates. (duplicated).

Coursey, D.G. and Alexander, J., 1968. 'African agricultural patterns and the sickle cell', *Science,* 160, 1474-5.

Creac'h, Paul, 1951. 'Sur quelques nouveaux sites et nouveaux industries pré-historiques d'Afrique occidentale française (note préliminaire)', *Conference report, Première Conférence Internationale d'Africanistes de l'Ouest (Dakar, 1945),* 2, 397-430.

Curson, H.H. and Thornton, R.W., 1936. 'A contribution to the study of African cattle', *Onderstepoort Journal of Veterinary Science, 7(2)* (Pretoria).

Dalziel, J.M., 1955. *The useful plants of West Tropical Africa* (2nd reprint).

Darlington, C.D., 1969. 'The silent millennia in the origin of agriculture', Ucko and Dimbleby 1969, 67-72.

Davies, Nina M., 1940. 'Some notes on the N.H. bird', *Journal of Egyptian Archaeology,* 26, 79-81.

Davies, Oliver, 1964. *The Quaternary in the coastlands of Guinea.*

Davies, Oliver, 1966. 'The Invasion of Ghana from the Sahara in the Early Iron Age', *Actas del V Congreso Panafricáno de Preistoria y de Estudío del Cuaternario* (Santa Cruz de Tenerife).

Davies, Oliver, 1968a. 'Mesoneolithic excavations at Legon and New Todzi', *Bull. Inst.Franc.Afr.Noire,* 30, 1147-94.

Davies, Oliver, 1968b. The origins of agriculture in West Africa', *Curr, Anthrop., 9(s),* 479-82.

Davies, Oliver, 1973. 'Excavations at Ntereso, Gonja, Northern Ghana, Final Report' (duplicated).

De Candolle, A., 1886. *Origin of cultivated plants* (2nd ed, 1959).

Deacon, H.J. and Deacon, Janette, 1963. 'Scott's Cave: a Late Stone Age site in the Gamtoos Valley', *Annals Cape Provincial Mus.III*, (Grahamstown), 96-121.

Delcroix, R. and Vaufrey, R., 1939. 'Le Toumbien de Guinée Française, *L'Anthropologie, 49*, 265-312.

Desplagnes, L., 1907. 'L'archéologie préhistorique en Guinée Francaise', *Bulletin de la Société de Géographie Commerciale* (Bordeaux).

De Wet, J.M.J. and Huckaby, P., 1967. 'The origin of *Sorghum bicolor;* distribution and domestication,' *Evolution*, 21(4), 787-802.

Dipeolu, O.O., 1974. Personal communication. (Lecturer, Department of Veterinary Pathology, University of Ibadan).

Doggett, H., 1965. 'The development of cultivated sorghums', in *Essays on crop plant evolution*, ed. Joseph Hutchinson, 50-69.

Doggett, H., 1970. *Sorghum.*

Drake, St Clair, 1959. 'The responsibility of men of culture for destroying the "Hamitic myth" ', *Présence africaine*, 24-5, 228-43.

Ehret, Christopher, 1967. 'Cattle-keeping and milking in eastern and southern African history: the linguistic evidence', *J.Afr.Hist.*, 8, 1-17.

Eyo, Ekpo, 1972. 'Rop rock shelter excavations 1964', *W.Afr.J.Archaeol.*, 2, 13-16.

Fagan, Brian, 1965. *Southern Africa.*

Fagan, Brian, 1966. 'Radiocarbon dates for sub-Saharan Africa IV, *J.Afri.Hist.*, 7, 495-506.

Fagan, Brian, 1967. *Iron Age Cultures in Zambia I*, London.

Fagan, Brian M. and Van Noten, Francis L., 1966. 'Wooden implements from Late, Stone Age sites at Gwisho Hot Springs, Lochinvar, Zambia', *Proc. Prehist.Soc.*, 32, 241-61.

Fagg, Angela, 1972. 'Pottery from the Rop rock shelter excavations of 1944 and 1964', *W.Afri.J.Archaeol.*, 2, 29-38.

Fagg, Bernard, 1944. 'Preliminary report on a microlithic industry at Rop rock shelter, Northern Nigeria', *Proc.Prehist.Soc.*, 10, 68-9.

Fagg, Bernard, 1972. 'Rop rock shelter excavations 1944', *W.Afr.J.Archaeol.*, 2, 13-16.

Faris, D.G., 1963. 'Evidence for the West African origin of *Vigna sinensis* (L) Savi' (Ph.D. thesis, University of California).

Filipowiak, M., Jasnosz, S. and Wolagiewicz, R., 1968. 'Polsbogwinejskie badarai archaeologiczne w Niani, w 1968r' (Les recherches archéologiques pologuinéennes à Niani en 1968), *Materiarty Zachodniopomorski*, 14, 578-648.

Flight, Colin, 1968. 'Kintampo 1968', *W.Afr.Archaeol.Newsl.*, 8, 15-19.

Flight, Colin, 1970. 'Excavations at Kintampo', *W.Afr.Archaeol.Newsl.*, 12, 71-3.

Ford, J., 1960. 'Distribution of African cattle', *Proceedings of the 1st Scientific Congress* (Salisbury, Rhodesia), 357-65.

Forde, C. Daryll, 1963. *Habitat, economy and society.*

Fouche, Leo, 1937. *Mapungubwe.* Vol.I (Cambridge).

Gabel, Creighton, 1974. *Boston University Archaeological Survey in Liberia.* Report submitted to the U.S. Educational and Cultural Foundation in Liberia (Duplicated).

Gardner, Guy A., 1963. *Mapungubwe.* Vol.II (Pretoria).

Gray, Richard, 1962. 'A report on the conference: third conference on African history and archaeology', *J.Afr.Hist.*, 3(2), 175-91.

Grove, A.T., 1970. *Africa South of the Sahara.*

Guébhard, P., 1907. 'Trois abris sous roche fouillés dans le Fouta - Djallon', *Bulletin de Géographic Historique et Descriptive 3*, 408-20.

Guillot, R. and Descamps, C., 1969. 'Nouvelles découvertes préhistoriques à Tiémassas (Sénégal), *Bull.Inst.Franc.Afr.Noire, 31* sér. B, 602-37.

Hamy, E.T., 1900. 'La grotte de Kakimbon à Rotoma près Konakry', *Conference report, Congrès Internationale d'Anthropologie et d'Archéologie Préhistorique*, 12.

Harlan, Jack R., 1971a. Personal communication.

Harlan, Jack R., 1971b. 'Agricultural origins: centers and noncenters', *Science*, 174, 468-74.

Harlan, Jack R., 1975. Personal communication.

Harlan, Jack R. and De Wet, J.M.J., 1973. 'On the quality of evidence for the origin and dispersal of cultivated plants', *Curr, Anthrop.*, 14 (1-2), 51-5.

Harlan, Jack and Stemler, Ann, 1972. 'The races of sorghum in `Africa'. Paper prepared for Burg Wartenstein Symposium 56 on the origin of African plant domesticates. (Duplicated).

Harrison, G.A., Weiner, J.S., Tanner, J.M. and Barnicot, N.A., 1964. *Human Biology.*

Hartle, D.D., 1966. 'Archaeology in Eastern Nigeria', *W.Afr.Archaeol.Newsl.*, 5, 13-17.

Hartle, D.D., 1968. 'Radiocarbon dates', *W.Afr.Archaeol.Newsl.*, 9, 73.

Hemardinquer, Jean-Jacques, Keul, Michael and Randles, W.G.L., 1967. *Sorgho. Documentation géographique et historique* (Paris).

Higgs, E.S., 1967a. 'Early domesticated animals in Libya', in Bishop and Clark 1967, 165-73.

Higgs, E.S., 1967b. 'Domestic animals', in McBurney 1967, 313-19.

Higgs, E.S. and Jarman, M.R., 1969. 'The origins of agriculture: a reconsideration', *Antiquity*, 43, 31-41.

Hill, Desmond, 1974. Review of Epstein's 'The origin of domestic animals in Africa', *W.Afr.J.Archaeol.*, 4, 189-98.

Ho, P.T., 1969. 'The Loess and the origin of Chinese agriculture', *American Historical Review*, 75, 1-36.

Holas, B., 1950. 'Notes préliminaires sur les fouilles de la grotte de Blandè', *Bull.Inst. Franc.Afr.Noire*, 12, 999-1006.

Holas, B., 1952. 'Note complémentaire sur l'abri sous roche de Blandè', *Bull.Inst., Franc.Afr.Noire*, 14, 1341-52.

Holas, B. and Mauny, R., 1953. 'Nouvelles fouilles à l'abri sous roche de Blandè (Guinée)', *Bull.Inst.Franc.Afr.Noire*, 15, 1605-17.

Hopkins, A.G., 1973. *An economic history of West Africa.*

Hubert, R., 1922, 'Objets anciens de l'Afrique occidentale', *Bulletin du Comité des Etudes Historiques et Scientifiques d'Afrique de l'Ouest Française*, 5, 382-99.

Hue, E., 1912. 'L'âge de la pierre à Fouta Djallon', *Bulletin de la Société Préhistorique Française*, 2.

Hugot, H.J., 1963. *Recherches préhistoriques dans l'Ahaggar Nordoccidentale 1950-1957.* Mem. C.R.A.P.E. I (Paris).

Hunter, J.M., 1966. 'River blindness in Nangodi, Northern Ghana', *Geographical Review*, 56, 398-416.

Inskeep, R.R., 1969. 'The archaeological background', in *The Oxford History of South Africa*, ed. Monica Wilson and Leonard Thompson, 1-39.

Jarman, M.R., 1969. 'The prehistory of Upper Pleistocene and Recent Cattle. Part I', *Proc.Prehist.Soc.*, 35, 236-66.

Joire, J., 1947. 'Amas de coquillages du littoral sénégalais dans le banlieu de Saint Louis', *Bull.Inst.Franc.Afr.Noire*, 9, 170-350.

Keimer, Ludwig, 1938. 'Sur l'identification de l'hieroglyphe N.H.', *Annales de la Service des Antiquités d'Egypte*, 38, 253-63.

Kennedy, R.A., 1960. 'Necked and lugged axes in Nigeria', *Antiquity*, 34, 54-8.

Kennedy-O'Byrne, J., 1957. 'Notes on African grasses - a new species of *Eleusine* from Tropical and South Africa', *Kew Bulletin*, 11, 65-72.

Kortlandt, Adriaan, 1972. *New perspectives on ape and human evolution* (Amsterdam).

Lambrecht, Frank L., 1964. 'Aspects of evolution and ecology of tsetse flies and trypanosomiasis in prehistoric African environment', *J.Afr.Hist.*, 5 (1), 1-24.

Lebeuf, A.M.D., 1969. *Les principautés Kotokos* (Paris).

Livingstone, Frank B., 1958. 'Anthropological implications of sickle cell gene distribution in West Africa', *American Anthropologist*, 60(3), 533-62.

McBurney, C.B.M., 1967. *Haua Fteah.*

MacNeish, R.S., 1965. 'The origin of American agriculture', *Antiquity*, 39, 87-94.

Marshall, J., 1931. *Mohenjo-Daro and the Indus Valley civilisation.*

Martin del Molino, A., 1965. 'Secuencia cultural en el Neolitico de Fernando Poo',

Trabajos de Preistoria del Seminario de Historia Primitiva del Hombre del Universidad de Madrid.

Mateus, A.De M., 1952. 'Nota preliminar Acerca da Estacao Prehistórica de Nhampasseré', *Conference Internationale d'Africanistes, Bissau, 1947,* 4 (Lisbon), 375-86.

Mauny, R., 1949. 'Etat actuel de nos connaissances sur la préhistoire de la colonie du Niger', *Bull Inst.Franc.Afr.Noire,* 11(1-2), 141-58.

Mauny, R., 1957. 'Buttes artificielles de coquillages de Joal-Fadioute', *Notes Africaines,* 7(75), 73-8.

Mauny, R., 1961. *Tableau géographique de l'Ouest africain au Moyen Age* (Dakar).

Mauny, R., 1967. 'L'Afrique et les origines de la domestication', in Bishop and Clark, 1967, 583-99.

Mauny, R., 1973. 'Datation au carbone 14, d'amas de coquillages des lagunes de Basse Côte d'Ivoire', *W.Afr.J.Archaeol.,* 3, 207-14.

Mehra, K.L., 1962. 'Natural hybridization between *Eleusine coracana* and *E.africana* in Uganda', *Journal of the Indian Botanical Society,* 41, 531-9.

Mehra, K.L., 1963a. 'Considerations on the African origin of *Eleusine coracana* (L) Gaertner', *Current Science,* 7. 300-1.

Mehra, K.L., 1963b. 'Differentiation of the cultivated and wild *Eleusine* species', *Phyton,* 20(2), 189-98.

Miège, J., 1948. 'Le Dioscorea esculenta Burkill en Côte d'Ivoire', *Revue Internationale de Botanique Appliquée et Agriculture Tropicale 28 (313, 314),* 144-55.

Morgan, W.B., 1962. 'The forest and agriculture in West Africa', *J.Afr.Hist.,* 3(2), 235-9.

Mori, F., 1965. *Tadrart Acacus: arte rupestre e culture del Sahara preistorico* (Turin).

Munson, Patrick J., 1968. 'Recent archaeological research in the Dhar Tichitt region of south-central Mauretania', *W.Afr.Archaeol.Newsl.* 10, 6-13.

Munson, Patrick J., 1970. 'Correction and additional comments concerning the Tichitt tradition', *W.Afr.Archaeol.Newsl.,* 12, 47-8.

Munson, Patrick J., 1971. 'The Tichitt tradition: a late prehistoric occupation of the southwestern Sahara' (unpublished Ph.D. thesis, University of Illinois).

Murdock, G.P., 1959. *Africa: its peoples and their culture history* (New York).

Nicholson, B.E., 1971. *The Oxford Book of Food Plants.*

Nunoo, R.B., 1948. 'A report on excavations at Nsuta Hill, Gold Coast', *Man,* 48, 72-6.

Odner, Knut, 1972. Excavations at Narosura, a Stone Bowl site in the southern Kenya Highlands, *Azania,* 7, 25-92.

Parkington, John, 1974. 'Relationships between farmers, pastoralists and hunter-gatherers in sub-Sahara Africa'. Paper presented to meeting of Africanist archaeologists, Cambridge, 16 December.

Parkington, J. and Poggenpoel, C.,1971. 'Excavations at De Hangen 1968', *South African Archaeological Bulletin,* 26, 3-36.

Payne, W.J.A., 1964. 'The origin of domestic cattle in Africa', *Empire Journal of Experimental Agriculture,* 32(126), 97-113.

Phillipson, D.W., 1968. 'The early Iron Age site of Kapwirimbwe, Lusaka', *Azania,* 3, 87-105.

Phillipson, D.W., 1970a. 'Notes on the late prehistoric radiocarbon chronology of eastern southern Africa', *J.Afr.Hist.,* 11(1), 1-5.

Phillipson, D.W., 1970b. 'Excavations at Twickenham Road, Lusaka', *Azania,* 5, 77-118.

Phillipson, D.W., 1975. 'The chronology of the Iron Age in Bantu Africa', *J.Afr.Hist.,* 16(3), 321-43.

Phillipson, D.W., 1976. Personal Communication.

Portères, Roland, 1951. '*Eleusine coracana* Gaertner', *Bull.Inst.Franc.Afr.Noire,* 13, 1-78.

Portères, Roland, 1962. 'Berceaux agricoles primaires sur le continent africain', *J.Afr.Hist.,* 3, 195-210.

Portères, Roland, 1972. Papers prepared for Burg Wartenstein Symposium 56 on the origin of African plant domesticates (Duplicated).

Posener, G., Saulneron, S., and Yoyotte, J., 1959. *Dictionnaire de la civilisation Egyptienne* (Paris).

Posnansky, Merrick, 1968. 'Bantu genesis: archaeological reflections', *J.Afr.Hist.*, 9(1), 1-11.

Posnansky, Merrick, 1969. 'Yams and the origins of West African agriculture', *Odu*, 1, 101-7.

Purseglove, J.W., 1972. 'The origins and migrations of crops in tropical Africa'. Paper prepared for Burg Wartenstein Symposium 56 on the origin of African plant domesticates. (Duplicated).

Reed, Charles, 1960. 'A review of the archaeological evidence on animal domestication in the prehistoric Near East', in *Prehistoric investigations in Iraqui Kurdestan*, ed. J. Braidwood and Bruce Howe (Chicago), 119-45.

Reed, Charles, 1969. 'The pattern of animal domestication in the prehistoric Near East', in Ucko and Dimbleby, 1969, 361-80.

Renfrew, Colin (ed.), 1973. *The explanation of culture change.*

Robinson, K.R., 1961. 'An early Iron Age site from the Chibi District, Southern Rhodesia', *South African Archaeological Bulletin*, 16, 75-102.

Robinson, K.R., 1966. 'A preliminary report on the archaeology of Ngonde, northern Malawi', *J.Afr.Hist.*, 7(2), 169-88.

Robinson, K.R., 1970. *The Iron Age of the southern lake area of Malawi* (Publication 8, Dept of Antiquities, Malawi).

Rosenfeld, Andree, 1972. 'The microlithic industries of Rop Rock Shelter', *W.Afr.J.Archaeol.*, 2, 17-28.

Roubet, C., 1971. 'Sur la definition de la chronologie Néolithique de Tradition Capsienne', *L'Anthropologie*, 75, 553-74.

Sassoon, Hamo, 1967. 'New views on Engaruka, Northern Tanzania', *J.Afr.Hist.*, 7(2), 201-17.

Sassoon, Hamo, 1968. 'Excavations of a burial mound in Ngorongoro Crater', *Tanzania Notes and Records*, 69, 15-32.

Sassoon, Hamo, 1971. 'Excavations at Engaruka, an Iron Age archaeological site in Tanzania', *National Geographical Society Research Reports, 1965 Projects*, 221-30.

Sauer, Carl O., 1952. *Agricultural origins and dispersals* (New York).

Schweitzer, F.R. and Scott, Katharine J., 1973. 'Early occurrence of domestic sheep in sub-Saharan Africa', *Nature*, 241 (5391) 1, 547.

Seddon, David, 1968. 'The origins and development of agriculture in East and Southern Africa', *Curr.Anthrop.*, 9(5), 489-94.

Seligman, C.G., 1930. *Races of Africa.*

Seligman, C.G., 1934. *Egypt and Negro Africa.*

Shack, William A., 1966. *The Gurage. A people of the Ensete culture.*

Shaw, Thurstan, 1944. 'Excavations carried out in the cave known as 'Bosumpra' at Abetifi, Kwahu, Gold Coast Colony', *Proc.Prehist.Soc.*, 10, 1-67.

Shaw, Thurstan, (ed.), 1967. 'Terminology', *W.Afr.Archaeol.Newsl.*, 7, 9-43.

Shaw, Thurstan, 1969. 'The late Stone Age in the Nigerian forest', *Actes Première Colloquuim International d'Archéologie Africaine*, ed. J.P. Lebeuf (For Lamy), 364-74.

Shaw, Thurstan, 1972. 'Early agriculture in Africa', *J.Hist.Soc.Nigeria*, 6(2), 143-191.

Shaw, Thurstan, 1973. 'Finds at the Iwo Eleru rock shelter, Western Nigeria', *Actes VI Congrès Panafricain de Préhistoire et d'Etudes du Quaternaire, Dakar, 1967*, ed. H.J. Hugot, 190-2, 505.

Shinnie, Peter, 1967. *Meroe.*

Simoons, Frederick J., 1965. 'Some questions on the economic prehistory of Ethiopia', *J.Afr.Hist.*, 6(1), 1-12.

Smith, A.B., 1973. 'Domesticated cattle in the Sahara and their introduction into West West Africa. Paper submitted to the IXth International Congress of Anthropology and Ethnography, Chicago.

Smith, A.B., 1974. 'Preliminary report of excavations at Karkarichinkat Mali, 1972', *W.Afr.J.Archaeol.* 4, 33-55.

Smith, A.B., 1975. 'Radiocarbon dates from Bosumpra Cave, Abetifi, Ghana', *Proc. Prehist.Soc.*, 41, 179-82.

Smith, H.S., 1969. 'Animal domestication and animal cult in dynastic Egypt', in Ucko and Dimbleby, 1969, 307-14.

Soper, R.C., 1965. 'The Stone Age in Northern Nigeria', *J.Hist.Soc.Nigeria,* 3(2), 175-94.

Steward, Julian H., 1949. 'Cultural causality and law: trial formulation of the development of early civilisations', *American Anthropologist,* 51, 1-27.

Strabo, 1967. *Geography, Book 17* (trans. H.L. Jones, Loeb edn).

Summers, R., 1958. *Inyanga.*

Sutton, John, 1974. 'The aquatic civilisation of Middle Africa', *J.Afr.Hist.,* 15(4), 527-46.

Szumowski, G., 1956. 'Fouilles de l'abri sous roche de Kourounkorokale', *Bull.Inst. Franc.Afr.Noire,* 18 sér. B, 462-508.

Tosi, Maurizio, 1973. 'Early urban evolution and settlement patterns in the Indo-Iranian borderland', in Renfrew, 1972, 429-46.

Ucko, Peter J. and Dimbleby, G.M., (eds), 1969. *The domestication and exploitation of plants and animals.*

Vaufrey, R., 1946. 'Le Néolithique de tradition capsienne au Sénégal', *Rivista di Scienze prehistoriche,* 1.

Vavilov, H., 1951. 'The origin, variation, immunity and breeding of cultivated plants', *Chronique de Botanie,* 131, 1-364.

Vishnu-Mittre, 1968. 'Prehistoric records of agriculture in India', *Transactions of the Bose Research Institute,* 31(3), 87-106.

Vogel, Joseph O., 1969. 'On evidence of early agriculture in southern Zambia', *Curr. Anthrop.,* 10(5), 524.

Vogel, Joseph O., 1971. Personal communication.

Wai-Ogosu, Bassey, 1973. 'Archaeological reconnaissance of Upper Volta' (unpublished Ph.D. thesis, University of California, Berkeley).

Webb, M.C., 1968. 'Carneiro's hypothesis of limited land resources and the origins of the state: a Latin Americanist's approach to an old problem', *South Eastern Latin Americanist,* 12(3), 1-8.

Wendorf, F., 1971. Personal communication.

Wendorf, F., Said, R. and Schild, R., 1970. 'Egyptian prehistory: some new concepts', *Science,* 169, 1161-71.

Werth, E., 1937. 'Zur geographie und geschichte der hirsen', *Angewandt Botanik,* 19, 42-88.

Wiesenfeld, E.L., 1967. 'Sickle cell trait in human biological and cultural evolution', *Science,* 157, 1134-40.

Willett, Frank, 1962. 'The microlithic industry from Old Oyo, Western Nigeria', *Actes IV Congrès Panàfricain de Préhistoire et d'Etudes du Quaternaire, Léopoldville, 1959,* 2, 261-72.

York, R.N., 1974. 'Excavations at Dutsen Kongba near Jos, Nigeria (Preliminary notice)', *Nyarre Akuma,* 4, 17-20.

Zeuner, F.E., 1963. *A history of domesticated animals.*

BRIDGET ALLCHIN

6 Hunters, pastoralists and early agriculturalists in South Asia

South Asia is the term used today for what used to be called India, or Greater India: the great triangular peninsula to the south of the Himalayas and the Hindu Kush. Today it includes a number of national entities, India, Pakistan, Nepal, Sri Lanka, etc., but retains a very strong overall cultural identity comparable to that of Europe, China or South-East Asia. Bounded on the north-west and north-east by two of the highest mountain ranges in the world, and on the south-west and south-east by the ocean, South Asia is an exceptionally clearly defined major geographical region. The term Indian sub-continent is apt as it suggests both internal diversity and over-riding unity; also because the name India - deriving through Greek from the Sanskrit *Sindhu* and Persian *Hindush,* names of the Indus river and its valley - no longer applies to the Indus region, now almost entirely in Pakistan.

As well as being a well-defined entity, the Indian sub-continent is a meeting-ground of Western Asiatic conditions and peoples on the one hand, and those of South-East Asia on the other. The desert and semi-desert environment of so much of Western and Central Asia - the environment in which oases and great rivers play such an important part in human life and cultural development, and in which man appears to have made his first ventures into urban life - extends across the north-western mountain wall into Pakistan and West India. Thus the Thar desert is an extension of the Saharan-Persian-Arabian desert belt, and shows many of its characteristics. It is dissected by the narrow fertile corridor of the Indus, as the Egyptian desert is dissected by the Nile, and the Mesopotamian desert by the Tigris-Euphrates.

Arid conditions extend eastward to the Aravalli hills, one of the major geographical and cultural divides within the sub-continent. Its north-eastern corner, Bengal, Assam, and Bhutan, presents a complete contrast climatically, and forms a link with the South-East Asian region of high rainfall and tropical forest, and with South China, with which it is the main corridor of cultural contact, a tortuous corridor, due to the density of the forests, and the many mountain ranges which cut across it running from north to south. High rainfall, mountains and forests extend sporadically down the eastern wall of the Indian peninsula plateau - the Eastern Ghats - and up the western coastal plain and Western Ghats as far as Bombay. A corridor of low rainfall extends from the main western Dry Zone down the western side of the peninsula plateau (fig. 36). Thus the two regions of low and high rainfall respectively interdigitate in South Asia.

The internal diversity of the sub-continent, geographical, ethnic, and cultural in every sense of the term, is immense, as all readers of Kipling must be aware. The environments it provides range from the arid desert of the north-west, with great seasonal and daily variations of temperature, to the tropical rain forest of the extreme east and the south-west coast, and to the high glaciated valleys of the Himalayas. All these regions of extreme conditions are inhabited by peoples whose way of life is adapted to their environment : semi-nomadic herdsmen with camels and goats in the desert margins, growers of rice and coconuts in tropical, coastal regions such as Kerala, and so on (Subbarao, 1958; Spate, 1957).

Between the regions of extreme climate in the west and east lie the vast and fertile alluvial plains of north India, with steadily increasing rainfall as one moves eastward, comprising one of the most densely populated rural areas of the world, parts of which produce four cereal crops per year. Here traditional farming methods are highly sophisticated, and rural society both complex and conservative (Wiser and Wiser 1973). Immediately to the south lies the much less densely populated hill and forest belt of Central India where all kinds of older or more specialized ways of life linger on. Here are communities who traditionally live by hunting and gathering, or by slash-and-burn agriculture, or who maintain other highly individual ways of life in relative isolation from the mainstreams of Indian historical and cultural development. South again are the somewhat less intensively farmed agricultural lands of Maharastra and the southern Deccan, the highly productive Tamil plain, and the tribal peoples who inhabited the wild, forest regions of the Eastern and Western Ghats (Allchin B. 1966). All these tribal peoples of South and Central India, are of great interest to the archaeologist, as are the nomadic herdsmen of the West, who still follow their yearly migrations alike through the arid lands of Rajasthan and the intensely cultivated plains and industrial developments of Gujarat, and still maintain their identity and individuality as communities as they do so (Majumdar 1961) (fig. 37).

Before we look more closely at some of these communities, and consider what light they can shed on the archaeological questions we are considering, we must look briefly at the early prehistory of the sub-continent as a whole. In Lower Palaeolithic times it fell within the hand-axe industry province, comprising most of Europe, western Asia, a small part of south Russia and Central Asia, and the whole of Africa (Bordes 1968). Chopper-chopping tool industries, predominant throughout East and South-East Asia, as discussed elsewhere in this volume appear to a limited extent in certain regions of India rather as they do in Europe. Middle Palaeolithic industries of the arid parts of the sub-continent, west of the Aravalli Hills, have the character of a regional variant of the complex of Mousterian industries extending from the western Mediterranean to the Pamirs. East of the Aravallis their character is somewhat

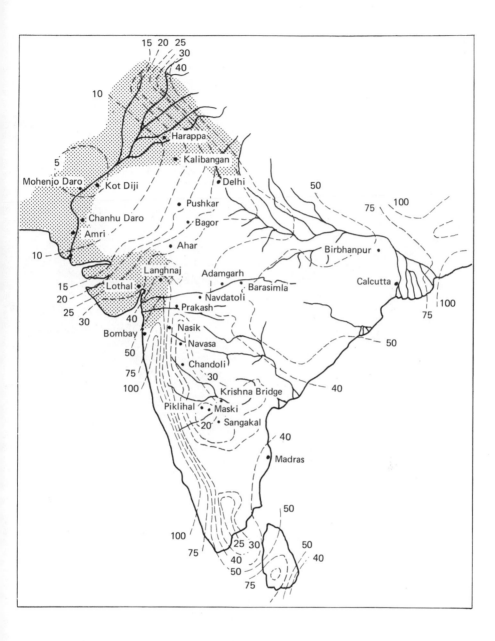

Figure 36. The Indian sub-continent, showing rainfall and principal archaeological sites mentioned in the text. The Harappan area is shaded. Scale: 1cm = c.400km.

Figure 37. Bardwal, Gujarat. These people are nomadic pastoralists. The women and old men move to a new camping place and set up camp and begin cooking the evening meal, and younger men follow more slowly with the flocks and herds, allowing them to graze as they go *(photograph: Bridget Allchin)*.

different. The Mousterian technique of striking flakes and blade-flakes from prepared cores of various kinds still forms the technological basis of the industries, but there are fewer recognizable tool types, such as points, keeled scrapers, burins etc., of traditionally established forms, such as characterize the Mousterian. In this respect, in their antistyle, these industries resemble the chopper-chopping tool industries of East and South-East Asia.

Upper Palaeolithic industries, so far found only in limited regions of South Asia, whenever they occur show clear Western Asiatic affinities (Allchin B., 1973). They appear to be a principal, direct ancestor of the ubiquitous Mesolithic industries which occur in profusion throughout the sub-continent (Allchin B. and Goudie 1974). Another direct ancestor, apparently, especially of the Mesolithic of south India (figs. 38-9) is the prepared core and flake technique of the Middle Palaeolithic, which continues on a reduced scale to be one of the basic methods of microlith making (Allchin B. and F.R. 1968, Ch.4). The extent to which past climates have varied from that of the present, the nature of these variations, their relationship to climatic change elsewhere in the world, and to phases of the Indian Stone Age are beginning to be investigated in the Indian sub-continent, and in the last five years some positive evidence has begun to come to light (Goudie, Allchin B. and Hegde 1973, and Singh, 1971).

The Chalcolithic cities of Pakistan and west India, the Indus valley or Harappan culture and its immediate antecedents, belong essentially to the West Asiatic or fertile crescent urban complex, (Childe, 1956). Its influence extends widely throughout much of the western parts of South Asia, and it is now becoming clear that there are cultural frontiers beyond which more rustic village cultures with their own distinctive characters existed alongside it. Many of these cultures, whether in Himalayan valleys, in the eastern plains, the Deccan or south India co-existed with the pre-Harappan, Harappan and post-Harappan cultures of the west, and in some cases there is evidence of contact, probably trade, between them, (Allchin B and F.R. 1968, Chs.5, 6 and 7). Settlements outside the direct Harappan sphere of influence on both the east and south have strong regional characters. They stem from the cultures of the indigenous peoples of the regions, demonstrated, for example, in south India by the continuity of the stone blade industries of Mesolithic and Neolithic cultures. External stimuli must also have played an important part in their development, as evidenced by cultural traits such as the stone axe types of eastern India, many of which are common to South-East Asia and South China. In more general terms the material culture of the peninsula has affinities both with the east and with the west.

C14 dates ranging back to the 23rd century b.c., so far obtained for the pre-Harappan cultures of the west, and for the southern Neolithic, suggest that they do not extend back in time anything like to so far as either the earliest settlements in Western Asia, or in South-East Asia. It is quite clear, however, that in no region of the Indian sub-continent, west, east or south have settlements which come near to representing the first experiments in agriculture or animal husbandry yet been investigated. Pre-Harappan settlements such as Kalibangan, Kot-Diji and Amri clearly belong to a well established tradition with roots going far back within the region itself. The same may be said of the small number of southern Indian Neolithic settlements excavated, in spite of their more rustic character. Some of the traits such as axe types and pottery found in eastern India have a long antiquity

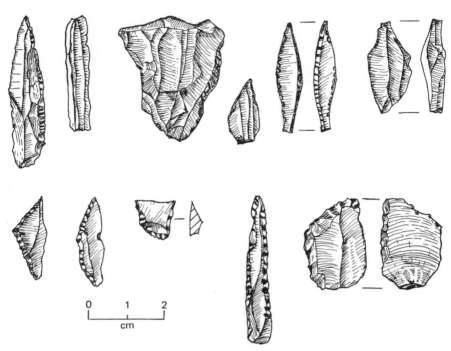

Figure 38. Adamgarh Cave: Mesolithic tools.

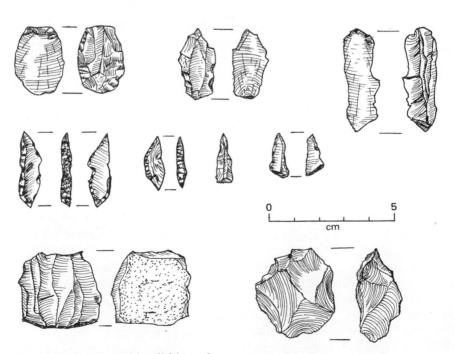

Figure 39. Langhnaj: Mesolithic tools.

further east, but here the picture is in all respects less clear than in the west and south.

What then can we say of the beginnings of agriculture or pastoralism in the Indian sub-continent, and their relationship to a hunting and gathering way of life?

As regards agriculture, Neolithic and Chalcolithic settlements based upon mixed agriculture, including cereal cultivation and animal husbandry, and upon the use of stone tools sometimes augmented by small quantities of copper or bronze have been found in many regions of the sub-continent. Settlements in the Harappan province during the pre-Harappan period show distinct individual and regional differences, particularly in terms of pottery. These differences are minimized during the Harappan period proper (c.2300 to 1600 BC), when ceramics, brick sizes, town planning and many other traits tend to become standardized throughout the province. The province as a whole is characterized by low rainfall, and generally arid conditions, as already indicated, and the settlements are invariably associated with rivers, either snow-fed or rising in regions of higher rainfall, which flow through the arid regions providing water throughout the year, and flooding fairly extensively so as to provide a kind of natural irrigation. The flood waters also bring down large quantities of silt which is deposited on the flooded land and greatly increases its fertility. Thus their economy rests upon the exploitation of a particular, highly specialized type of environment.

Both pre-Harappan and Harappan farmers practised a fairly complex system of agriculture. The main crops were wheat, barley, pulses and cotton, and these were cultivated with the aid of a wooden plough drawn by draught oxen of the type still extensively used in south Asia. They also used two-wheeled ox carts very similar to those of today. Numerous clay models of carts, cattle and other animals have been found in excavations and from these and from the beautiful carved steatite seals we know that both *bos indicus* (humped Indian cattle) and other varieties of cattle were kept, and it appears that dogs, sheep, goats, camels and elephants were also domesticated. Houses were square, the larger built as a series of rooms looking in upon a central courtyard, with no windows in the outside walls. Unbaked mud brick was the principal building material and baked brick was used for important buildings, bathrooms, and drains during the classical Harappan period. The general concept of a settlement was one of a concentrated area of occupation with intersecting streets and lanes between houses or blocks; in the Harappan period proper the plan became a regular grid pattern, and gave way again to irregularities with the collapse of unifying authority. Outstanding features of the culture are its highly sophisticated wheel-thrown pottery (fig. 40), much of it decorated with painted patterns; the stone blade industry utilizing chert often transported over long distances; the highly developed jeweller's craft, combining semi-precious stones and small quantities of gold. A small quantity of copper tools and vessels have been found at Harappan sites but all types of heavy tools, whether of stone, copper or alloys of copper are notable by their absence. The Harappan script, which is still unread, is represented only by very short inscriptions, most of them evidently of a rather specialized nature, being on steatite seals (Wheeler, 1959).

During the Harappan period a remarkable uniformity of material culture was achieved throughout the whole province, suggesting powerful and effective political and economic control. This declines in the post-Harappan period (after c.1700 B.C.) and there is a return to regionalism. Throughout, however, the settlements remain

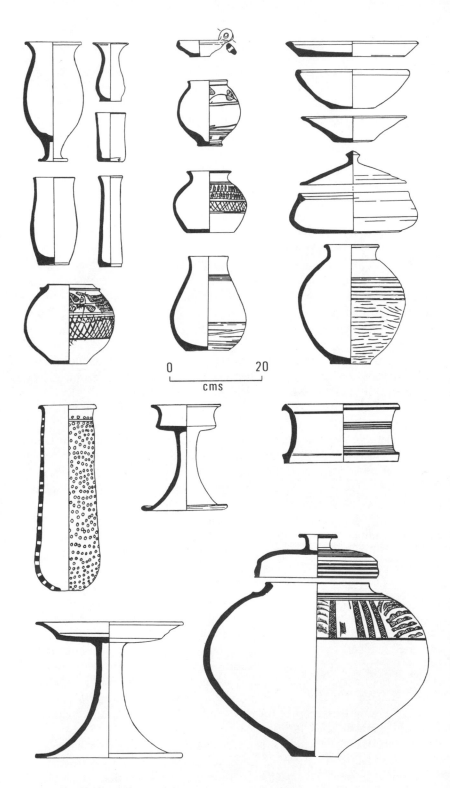

Figure 40. Harappa: pottery types.

little more than large villages, comparable in size to villages in the region today. The largest sites, such as Mohenjo Daro and Harappa, are comparable to small towns in terms of estimated population density (Lambrick, 1964:Ch.6), but small cities might better describe their status. All the settlements are widely separated, far more so than their needs in terms of accessible cultivable land could demand. This indicates a low density of population, and also suggests that each served as a centre for a wide area, probably inhabited by hunting or pastoral peoples. Nomadic pastoralists form an important element in the rural population of Pakistan and western India today, occupying large areas in Rajasthan and Sind, for example, too arid for anything but the most ephemeral attempts at cultivation. Even in intensively cultivated regions such as the plain of Gujarat nomadic herdsmen successfully move through village lands in the course of their yearly migrations, and are welcomed by the sedentary agricultural population who pay them a small fee to pen their animals overnight on areas'that need manuring. Unlike Central India there are no communities in western India today who depend solely on hunting, although many people at all levels of society do hunt wild game when they have the opportunity, and in parts of Rajasthan Nilgai (large antelope not unlike Eland in appearance) are found in fairly large numbers and are a popular source of food.

Settlements belonging to the Harappan complex extend round the northern and southern margins of the Thar desert, as well as along the major rivers that dissect it. In the north they are found as far east as the Jamuna river on the boundary between the Punjab and Uttar Pradesh, and somewhat beyond. On the south they follow the coast into the two peninsulas of Cutch and Kathiawar, and down the coastal plain of mainland Gujarat to the Tapi estuary. Most of these belong to the later part of the Harappan or to the post-Harappan phase (Kirk, 1975). Contemporary Chalcolithic settlements such as Ahar on the eastern borders of the desert are outside the Harappan province, and belong to an independent tradition. So too do the Chalcolithic settlements of Maharastra (Sankalia 1974). Those that have been excavated are contemporary with the post-Harappan, but there are indications that settlement in the region extends back to earlier times. This is also an economy based upon a wide range of domestic animals, wheat and pulses, but, as at the present time, cultivation must have depended wholly upon the local rains instead of largely upon inundation as that of the Harappans did. The stone blade industries of these sites are related to those of the Mesolithic cultures of the region. In eastern India all the early settlements excavated show evidence of rice cultivation and at some of them remains of rice and fish have been found, suggesting a diet like that of Bengal and Bangladesh today.

The south Indian neolithic culture of the southern Deccan plateau (Mysore State, southern Maharastra and western Andhra Pradesh) has a decided individuality of its own (Allchin F.R. 1963). The earliest C14 date for its lowest levels is c.2300 bc. The principal settlements are located on the granite hills of the region, the sides of which are terraced with dry stone retaining walls behind which earth and detritus from the rocky slopes accumulated. On these terraces round huts were built with frames of wooden poles supporting wattle and daub walls. One or two huts were built on each terrace, the settlement in some cases extending in a series of steps from the pediment of the hill to a height of several hundred feet above the plain. Layers of accumulated occupation debris and mud floors indicate a continuity of some centuries before the villages moved down onto the plains, a process which seems to have begun with the

Iron Age in approximately 1000 B.C. The Neolithic culture is based primarily upon large herds of humped Indian cattle. Vast quantities of fragmented bones indicate both that some of the cattle at every site were domesticated, and that they formed an important source of food, augmented by smaller numbers of sheep, goat and various game animals. Millet was evidently cultivated on a small scale, and flaked and ground axes of basalt, and boldly-shaped, well-fired grey or buff hand-made pottery are prominent features. The stone blade industry is closely related to that found at Mesolithic sites in the region. Small quantities of copper and bronze are associated with the latest phases of the culture. Terra cotta figurines are predominantly of humped cattle, and so are the numerous rock drawings and bruisings associated with Neolithic sites.

Cattle are also the predominant theme of the second major type of site associated with the culture. These are the ash mounds, great platforms of vitrified cow dung which seem to have formed the bases of cattle pens surrounded by stockades of palm trunks. Occupation debris here consists of small quantities of Neolithic pottery like that at the hill settlements, and more cattle bones. Possibly these are the sites where the wild cattle of the Deccan were impounded and tamed for domestic use. The interesting question regarding this culture is how far can it be attributed to incoming pastoral peoples who settled in the peninsular plateau, and how far to indigenous hunting peoples who learnt to domesticate the cattle of the region upon which they also preyed as hunters?

We must think of all these settled communities against a background of Mesolithic hunting peoples extending as an ethnic and cultural continuum throughout South Asia, among which the settlements were like islands. Until the early decades of this century, and in some cases right down to the present day, communities or tribes whose economy and life style were based upon hunting and gathering were and are to be found in the more remote, and less cultivatable, hill and forest regions of Central and South India. Examples of such people who have been well described by anthropologists are the Baiga of Central India (Elwin 1939) the Chenchu of the Eastern Ghats (Fürer Haimendorf 1943) and the Veddas of Ceylon (Seligman and Seligman 1911). In each case these people retained their traditional way of life, marrying almost exclusively among themselves. Their traditions included a limited amount of contact and trade with other communities, either through attending village markets, or through itinerant traders. In this way they sold honey, animal skins, baskets and other products of the wild, and bought small quantities of cereals, cloth, tobacco and above all iron axes and knives. Iron arrow heads they are generally said to have made from small pieces of scrap iron. During the nineteenth century individuals from these communities were already going to work as occasional labourers, building roads, etc., and they may well have done so from much earlier times. There are records of the kings of Candy being supported by contingents of some hundreds of Vedda bowmen in their wars against invaders (fig. 41). The Bhils, a group of tribes in western Central India (Majumdar 1961:Ch.4), who generally practise rather elementary forms of agriculture along with hunting, gathering forest products, and casual labour, are known to have provided contingents of bowmen to take part in the Maratha wars of the seventeenth and eighteenth centuries.

Under the continual pressure of expanding agricultural populations, prepared to clear the forests, plough, irrigate and generally transform the countryside, many

Figure 41. Vedda bowmen, Sri Lanka. The Veddas were until recently hunters and gatherers, each group moving constantly in a series of regular migrations within their own forest territory *(photograph: Royal Anthropological Institute of Great Britain and Ireland (Photograph Collection); copyright reserved).*

communities of hunters and casual cultivators have been forced to give way, and relinquish their extensive hunting grounds to timber contractors and pioneer farmers. They have had to adapt themselves to living in closer contact with a more complex society, and they have tended to do this not as individuals but as communities. Groups of 'tribal' families are to be found on the outskirts of many Indian towns, in settlements which try to preserve the character of the villages they have left. Many make baskets, sleeping mats and screens of reeds or withies to provide privacy in the urban courtyards of the better-off. Others work as labourers, and a few are reduced to begging. Such groups generally maintain contact with those remaining in the home territory, and regard themselves as part of the same community especially for the purpose of arranging marriages. They may return from time to time for important occasions and religious ceremonies.

The absorption of communities rather than individuals into village or urban society is a characteristic feature of the sub-continent as a whole; a feature which distinguishes it from the rest of the world, and of which there are historical and literary records going back for many centuries. This system is closely related to that of caste. A caste is a hereditary, endogamous group which carried out a certain function or group of functions in traditional Indian society. These functions have been modified and extended with the passing of time. The first mention of the division of society into major caste groups goes back to the Purusha Sukta of the Rigveda (c. 1000 BC). Since then many new groups and communities have been absorbed or added to the structure, and the barriers between groups have become rather vague for all purposes except marriage; under the impact of modern technology they are tending to be less and less regarded for all practical purposes. The concept of absorption of groups rather than individuals, however, remains a basic one (Kosambi 1956).

As we have already indicated in respect of western India the practice of maintaining economic and social relationships between groups rather than individuals applies equally to herdsmen and pastoralists as it does to hunters or slash-and-burn cultivators. Throughout the sub-continent today there are communities who specialize in herding one or more variety of animals, camels, sheep, goats, cattle, water buffalo etc. The way this is done varies greatly according to the nature of the region and to local practice. Some herdsmen are attached to villages in a subordinate capacity, and simply take the animals of village farming families out to graze each day, bringing them back to their owners in the evening. Others take large herds of breeding cattle and young stock to graze in areas of hill and open woodland remote from village settlements for periods of weeks or months. Others again are the owners of flocks and herds with which they move in a series of yearly migrations, often covering hundreds of miles. They may combine this with selling young stock at various suitable points in their itinerary and selling milk, butter, woollen textiles etc. in the markets of towns and villages. Various communities of herdsmen like the Bardwal in Gujarat and south Rajasthan fall into this category. When in the vicinity of major railway junctions they sell large numbers of lambs to dealers from Bombay and other cities who take them away by rail. Young cattle are sold to local farmers as draught oxen and milking cows, either privately or at annual fairs. Such fairs usually combine a commercial and religious purpose, rather as fairs in Europe once did and sometimes still do, and are a very ancient feature of Indian rural life. That at Pushkar in eastern Rajasthan, one of the largest in India, takes place in the autumn and is associated with one of the most important places of pilgrimage in the sub-continent, the temple of Brahma at Pushkar Raj (Imperial Gazetteer of India, 1968, vol.21, 1).

Nomadic herdsmen who own their own animals usually have a home base somewhere on their route where old people may remain permanently, and where they have small holdings of cultivatable land. The west Indian groups we have discussed are in this category, and so are the Kuchi peoples of Sind and Afghanistan. They return to their lands at seed time and harvest, leaving them, in some cases, to be guarded by some of the members of their community while the others are away with the animals. Young families usually go with the herds, and small children may be seen riding on the animals in panniers together with chickens, puppies and other livestock. Some of these peoples combine acting as carriers of goods with their nomadic life. The Banjara of the Deccan and south India exemplify this. In dress, physical appearance and life style they are quite distinct from the south Indian village population, and are said to have come from the Indus region following the advance of the Mogul armies as carriers of baggage and supplies. They still act as carriers of all sorts of goods, and sometimes also work as labourers. Attempts have been made in recent years to settle them and their livestock in forest areas which are in process of being brought under cultivation. Carrying of goods with the aid of animals is an aspect of South and Central Asian life which has declined with the introduction of railways and lorry transport, but has been of great importance in the past. The organization of large caravans of bullock carts and pack animals of all kinds was obviously intimately connected with the movement and sale of animals and herding communities, and both formed part of a vast socio-economic network.

We have already pointed out how nomadic herdsmen form an important element of rural life in India and Pakistan today, including the old province of the Harappan culture. There is every reason to suppose that they did so in Harappan times, and that they played an important part in the economy and organization of the Harappan world. In the same way there is every reason to suppose that relations with both hunting and herding communities played an important part in the life of the early settlements of the Deccan and south India. The similarity of the blade traditions of Mesolithic hunters and settled peoples clearly indicates this, and there are other indications of contact in rock art, material culture and animal remains at many sites, and as we have indicated, modern practice accords with the archaeological record.

A major problem archaeologically is to distinguish between the cultural remains of hunters and nomadic pastoralists, particularly when we bear in mind that many pastoralists were undoubtedly also hunters. The stone blade industries of Neolithic and Chalcolithic sites (figs. 42-3), while closely resembling those of the Mesolithic in terms of basic technology and choice of raw materials, have been shown to differ from them consistently in terms of the relative proportions of various tool types : utilized but unretouched blades are more plentiful in settled cultures, and reworked artifacts such as lunates, triangles and scrapers of various types, whether made as blades or flakes, are more common at Mesolithic sites (fig. 44) (Allchin, F.R. and B., 1974). It has not so far been possible to draw any such distinction between the stone blade industries of pastoralists and hunters. At the many Mesolithic sites recorded throughout South Asia stone blade industries are almost always the principal and often the only distinguishing feature. Such sites can be divided into occupied caves

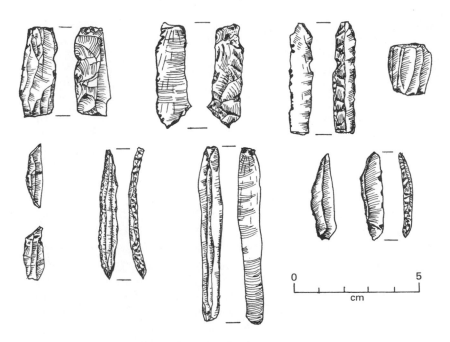

Figure 42. Nevasa and Chandoli: Chalcolithic stone-blade industry.

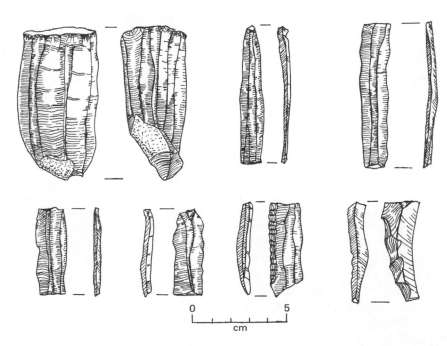

Figure 43. Harappan stone-blade industry.

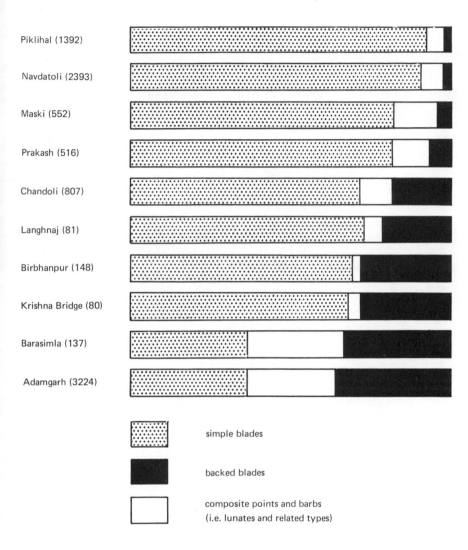

Piklihal (1392)

Navdatoli (2393)

Maski (552)

Prakash (516)

Chandoli (807)

Langhnaj (81)

Birbhanpur (148)

Krishna Bridge (80)

Barasimla (137)

Adamgarh (3224)

simple blades

backed blades

composite points and barbs
(i.e. lunates and related types)

Figure 44. Stone-blade industries from Neolithic and Chalcolithic settlements, Piklihal, Navdatoli, Maski, Prakash, Chandoli; and Mesolithic living sites and working floors, Langhnaj, Birbhanpur, Krishna Bridge, Barasimla, Adamgarh, showing percentages of artifact types.

or rock shelters; factory sites, often extensive and showing evidence of continued use over a long period of time, both before and after the Mesolithic; smaller surface sites, generally on rising ground, hillocks or spurs commanding a good view of the surrounding countryside. The last appear to have been living or camping places, and resemble situations favoured by hunting peoples in recent times for siting their huts.

A certain number of rock shelters and caves have been excavated, mainly in Central India, and although some of these have been found to contain only very shallow deposits, or to have been cleared or seriously disturbed by later occupants - often religious ascetics seeking to escape from the world - others have been found to have undisturbed occupation debris of sufficient depth to contain interesting cultural material. Quantities of microliths are almost always found, frequently accompanied by a few pot sherds in the upper layers, pieces of haematite corresponding to that used for drawing animals and human figures on the walls, and fragmented animal bones. At one such group of rock shelters, Adamgarh in Central India, where a very rich microlithic industry was found, an analysis of the animal bones showed that the following species of wild animals were present, and had probably been used as food: hare, porcupine, monitor lizard and three species of deer. There were also remains of pig, sheep, goat, water buffalo and humped Indian cattle, all of which with the exception of sheep and goat are generally considered indigenous to the region, and bones of the domestic dog were also found (Joshi 1968). The Mesolithic levels at Adamgarh have been dated by C14 to the mid-fifth millennium bc. Thus it appears that in central India at this time there were pastoral people who hunted a variety of animals - probably with the aid of bows and arrows armed with composite points and barbs built up from the varied range of microliths present at this and many similar sites. These people kept dogs and flocks of sheep and goats, and possibly also cattle, buffalo and pig. A detailed study of the bones might show whether any of these species had undergone the type of structural change sometimes associated with domestication. Here, however, there are further problems, for even today certain species of domestic animals, notably pig, buffalo and elephant, frequently interbreed with their wild representatives. Elephants are reputed never to mate in captivity, and the cows are therefore released into the jungle in Mysore, for example, where they mate with wild bull elephants.

Again at Bagor, a small settlement excavated in eastern Rajasthan, it appears that the transition from a hunting and gathering economy to one which included domestic animals and perhaps small-scale cultivation can be demonstrated through three phases of occupation ranging in date from c. 4000 BC to 6000 BC (Misra 1973). This means that the transition was made at this particular site during the Harappan period. Similarly the earliest occupation levels excavated at a number of Chalcolithic settlements in Baluchistan, dating back as far as the fifth millennium BC, appear to represent sporadic occupation by nomadic pastoralists, while the succeeding levels appear to represent continuous settlement. All this evidence suggests that nomadic pastoralists inhabited the relatively dry region extending from Baluchistan to western central India long before the earliest dates (second half of the third millennium bc) so far obtained for the pre-Harappan and other early settled cultures. It remains to be seen whether the earliest settlements based on cultivation and a mixed agricultural economy extend back to a comparably early date. It seems highly likely that they will be pushed back to the fifth millennium or even further.

The whole of this paper has been a summary of problems rather than of conclusions : anything else at this stage would be misleading. I hope I have been able to give some indication of the size and varied nature of the Indian sub-continent, or South Asia, and of the importance of both the physical geography and the modern ethnography in gaining a proper understanding of its archaeological past. Through them one can begin to reconstruct ecological patterns and the interrelationships of communities from what would otherwise be mere catalogues of finds.

REFERENCES

Allchin, B., 1973. 'Blade and Burin industries of West Pakistan and Western India', in *South Asian Archaeology,* ed. N. Hammond, 1973, 39-50.

Allchin, B., 1966. *The Stone Tipped Arrow.*

Allchin, B. and F.R., 1968. *The Birth of Indian Civilization.*

Allchin, B. and F.R., 1974. 'The relationship of Neolithic and later settled communities with those of Late Stone Age hunters and gatherers in peninsular India', in *Indian Society, Historical Beginings, In Memory of D.D. Mosambi,* ed. R.S. Sharma, 1974 (Delhi), 45-66.

Allchin, B. and Goudie, A., 1974. 'Pushkar : prehistory and climatic change in western India', *World Archaeology, 5(3),* 358-68.

Allchin, F.R., 1963. *Neolithic Cattle Keepers of South India.*

Bordes, F., 1968. *The Old Stone Age.*

Childe, V.G., 1956. *New Light on the Most Ancient East.*

Elwin, V., 1939. *Baiga.*

Fürer Haimendorf, C. von, 1943. *The Chenchu.*

Goudie, A., Allchin, B. and Hegde, K.T.M., 1973. 'The former extensions of the Great Indian Sand Desert', *Geogr. 139(2),* 243-57.

Imperial Gazetteer of India, 1908, vol.21.

Joshi, R.V., 1968. 'Late Mesolithic Cultures in Central India' in *La Prehistoire, Problèmes et Tendances, 1968* (Paris), 245-54.

Kirk, W., 1975. 'The role of India in the diffusion of early culture', *Geogr., 141(1),* 19-34.

Kosambi, D.D., 1956. *An Introduction to the Study of Indian History* (Bombay).

Lambrick, H.T., 1964. *Sind* (History of Sind Series, vol.1)(Hyderabad).

Majumdar, D.N., 1961. *Races and Cultures of India* (4th edn).

Misra, V.N., 1973. 'Bagor - a late mesolithic settlement in north-west India', *World Archaeology, 5(1),* 92-110.

Sankalia, H.D., 1974. *Prehistory and Protohistory of India and Pakistan* (Poona).

Seligman, C.G. and B.Z., 1911. *The Veddas.*

Singh, G., 1971. 'The Indus Valley culture seen in the light of post-glacial and ecological studies in north-west India', *Archaeology and Physical Anthropology in Oceania,* 6(2), 177-89.

Spate, D.H.K., 1957. *India and Pakistan : a general and regional geography.*

Subbarao, B., 1958. *The Personality of India* (2nd edn).

Wheeler, M., 1959. *Early India and Pakistan.*

Wiser, W. and C., 1973. *Behind Mud Walls 1930-1960* (Berkeley).

I. C. GLOVER

7 The Hoabinhian: hunter-gatherers or early agriculturalists in South-East Asia?

WHAT IS THE HOABINHIAN?

The term Hoabinhian entered the literature of archaeology at the First Congress of Prehistorians of the Far East, meeting in Hanoi in 1932, (Matthews 1966: 86) where, following spectacular discoveries by French archaeologists in the limestone caves of Tonkin, it was described as a culture composed of implements, flaked with a rather primitive technique, usually split river pebbles worked often on only one face, including discs, short axes, almond-shaped tools and with many hammer and grinding stones and bone tools. Three stages of the Hoabinhian culture were claimed: I, with large and crude flaked tools only; II, smaller core tools, a few used flakes and occasionally pebbles with ground edges; and III, dominated by edge-ground tools and with some pottery, usually with cord impressions.

Unsatisfactory as the definition so obviously is, the term has survived as an accepted name for a considerable number of cultural assemblages and stone tool collections widely distributed in South-East Asia and which have some basic resemblance to each other. But it is a term which 'ignores significant differences rather than emphasising precise similarities' (Matthews 1961: 1) and if it were not so well established, it would be better to drop it. Gorman (1971: 300), following Clarke (1968: 357), has recently described the Hoabinhian as a 'technocomplex' rather than a culture, taking into account its long life, wide distribution, and the rather varied composition of Hoabinhian assemblages which nevertheless reflect some common ecological adaptations.

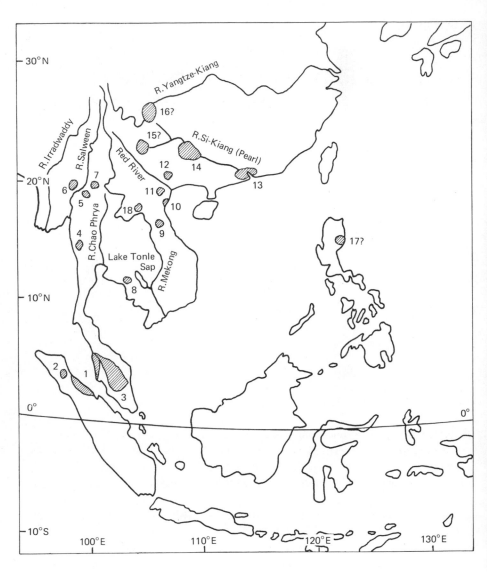

Figure 45. Principal Hoabinhian sites, or areas of site concentration. Sites whose attribution to the Hoabinhian is not yet certain are indicated by a question mark after the number.

1. Malacca Strait shell middens
2. Lho' Saumaweh (Aceh) surface sites
3. Malayan caves
4. Ongba Cave, Sai Yok, and other Kwai Noi sites
5. Spirit Cave and the Banyan Valley sites
6. Padah-lin Caves
7. Tham Nguang Cham
8. Laang Spean
9. Quang Binh
10. Da But and other Tonkin shell middens
11. Hoabinh Caves
12. Bacson Caves
13. Kwangtoung shell middens
14. Kwangsi Caves
15. Yunnan Caves
16. Sechwan surface sites
17. Pintu Cave, Luzon
18. Tam Hang and the central Mekong sites, Laos

Figure 46. Sukajadi Kec., Northern Sumatra: north-west face of Hoabinhian shell midden *(photograph: E. Edwards McKinnon).*

DISTRIBUTION

Assemblages which are called Hoabinhian have an enormous geographical spread: from Burma (and perhaps even Assam) to Vietnam, from South China to North Sumatra (very roughly 1,200 x 1,800 miles), or from Wales to the Russian border and from Central Sweden to Sicily, and it is not surprising to find considerable regional differences - for instance in north coastal Sumatra unifacially flaked andesite pebbles are known from shell middens and surface scatters; in Malaya, flat bifacially-flaked oval tools dominate, and in North Vietnam so-called 'short-axes' are common. But typological analysis is so poorly developed that no precise comparisons can be made, and in any case, I do not want to discuss sequences and artifact types here.

Basically, there are two sorts of sites: 1. Caves in the limstone karst formations so common in South-East Asia; and 2. Coastal and riverine shell middens, particularly along both sides of Malacca Strait, and in the Red River Delta of North Vietnam and south along the Annam coast. Gorman (1971: 306-10) argued that this dichotomy reflected two separate ecological orientations, upland karst/riverine, and coastal. But I believe that this distribution reflects only the visibility of sites to archaeologists. The limestone is primarily away from the coasts and contains caves; shell middens stand out above ground level and have usually been commercially exploited and so come to the notice of archaeologists (figs. 45-6).

It is difficult to do more than estimate the number of Hoabinhian sites so far investigated; perhaps 2-3 in Burma, 6 in Thailand, 25 in Malaya, 5-6 in Sumatra, 1 in Cambodia, 2 in Laos, 100 in Vietnam and more than 20 in China; perhaps 120-60 in all. I should also say that quite recently some sites in North Luzon, Philippines (Peterson 1974: 28), have produced material closer to Hoabinhian than to the flake traditions (Glover 1973) which predominate in Island South-East Asia. But the occasional references which have been made to Hoabinhian tools in Java, Borneo, and elsewhere in Indonesia (e.g. in van Heekeren 1972: 100-6) outside North Sumatra, are not yet justified in my opinion. Finally, it should be pointed out that within its area of distribution, the Hoabinhian is so far the only recognized post-Pleistocene, pre-neolithic tradition.

CHRONOLOGY

The first Hoabinhian assemblages rather puzzled archaeologists - in Malaya the bifacially-flaked pebbles were rather tentatively called 'palaeoliths' when they started to appear late in the last century because of their obvious resemblance to European handaxes. But on the other hand it was felt that they were the not-too-ancient tools of negrito aborigines, the broken groups of which still lived in the jungles of upland Malaya, Thailand, the Philippines and in the Andamans. In China also, Teilhard de Chardin first described finds from the caves of Kwangsi as 'purely palaeolithic', and in Vietnam, Mansuy and Colani, in the early stages of their research, both believed that their cave finds were Peistocene in age. Later however, it was realised that the cave fauna of South China and Tonkin was entirely modern with no extinct species and, on the advice of geologists, the South Chinese and the Hoabinhian cave finds were put into the post-Pleistocene period. As late as 1964 Matthews in a survey of the Hoabinhian summarized it as follows: 'a distinctive culture, based on a hunting and gathering economy, with flaked stone artefacts made primarily on pebbles. It was a mesolithic culture in that it exhibited no evidence of agriculture. The rather inadequate faunal data would seem to indicate a post-Pleistocene date' (1966: 94).

Since then, new sites have been excavated by Dunn (1964) at Gua Kechil and elsewhere (Al Rashid 1973) in Malaya; by Gorman (1971) at Spirit Cave and Banyan Valley and by Sørensen (1973) at Ongba Cave, all in Thailand; by U. Aung Thaw (1971) at Padah-Lin in Burma; by the Mourers (1970) at Laang Spean in Cambodia, and three cave excavations made in North Vietnam in the early 1960s have come to the notice of Western archaeologists (Boriskovsky 1969/70, Davidson 1973). Some carbon dates are also now available, which suggest that the Hoabinhian spans the Pleistocene-Recent boundary and continues in some areas into quite recent times. The oldest date is from Padah-Lin of 11,450 ± 200 bc (R-2547/5-B), and dates of c. 9000-10,000 bc have come from Thailand, and 4,000-5,000 bc from Cambodia. Hoabinhian terminal dates of 5000 bc and 2800 bc have been proposed respectively for Spirit Cave and Gua Kechil, while in Malaya a survival into historical times is claimed (Al Rashid 1973: 90). Gorman suggests that the earliest Hoabinhian phase so far recognized may be close to 14,000-15,000 bc (fig. 48).

Associations with agriculture have also been proposed, but first I want to say something about South-East Asian hunter-gatherers, and ideas concerning the development of agriculture in South-East Asia.

SURVIVING HUNTER-GATHERERS IN SOUTH-EAST ASIA

Today, or in the quite recent past, communities of hunting and collecting people have survived in many parts of the region, but information on them is scattered and incomplete, and there has been no extensive and systematic modern field research with any community, and directed towards ecological relationships, such as that of Lee (1972) and Silberbauer (1972) with the Bushmen, Turnbull (1965) with the Pygmies, Woodburn (1968, 1971) with the Hadza, all in Africa, and many others in Australia and North and South America. Books such as *Man the Hunter* (Lee and De Vore 1968) and *Hunter-gatherers Today* (Bicchieri 1972) scarcely mention South-East Asia, and it required the astonishing discovery of the stone-using Tasaday (Fernandez and Lynch 1972) in the forests of Cotabatu province, Mindanao, Philippines, to bring South-East Asian collectors to the attention of modern ethnographers. This lack of detailed study is unfortunate because these groups have existed in a variety of environments and a better understanding of their adaptations might provide a valuable balance to generalizations about pre-agricultural peoples in other parts of the world. Some of the published data were collected in a short paper I wrote a few years ago (Glover 1971) and I summarize here a few points from it, and make some corrections and additions.

Best known are the people of the Andaman Islands, the Negritos, Senoi and Malayan Aborigines of Malaya and South Thailand, the Kubus, Orang Batin and other small groups of central and east Sumatra, possibly the Toala of South-West Sulawesi, the Punan and Penan of Borneo, and some groups in North-East Thailand, variously called Yumbri, Mrabri, Khon Pa and Phi Tong Luang, and the Tasaday of the Philippines. The correct identification of these forest groups is difficult; many names in the literature are reference terms, often derogatory, given by nearby villagers, such as *sakai* and *kubu*, and others mean no more than 'jungle dwellers' in various local languages, e.g. *khon pa, orang utan* and *toala*.

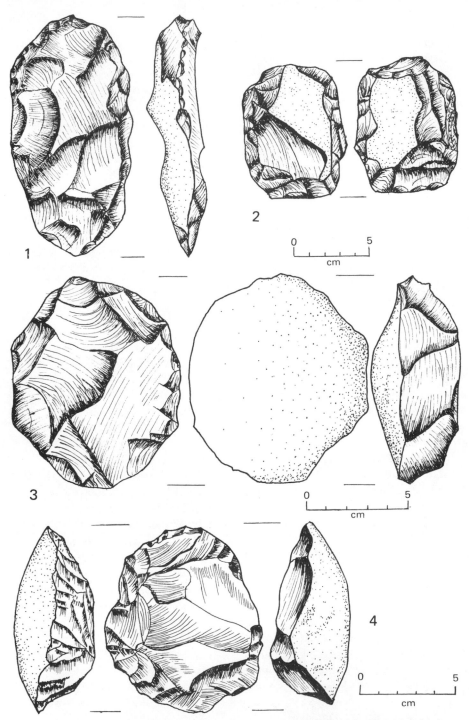

Figure 47. Some Hoabinhian flaked stone tool types. 1-2. Pebble chopping-tools; a. bifacial working at ends only, b. bifacial around entire margin. Both from Gua Debu, Kedah, Malaya *(after Collings 1936)*. 3. Unifacial pebble chopper, Hoabinh Province, Vietnam *(after Matthews 1964)*. 4. Hornfels chopper or scraper, Laang Spean, Cambodia *(after Mourer 1971)*. Hornfels short axe, Laang Spean, *(after Mourer 1971)*. 6-7. Hornfels choppers, Laang Spean *(after Mourer 1971)*. 8-12. Hornfels flakes, Laang Spean *(after Mourer 1971)*.

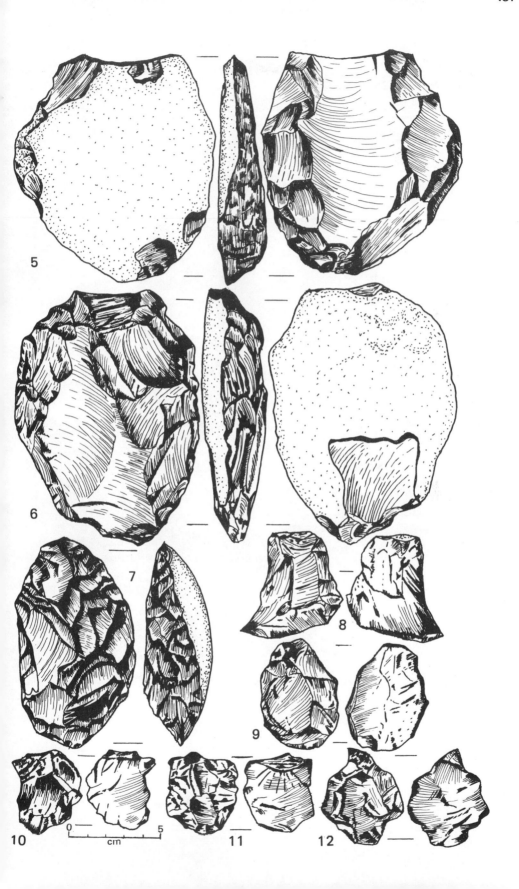

Figure 48. Laang Spean, Cambodia: cave site with Hoabinhian occupation
(photograph: R. Mourer).

The hunter-gatherers of South-East Asia belong to a variety of racial groups although there is little agreement on how to classify them. The Andaman Islanders, Semang of Malaya and South Thailand, together with the Aeta of the Philippines are usually called Negrito; the Senoi, Kubu and Toala have, though the term is not accepted today, been described as Veddoid, with the implication that they are relicts of a pre-Mongoloid, non-Negrito population of South-East Asia; while the groups of the Nam Wa valley in North-East Thailand, the Aboriginal Malay (or Jakun), Punan and Penan and the Tasaday are largely or completely Mongoloid. Of these peoples, the Negritos of the Andamans, the Kubus of Sumatra between Djambi and Palembang, and the nomads of the Nam Wa valley and the Tasaday depend most on hunting and collecting, although all of these people, except the Tasaday, obtain some artifacts, especially iron, and sometimes food from surrounding agricultural populations in exchange for forest products, such as matting, rattan, camphor and beeswax (fig. 49).

The Tasaday came to the notice of the outside world only in 1966 when their existence was reported to Filipino anthropologists by Dafal, a hunter from another social group. They appear to be the most isolated of known South-East Asian forest peoples and provide a contrast in important details with the other groups mentioned here. In the first place, they form a small patrilocal, exogamous band of 26 persons (13 adults and 13 children) permanently resident (as far as the data indicates) in a group of three caves at about 1380 m above sea level in mountainous rain forest. Study of their language suggests that the Tasaday have been isolated from neighbouring lowland groups for several hundred years, but it seems that they are in irregular contact with other small forest bands with whom they exchange wives. The Tasaday are food collectors more than hunters, depending on wild yams, fruits, palm and bamboo shoots and wild bananas as staple foods and obtaining their protein from crabs, fish, frogs and tadpoles of the mountain streams. Deer, wild pig and monkey are common in the forest but not regularly hunted, and the presence of many rarely used plant foods, important elsewhere for South-East Asian collecting peoples, shows that the Tasaday environment offers a wide margin of security. Before 1966 the Tasaday had no metal tools, although now the *bolo* (bush knife), small knives, awls and wire are in common use. Their toolkit consisted of hafted stone pounders, edge-ground pebble axes, digging sticks, a fire drill, bamboo knives, vine slings and rattan for hafting. Traditional South-East Asian weapons, the bow and arrow, spear and blowpipe were not used, and traps and snares, if known, were little used.

Although the Tasaday have not been under observation for long, reports indicate that they do not range far from their base camp, and that foraging expeditions are limited to within an area of 25 km^2 around the caves, with individual expeditions usually covering less than 3 km^2. Three ecological zones are exploited, a freshwater stream 120 m below the cave, its banks and terraces, and upland forest which yields starch-storing palms as well as yams, bananas, rattans and small animals. On the data available (Fernandez and Lynch 1972: 309-11) it seems that men and women each spend about three hours a day on the food quest, visiting the stream or its banks every day, while the men climbed to the upland forest on only three of the seven days recorded. As with the !Kung Bushmen, the Hadza and many other surviving hunting societies recently studied, the Tasaday have abundant leisure, and have little need for techniques of food storage and preservation because their

Figure 49. Philippines: the Tasaday tribe. This stone-using group of 26 persons remained unknown until 1966 *(photograph: United Press International)*.

subsistence is assured and varies little throughout the year. The size of the Tasaday group is thought to be growing, but only slowly, and the investigators believe that they are operating well below the point where there is any pressure on their subsistence resources.

Some information is available for other South-East Asian hunters also, on the size and composition of groups, structure of camps, food sources, and hunting techniques. And we can say that most South-East Asian collectors conform reasonably well to the generalized idea of pre-agricultural society developed by recent hunter-gatherer anthropology. Absolute population densities are very low, local groups range in size from half a dozen to about 40 people, composition is usually mixed (i.e. no apparent unilineal descent group structure) and fluid. Camp groups, except among the Tasaday, are usually mobile, moving even when local resources are plentiful, but there are favoured camping localities regularly visited to exploit seasonal resources. There is no formal authority structure, and camping groups may split and move to avoid conflict and for other social reasons, as well as to make the most efficient use of scattered food sources. Individuals may regard themselves as belonging to a certain area, and while specific resources such as fruit trees may be owned, local groups do not exercise exclusive rights over clearly defined territories.

Stone tools generally fall within Binford's (1973: 242-4) 'expedient' rather than 'curated' technology, with obvious problems for the typologically-minded archaeologist. And very great use is made of perishable organic resources, although not necessarily more than in other parts of the world. But superficial (although very valuable) accounts of the camps of the Mrbrai forest collectors in Thailand (Velder 1963: 185-8) suggest that some of these people would be archaeologically almost unrecognizable.

We must also admit that for no single group, not excepting even the Andaman Islanders, is there sufficient well-documented and first-hand data to enable us to reconstruct a functioning, integrated community and to understand how they had maintained their way of life for thousands of years, in contact with, and often in competition with, more aggressive and expanding agricultural peoples. As a very crude generalization we can say that these people survived in areas remote from centres of the 'great traditions' of South-East Asia in the lowland river valleys of the monsoon zone, and which were also not immediately attractive to agriculturalists; they are found particularly in the equatorial rain forests of Sumatra, Malaya, South Thailand, Borneo or else in isolated islands such as the Andamans, or the mountains of Mindanao and on the Thai-Laos border. But I think the explanation is not so simple. Until the comparatively recent intensification and expansion of agriculture in South-East Asia, perhaps triggered off by European colonial interferences (cf. Hanks 1972: 72-147 and Geertz 1963), these collecting peoples seem to have maintained a fairly stable way of life, in many cases sharing the same territory with, and interdependent with agriculturalists.

MODELS FOR THE DEVELOPMENT OF AGRICULTURE IN SOUTH-EAST ASIA

Today, in terms of the number of people dependent on it, South-East Asian agriculture is dominated by labour-intensive wet rice farming, monocultural and neotechnic in both Wolf's (1966) and Harris's (1973a) terminology. But this is really quite a recent development, as Spencer (1966), Hanks (1972) and Geertz (1963) have shown. Traditional South-East Asian agriculture has emphasized vegetatively reproduced root crops, especially yams (*Discorea* sp.) and taro (*Colocasia* and *Alocasia* sp.), bananas (*Musa* sp.), and tree fruits, but it seems quite probable that some cereals, such as Job's tears (*Coix lachryma jobii*), rice (*Oryza sativa*), and foxtail millet (*Setaria italica*) are ancient, perhaps original, cultigens within eastern Asia, south of the Yangtze River.

There are two strategies for agriculture in South-East Asia quite opposed in principle, and which are both dependent on the characteristics of the humid tropical ecosystems. In what Harris calls the palaeotechnic tropical agriculture, diverse assemblages of crops and animals are raised in structural and functional interdependence, mirroring the complex structure of the natural ecosystem. This pattern is characteristic of most shifting or swidden agriculture, with relatively low population densities, and is generally thought to be the form of primitive (early) South-East Asian agriculture. Certainly, the neotechnic, monocultural, intensive, fixed field agriculture which is typified in our area by wet rice cultivation or sweet potato gardens, as in parts of the New Guinea Highlands (Brookfield with Hart 1971: 111-14), requires dense local populations. And the change from the one to the other is understandable in terms of the Boserup model (see Spooner 1972) of agricultural intensification following population growth.

There are several sorts of traditional explanations for the development of South-East Asian agriculture. De Candolle (1883) and Vavilov (1951) both recognised South-East Asia as the area of origin of many cultivated plants but until recently most archaeological reconstructions of the region, very much under the influence of the Vienna *Kulturkreis* school, have favoured a combination of diffusion and invasion from China in the third millennium B.C. The appearance of pottery with edge-ground axes in middle and late Hoabinhian sites was supposed to reflect the influence of migrating neolithic mongoloid farmers from the north on the backward aboriginal inhabitants, who were variously seen as 'Veddoid' or 'Melanesoid' in race (see van Heekeren and Knuth 1967: 107-17). Carl Sauer (1952) proposed an ingenious hypothesis, that vegetatively reproduced crops were probably older than cereals and that South-East Asia, with its diverse wild plant resources, strongly seasonal climate, and long coast lines provided the perfect setting for the first development of sedentary fishing-farming communities. But this did little to shake the archaeologists' belief in diffusion and migration until the results of new excavations in the 1960s supported by C14 dates, and a sort of growing archaeological nationalism, combined to undermine all traditional interpretations. Sauer's hypothesis has been said to be founded 'not on evidence, but lack of it', and Mangelsdorf (1953: 422), reviewing Sauer's theory, has aptly said that 'if one sought as an exercise of the imagination, to design a completely untestable theory of agricultural origins and dispersals, it would be difficult to improve on this one'. I would also say, at the present state of archaeological knowledge, that an acceptance of some of the more extreme claims for the independent or very early development of pottery, ground edge tools, rice cultivation, (*pace* Solheim 1972: 145), bronze casting and even iron-working in South-East Asia (Bronson 1973) requires a certain faith - which, however, is not lacking.

Refinements of theory have certainly been made, notably by Chang (1970), Harris (1973a and 1973b), Gorman (1971 and 1973), and Higham (1972 and 1973), and I want to discuss a few points from these, before looking at the botanical and faunal remains from recently excavated South-East Asian sites in the light of some general hypotheses which have been advanced for the development of agriculture.

Chang (1970), starts with Li's (1970) distinction between four zones of concentration of East Asian cultivated plants - North China, South China, Southern Asia (= mainland South-East Asia) and the Southern Islands, but argues that South China is a 'buffer zone' and that two primary foci of cultivation can be found, North China and South-East Asia (which includes Li's two southern zones). The North Chinese early agriculture emphasized cereals (*Setaria* and *Pannicum* millets), whereas in South-East Asia roots and tubers and other vegetatively reproduced plants predominated. Chang does not try to provide any general explanation of the process, but broadly accepts Sauer's idea of South-East Asian fisherfolk utilizing bamboos, gourds, fish poisons and fibre-yielding plants, and tubers, water chestnut (*Eleocharis tuberosa*) and calatrop (*Trapa natans*) for subsistence. The concentration of marine resources would have enabled permanent settlements to develop in the early post-Pleistocene period, and the first cultivation was 'probably undertaken in little patches near individual homes'. Only small peripheral forest clearings were necessary and 'no tool more elaborate than a digging stick was used' (Chang 1970: 180). Chang cites Gorman's results from Spirit Cave, and his own from Taiwan, as at least supporting such a reconstruction.

Harris (1973a and b) has refined some of these arguments and in particular has pointed to the need for some sort of stress situation to develop before hunter-gatherers find it profitable to develop techniques of food production. This may take the form of changes in the natural environment independent of man, changes induced by man, population increase and competition for scarce resources induced by reduction in mobility. He argues cogently that different combinations of these factors, in different places, and at various times in prehistory have led to what he calls 'alternative pathways towards agriculture'. In South-East Asia, he argues that forested and wooded areas within the seasonally dry, intermediate tropical zone are the homelands of most tropical cultigens, and that fixed plot horticulture in small domestic gardens adjacent to houses probably represent man's earliest system of proto-cultivation in the tropics. These conditions would have been best suited to the cultivation of both vegetatively and seed-propagated plants, perennial climbers, shrubs and trees. Cereals and other herbaceous plants would have been more effectively grown in larger-scale clearings, swiddens, made especially for this purpose. The expansion from domestic to swidden plots may have resulted from population increase and/or inter-group warfare (Harris 1973a: 405). He adds that seed-crop swidden systems are ecologically less stable than vegecultural systems and are likely to have expanded territorially, gaining spatial ascendancy over vegeculture. That such a process has been happening into recent historic times in South-East Asia is well documented by Spencer (1966) in his study, *Shifting Agriculture in South-East Asia*.

Gorman (1973) argues that there is no real reason to accept the priority of vegeculture over seed cultivation in South-East Asia, and that rice may first have been cultivated in the lower piedmont areas of South China and South-East Asia together with taro and yams prior to 7000 B.C. The basis for his argument is complex, but seems to depend on the fact that when agricultural peoples moved into the islands of the western Pacific in the second millennium B.C. they apparently were not cultivating rice, but took with them traits (particularly stone and pottery types) derived from Lungshanoid, supposed rice cultivators of South China.

THE RECENT ARCHAEOLOGICAL EVIDENCE

Botanical remains from Spirit Cave, Thailand, have been cited as evidence in favour of an early and independent development of South-East Asian agriculture within the context of terminal Pleistocene and early Recent Hoabinhian culture.

The botanical remains include 12 genera of mainly seed-propagated plants: *Aleurites, Areca, Canarium, Cucumis, Lagenaria, Madhuca, Piper, Prunus, Terminalia, Trapa, Vicia* or *Phaseolus,* and *Pisum* or *Raphia.* The tentative identifications, and particularly the difficulty of the Bishop Museum botanists in distinguishing between *Pisum* or pea, and *Raphia* - a palm native to Africa and America (Burkill 1935 II: 1900-1) - has led to rejection, or severe doubt as to the value, of this evidence by some botanists, notably by Harlan and de Wet (1973).

Claims have been made, from the careful 'harvesting of domestically useful wild or semi-domesticated species' (Harris 1973a: 410) to assertions of the world's first agriculture (Solheim 1971: 339) on the basis of these finds. The botanists all seem to accept that it is very difficult to distinguish wild from cultivated varieties of these plants, but to my mind the most significant point is that this list represents plants, most of which, later, are certainly domesticated, and that it includes virtually nothing which remains wild, occasionally utilized, or altogether abandoned. This is remarkable when we think how many useful, but not domesticated, plants have been found in archaeological sites in Europe and the Near East: couch grass, field brassica, soft brome, shepherd's purse, *Chenopodium album,* hemp nettle, and many others. Jane Renfrew (1973: Ch.19) lists about 50 such species.

The faunal evidence from Hoabinhian sites is summarized by Gorman (1971), and in a recent paper Higham (1973) compares the finds of Spirit Cave, Banyan Valley Cave and Laang Spean. A large range of species is present, including pig, cattle, various deer, rhinoceros, several monkeys and carnivores, rats, porcupine, ground and flying squirrel, bats, freshwater fish, turtle and crabs and shellfish and lizards. No evidence of domestication (although caves may reflect only the hunting aspect of an otherwise agricultural economy)-but the wide range in species, which includes virtually all terrestrial animals (except some of the very large animals such as elephant and tapir) and many arboreal species suggests a broadly-based hunting economy, focussing on cervids, suids and primates, but not dominated by them. Gorman's compilation of the faunal reports from 26 Hoabinhian sites (1971: table 2) in Thailand, Malaya, Cambodia and Vietnam, further supports this interpretation, and Gorman specifically refers to the concept of a 'broad spectrum exploitation as pre-adaptation to early domestication'.

PRIME MOVERS FOR THE DEVELOPMENT OF AGRICULTURE IN SOUTH-EAST ASIA

If we accept Harris's argument for the need for some stress factor in hunting and collecting economies before agriculture can became an effective subsistence strategy, we must look for potential causes of stress in South-East Asian communities in the late Pleistocene and early Recent periods. There is no space to discuss the various models - Childe's (1936: 86-7) climatic change, Braidwood and Howe's (1960:

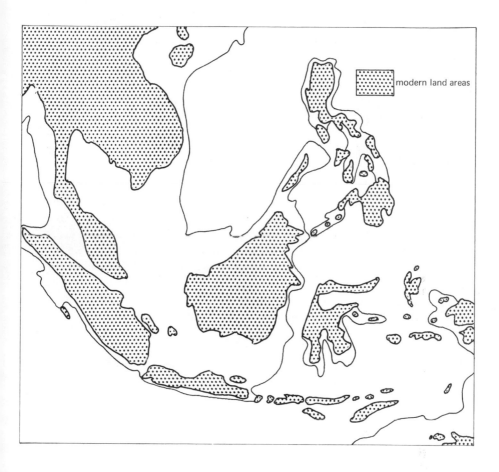

Figure 50. South-East Asia, showing the extent of the Sunda and Sahul Shelves likely to have been dry land at times of low sea level. The outer line follows the 200m submarine contour and roughly indicates the area of lowland plains exposed between 30,000 and 20,000 BP, and which was progressively drowned from 20,000 to 7,000/6,000 BP.

Although present estimates for glacial minima vary between − 100m and − 150m, because the outer edges of the continental shelves slope more steeply than the inner parts, the 200m submarine contour, because of its availability on published maps, is not significantly misleading on small-scale maps for the extent of land exposed at maximum low sea level in the Upper Pleistocene *(after Jennings)*. Scale:1cm = c.350km.

181-4) cumulative evolution, Binford's (1968) demographic stress, Flannery's (1968) 'positive feedback' model, or Bray's (1976) recent systems equilibrium model, which have been advanced as explanatory frameworks for the development of agriculture. Equilibrium models for hunter-gatherers are particularly fashionable at present and rather tend to overlook the fact that radical changes in social and economic systems *did* occur apparently at approximately the same time in Western Asia, Central and South America and, I believe, in North-East and South-East Asia, and all led by different routes, towards increased human populations dependent for the most part on cultivated plants. Unless we believe that such a development was inevitable, causes must be sought.

Here, I want to discuss just two possible stress-causing factors which may have been significant in stimulating adaptive changes in subsistence patterns in South-East Asia towards the end of the Pleistocene. The first, which has already been mentioned by Gorman (1971: 306-8), is the late Pleistocene marine transgression. At about 18,000-20,000 BP world sea levels were about 120-130 m below present, extensive areas of the Sunda shelf would have been dry land and Sumatra, Java, Borneo and Palawan were linked to the mainland. There is much dispute over the exact rate of the subsequent marine transgression, but by 10,000 years ago the sea seems to have been at 10-15m below present levels, and it reached them by about 8,000-5,000 years ago. Tectonic movements have certainly occurred during this time in South-East Asia, but are not thought to have been significant, except perhaps in Java and some of the islands on the Outer Banda Archipelago. If we accept these provisional figures, then we can say that at 20,000 years ago, Sundaland was about twice its present size, with a coastline about half the present one. By 5,000 years ago, when the present coastline had certainly appeared, the proportion of coast to land had increased by roughly a factor of four times. In addition, the proportion of highlands to lowlands has increased substantially. These estimates provide a crude indication of the extent of late Pleistocene-mid-Recent landform changes (fig. 50).

Recent discussions of the problems of agricultural origins tend to dismiss single 'prime movers' and in particular discount the importance of late Pleistocene climatic changes. In South-East Asia, Late Würm termperatures were only a few degrees (3-5°C) below present levels and may have had only a limited direct effect in depressing altitudinal vegetation zones in the upland areas. But if we accept Verstappen's (1975) argument that changes in the intensity and pattern of movement of the intertropical convergence zone (ITC) characterized Pleistocene climates, then greater aridity and greater seasonal variation in precipitation would have obtained in South-East Asia during cold phases in more extreme latitudes. Areas now under equatorial forest would have been smaller in extent, and monsoon forest and savanna characterized most of lowland South-East Asia at 20,000 years ago. The next 10,000 years saw reduction in the area of vegetation adapted to marked seasonal variation in rainfall as the ITC gained in strength and remained longer over South-East Asia. These changes, combined with the alteration in physical environment through flooding of the Sunda shelf, surely provided a massive dislocation of existing hunting communities, creating both demographic and resource availability stress of the sort envisaged by both Binford and Harris (fig. 51).

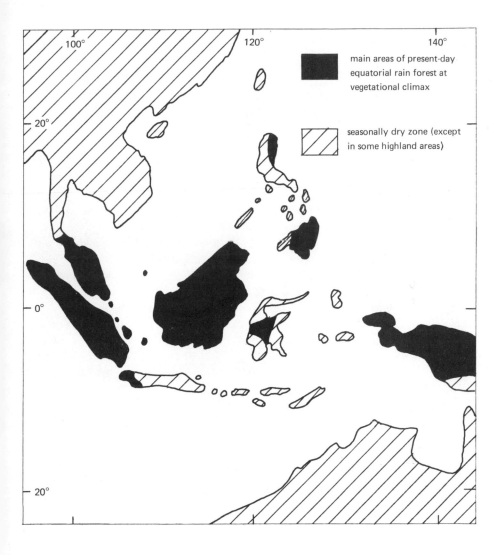

Figure 51. Present-day distribution of ever-wet, and occasionally seasonally dry vegetation, much simplified. At times of low sea level and colder temperatures such as during the Würm IV Period, these areas of equatorial rain forest are believed to have been reduced in size and the now flooded Sunda and Sahul Shelves would have been extensions of the seasonally dry zones of, respectively, mainland South-East Asia and Wallacea, and Australia and Papua *(after van Steenis)*.

DISCUSSION

What role in the economic transformation of South-East Asian society was played by those communities whose material remains we group together under the term Hoabinhian? The term Hoabinhian relates, in the first place, to distinctive assemblages of stone tools, and it is clear that consideration of these tells us little about the subsistence base of their makers. It is also clear that the level of archaeological research in South-East Asia has been, until quite recently, too primitive to answer this sort of question. The presence of surviving hunting peoples has been in one sense a handicap to achieving a better understanding of Hoabinhian culture, for they have provided a too ready, if poorly understood, framework into which to fit the archaeological finds. No Hoabinhian site has provided undoubted evidence of domesticated plant remains (but it must be recognized that they have only been searched for at one or two), and no site has contained the bones of domesticated animals. Apart from Gorman's finds at Spirit Cave and the controversial interpretations put on them by some writers there would be few internal grounds on which to reject Matthew's (1966: 94) characterization of the Hoabinhian as a post-Pleistocene, mesolithic culture based on hunting and gathering: the archaeological manifestation of the way of life still followed by these small, scattered communities of forest collectors such as the Semang and Tasaday.

Chronologically some Hoabinhian levels can now be put back into the very end of the Pleistocene, but the opening date of about 50,000 BP suggested by Solheim (1972: 149) lacks any empirical support. The end of Hoabinhian assemblages appears to vary depending on locality. In north Thailand Gorman has good evidence for its replacement by about 5000 B.C., but elsewhere much later dates are claimed: the third or early second millennium B.C. in south-western Thailand, the third millennium B.C. in Tonkin (but without any support from modern dating). In Malaya Hoabinhian types are replaced at Gua Kechil about 2800 B.C., but at other sites not far distant, Hoabinhian tools are said to overlie, and postdate, finds which can be rather securely attributed to the period of Indian religious and trading contacts of the early second millennium A.D.

Nevertheless, Gorman and others have presented rather strong arguments that an indigenous development of the techniques of plant and animal domestication took place in South-East Asia within the context of Hoabinhian cultures. Not only were the traditional root and tree crops of the region taken into cultivation, but rice (Gorman 1973), now the world's most important cereal crop, may also be a legacy of those early post-Pleistocene monsoon forest dwellers. So far there is nothing in the Hoabinhian material equipment to indicate clearly their economic orientations. Nor is the analysis of this equipment sufficiently advanced for us to discriminate between regional, temporal and functional variations of the Hoabinhian throughout South-East Asia. As Matthews (1966: 1) pointed out, Hoabinhian, 'is a term which ignores significant differences rather than emphasising precise similarities'. But unless we reject entirely the concept of the local development of plant and animal domestication in South-East Asia by the mid-Recent period, an idea which has considerable botanical support and for which good evidence from well-conducted excavations is slowly growing, and return to the notion that the arts of agriculture and settled village life were introduced into South-East Asia through the southward migration of mongoloid farmers whose cultural inheritance came ultimately from the 'nuclear area' of North China, then there is no alternative but to accept the fact that some groups within the too-broadly-embracing label of Hoabinhian Culture took those first steps towards changing the basis of their subsistence from entirely wild to managed, and finally.dependent, domesticated plants. At the same time, we must recognize that many, perhaps most groups, whose remains we class as Hoabinhian, were entirely collectors of wild foods and remained this way long after agricultural village settlements had appeared on the lowland river plains of South-East Asia; even in some places, after towns and proto-states had grown up, importing their models of religious and political organization from India and forging commercial links with places as far distant as the Mediterranean and North China.

Additional note on distribution of sites (see p.148)
In a recent paper Brandt (1976: 51) calls attention to another location for Hoabinhian sites in north-eastern Sumatra, on low hilly terraces behind the coastal plains, and he postulates a seasonal movement between these sites and the adjacent coastal and riverine shell middens. In a lecture given in 1925 P.V. van Stein Callenfels referred to 50 such open-air sites, apart from the middens, in the districts of Langkat and Serdang.

REFERENCES

Aung Thaw, U., 1971. 'The "neolithic" culture of the Padah-Lin Caves', *Asian Perspectives, 14*, 123-33.

Bicchieri, M.G. (ed.), 1972. *Hunters and Gatherers Today* (New York).

Binford, L.R., 1968. 'Post-Pleistocene adaptations', in *New Perspectives in Archaeology*, ed. L.R. and S.R. Binford, 1968 (Chicago), 313-42.

Binford, L.R., 1973. 'Interassemblage variability - the Mousterian and the "functional" argument', in *The Explanation of Culture Change*, ed. C. Renfrew, 1973, 227-54.

Boriskovsky, P.I., 1969/1970. *Vietnam in Primeval Times*, Chs. IV and V, trans. from Russian in *Soviet Anthropology and Archaeology, 8(3)*, 214-57.

Braidwood, R.J. and Howe, B., 1960. *Prehistoric Investigations in Iraqi Kurdistan* (Chicago).

Brandt, R.W., 1976. 'The Hoabinhian of Sumatra: some remarks', *Modern Quaternary Research in Southeast Asia, 2*, 49-52.

Bray, W.M., 1976. 'From predation to production: the nature of agricultural evolution in Mexico and Peru', in *Problems in Social and Economic Archaeology*, ed. G. de G. Sieveking, I.H. Longworth and K.E. Wilson, 1976, 73-95.

Bronson, B., 1973. 'Prehistory and early history of Central Thailand with special reference to Chansen'. Paper delivered to *London Colloquy on Early Southeast Asia*, September 1973 (duplicated).

Brookfield, H.C., with Hart, D., 1971. *Melanesia: a geographical interpretation of an island world*.

Burkill, I.H., 1935. *A Dictionary of the Economic Products of the Malay Peninsula*.

Candolle, A. de, 1883. *Origine des plantes cultivées* (Paris).

Chang, K.C., 1970. 'The beginnings of agriculture in the Far East', *Antiquity, 44*, 175-85.

Childe, V.G., 1936. *Man Makes Himself*.

Clarke, D.L., 1968. *Analytical Archaeology*.

Davidson, J.H.C.S., 1973. 'Archaeology in Vietnam since 1954'. Paper delivered to *London Colloquy on Early Southeast Asia*, September 1973. (Duplicated).

Dunn, F.L., 1964. 'Excavations at Gua Kechil, Pahang', *Journal of the Malaysian Branch of the Royal Asiatic Society, 37*, 87-124.

Flannery, K.V., 1968. 'Archaeological systems theory and early Mesoamerica', in *Anthropological Archaeology in the Americas*, ed. B.J. Meggars, 1968 (Washington), 67-87.

Fernandez, C.A. II and Lynch, F., 1972. 'The Tasaday: cave, dwelling food gatherers of South Cotabato, Mindanao, *Philippines Sociological Review 20(3)*, 279-330.

Geertz, C., 1963. *Agricultural Involution: the process of ecological change in Indonesia* (Berkeley and Los Angeles).

Glover, I.C., 1973. 'Settlements and mobility among the hunters-gatherers of South-east Asia', in *Man, Settlement and Urbanism*, ed. P. Ucko, R. Tringham and G.W. Dimbleby, 1971, 157-64.

Glover, I.C., 1973. 'Late Stone Age Traditions in Southeast Asia', in *South Asian Archaeology*, ed. N. Hammond, 1973, 51-65.

Gorman, C.F., 1971. 'The Hoabinhian and after: subsistence patterns in Southeast Asia during the Late Pleistocene and early Recent periods', *World Archaeology, 2(3)*, 300-20.

Gorman, C.F., 1973. '*A priori* models and Thai Prehistory: a reconsideration of the beginnings of agriculture in Southeastern Asia'. Symposium: Origins of Agriculture. Ninth I.C.A.E.S., Chicago. (Duplicated).

Hanks, L.M., 1972. *Rice and Man: agricultural ecology in Southeast Asia* (Chicago).

Harlan, J.R. and de Wet, J.M.J., 1973. 'On the quality of evidence for origin and dispersal of cultivated plants', *Curr.Anthrop., 14 (1-2)*, 51-61.

Harris, D.R., 1973a. 'The prehistory of tropical agriculture: an ethno-ecological model', in *The Explanation of Culture Change,* ed. C. Renfrew, 1973, 391-417.

Harris, D.R., 1973b. 'Alternative pathways towards agriculture'. Symposium: Origins of Agriculture. Ninth I.C.A.E.S., Chicago. (Duplicated.)

Heekeren, H.R. van, 1972. *The Stone Age of Indonesia* (2nd edn) (The Hague).

Heekeren, H.R. van and Knuth, E., 1967. *Sai Yok, Archaeological Excavations in Thailand, Vol.I* (Copenhagen).

Higham, C.F.W., 1972. 'Initial model formulation in *Terra Incognita*', in *Models in Archaeology,* ed. D.L. Clarke, 1972, 453-76.

Higham, C.F.W., 1973. 'Economic changes in prehistoric Thailand'. Symposium: Origins of Agriculture. Ninth I.C.A.E.S., Chicago. (Duplicated.)

Jenning, J.N., 1971. 'Sea level changes and land links', in *Aboriginal Man and Environment in Australia,* ed. D.J. Mulvaney and J. Golson (Canberra).

Lee, R.B., 1972. 'The !Kung Bushmen of Botswana', in Bicchieri 1972, 326-68.

Lee, R.B. and de Vore, I (eds.), 1968. *Man the Hunter* (Chicago).

Li, H., 1970. 'The origin of cultivated plants in Southeast Asia', *Economic Botany, 24,* 3-19.

Mangelsdorf, P.C., 1953. 'Review of "Agricultural Origins and Dispersals" by Carl O. Sauer', *American Antiquity, 19(1),* 87-90.

Matthews, J.M., 1961. *A Checklist of 'Hoabinhian' sites excavated in Malaya 1860-1939* (Singapore).

Matthews, J.M., 1964. *'The Hoabinhian in Southeast Asia and Elsewhere'* (Ph.D. Thesis, Australian National University, Canberra; unpublished).

Matthews, J.M., 1966. 'A review of the Hoabinhian in Indo-China', *Asian Perspectives, 9,* 86-95.

Mourer, C. and R., 1970. 'The prehistoric industry of Laang Spean, Province of Battambang, Cambodia', *Archaeology and Physical Anthropology in Oceania, 5(2),* 128-46.

Mourer, C. and R., 1971. 'Prehistoric research in Cambodia', *Asian Perspectives, 14* (1973 for 1971).

Peterson, W., 1974. 'Summary report of two archaeological sites from N.E. Luzon', *Archaeology and Physical Anthropology in Oceania, 9(1),* 26-35.

Al Rashid, 1973. 'Malaysian prehistory: a review', in *Radiocarbon and Indian Archaeology,* ed. D.P. Agrawal and A. Ghosh, 1973 (Bombay: Tata Institute of Fundamental Research), 88-95.

Renfrew, J., 1973. *Palaeoethnobotany.*

Sauer, C.O., 1952. *Agricultural Origins and Dispersals* (American Geographical Society, Bowman Memorial Lectures ser. 2, New York).

Silberbauer, G.B., 1972. 'The G/wi Bushmen', in Bicchieri 1972, 271-325.

Solheim, W.G.II, 1971, 'New light on a forgotten past'. *National Geographic, 139(3),* 330-9.

Solheim, W.G.II, 1972. 'Northern Thailand, Southeast Asia and World Prehistory', *Asian Perspectives, 13* (for 1970), 145-57.

Sørensen, P., 1973. 'Prehistoric iron implements from Thailand', *Asian Perspectives, 16(2),* 134-73.

Spencer, J.E., 1966. *Shifting cultivation in Southeastern Asia,* University of California Publications in Geography, vol. 19, Berkeley, Cal.

Spooner, B. (ed.), 1972. *Population growth: anthropological implications* (Cambridge, Mass.).

Turnbull, C., 1965. *The Wayward Servants: the two worlds of the African Pygmies* (New York).

van Steenis, C.G.G.J., 1961. 'Preliminary revisions of Malaysian Papilionaceae', *Reinwardtia, 5 pt IV,* 420-9.

Vavilov, N.I., 1951. *The Origin, Variation, Immunity and Breeding of Cultivated Plants* (New York).

Velder, C., 1963. 'A Description of the Mrbrai Camp', *Journal of the Siam Society, 51(2),* 185-8.

Verstappen, H.Th., 1975. 'On palaeoclimates and landform development in Malesia', *Modern Quaternary Research in Southeast Asia, 1,* 3-35.

Wolf, E.R., 1966. *Peasants* (New Jersey).

Woodburn, J., 1968. 'An introduction to Hadza ecology; and stability and flexibility in Hadza residential groupings', in Lee and DeVore 1968, 49-55 and 103-10.

Woodburn, J., 1971. 'Ecology, nomadic movement and the composition of the local group among hunters and gatherers: an East African example and its implications', in *Man, Settlement and Urbanism,* ed. P.Ucko, R.Tringham and G.W.Dimbleby, 193-206.

JIM ALLEN

8 The hunting Neolithic: adaptations to the food quest in prehistoric Papua New Guinea

New Guinea is an island some 2,400 km long, which for the majority of its length is less than 500 km wide. Across this relatively narrow front, however, altitude varies from sea level to beyond 4,500 m with the high mountains not merely isolated peaks, but part of a central cordillera which runs for most of the length of the country. Thus while climatically the entire island lies within the humid tropics, it contains significant areas of montane and alpine vegetation. Within 6 degrees of the equator some mountains are high enough for ice to form permanently, and for frosts to be widespread. Rainfall varies within the island between 100 and 500 cm per annum depending on location, and likewise rainfall patterns differ, moving from continuously heavy to continuously light on the one hand, to a variety of strongly seasonal patterns on the other. Other climatic factors also show strong variation. For example, evaporation rates, normally governed by high humidities and cloud cover, are for the most part low, but the Port Moresby area, with a mean annual average of 7 hours sunshine per day, has evaporation rates in excess of the rainfall, with consequent effects on the vegetation patterns. The variation in environments is perceived by the Melanesians in terms of the most readily observable features, particularly vegetation, and while New Guinea can be said to be 90 per cent forest, such a statement obscures the diverse nature of the country's vegetation, and the distinct types which occupy particular habitats, ranging from the coastal swamps to the alpine grassland zones, each with their particular range of resources.

The physical background of the country combines with two other facts to provide an almost unique situation for archaeological and anthropological research. The first of these is that European colonization of the country began little more than a century ago and in many areas has only made imperceptible inroads into traditional subsistence strategies; the second is that 100 years ago there existed a landmass in excess of 850,000 square kilometres, populated at a conservative estimate by 2,500,000 people (Brookfield with Hart 1971:1v, 65-8) who neither traded nor manufactured any metal implements, but who, in the main, derived their food from horticultural practices of various sorts. In this sense New Guinea remains a living neolithic country of great diversity, but one in which archaeologists provided with the twin data sources of ethnography and archaeology are being forced to reconsider premises concerning the social and economic development of man which have for too long been taken for granted by many prehistorians. Despite the altered economic emphases of such constructs as savagery/barbarism versus palaeolithic/ neolithic versus hunter-gatherer/food producer, the basic dichotomy between the two behaviour patterns and its implications for the social evolution of man have been seen as sufficiently profound as to be labelled a revolution if not, indeed, a revelation. It is therefore somewhat disconcerting to be confronted with an entire country whose ethnography reflects a wide range of subsistence strategies varying from almost complete hunting and collecting to intensive agricultural practices providing almost all the required food. It seems clear that in the main, adaptations to the food quest in New Guinea depend upon local environments and their localized resources, although strategies need not necessarily be conditioned solely by environmental advantages and constraints; the whole gamut of observable social values offers indications of caution towards the naive models of prehistory.

FOOD

In traditional New Guinea, animal husbandry is confined to the cassowary which is tamed but not bred, the dog which may or may not be eaten depending on the locality, the chicken and the pig. Of these, only the cassowary is indigenous to New Guinea, and only the pig appears to contribute in any significant way to the diet; even with the pig, its contribution to the ritual aspects of life would appear to be equally as important as its contribution as a food source. It is the plants which form the basis of life for New Guinea man.

At contact the majority of the New Guinean population subsisted on gardens growing a variety of starchy tubers as staple crops. These tubers, taro, yam and sweet potato, together with bananas and subsidiary crops such as sugar cane, other fruits and nuts, and green vegetables, present at face value a deceptively simple picture. For example, the Tsembaga people alone possess 90 varieties of the three basic tubers, and grow a further 174 locally-named plants in gardens, in addition to silviculture outside gardens and the added exploitation of over 200 non-domesticated trees, shrubs, vines, fungi and epiphytes from a number of ecological zones (Rappaport 1968: 42-56, 271-7). In a recent review of ethnobotanical literature Powell listed 650 species of plants representing 378 genera and 134 families used for food, poisons and medicines and as raw materials for a variety of other tasks in New Guinea, and such a list can be considered far from exhaustive (Powell, in press).

Of the tubers, the sweet potato, *Ipomoea batatas,* is the staple for a large number of people in New Guinea, but is restricted as a first crop mainly to the highlands regions. A plant of tropical American origin, it had certainly diffused across the Pacific prior to the arrival of Europeans, being well established in New Zealand and other areas of the central Pacific when Europeans arrived. Until recently the sweet potato in New Guinea was generally accepted to have arrived there via South-East Asia, where it was taken by the Portuguese and Spanish in the fifteenth and sixteenth centuries A.D. (Yen 1971a), but recent archaeological research in New Guinea, discussed below, has revived the theory that it may have diffused across the Pacific to New Guinea at an earlier date. Taro, *Colocasia esculenta,* the fundamental crop of rain forest swidden gardening, appears to have been the most important staple in prehistoric New Guinea prior to the arrival of the sweet potato and is usually considered to be an 'ancient' introduction together with the yams, principally *Dioscoria alata* and *D. esculenta,* which may have been preferred in drier situations. Taro is thought to have been initially domesticated in western Indonesia or India, and the two yams in Indo-China (Brookfield with Hart 1971: 82). Among the lesser crops also introduced into prehistoric New Guinea can be listed bananas of the Eumusa section, various beans such as *Psophocarpus tetragonolobus, Lablab niger,* and *Phaseolus lunatus,* and the gourd, *Lagenaria siceraria* (Powell, in press).

While the most important staples grown in gardens today have been introduced from outside New Guinea, an impressive list of indigenous domesticated plants can be be added to them. This list includes other tubers, *Cordyline terminalis, Pueraria lobata,* and perhaps some of the lesser yams *Dioscoria bulbifera, D. nummularia, D. pentaphylla,* and *D. hispida;* sugar cane *(Saccharum officinarum)* and the edible pitpits *Saccharum edule* and *Setaria palmifolia;* the fe'i banana of the Australimusa section; a range of green vegetables including *Rungia klossii, Hibiscus manihot, Oenanthe javanica, Commelina spp., Solanum nigrum,* and possibly the *Amaranthus spp.* Of the pandanus species, coastal forms are pan-tropical, but some montane forms are indigenous to New Guinea. The coconut and breadfruit are considered by some authorities to have been domesticated in the Melanesian area. Last but not least the sago palm *(Metroxylon spp.)* is also cultivated, but its exploitation in its wild state remains today extremely important and widespread. An enormous number of non-domesticated indigenous plants are also exploited, amongst which the mangrove species and *Cycas spp.* on the coast seem likely to have been more important as food sources in the past (Brookfield with Hart 1971: 82-3; Yen 1971b: 4 and 1973; Powell, in press).

Along with the variety of domesticated crops in New Guinea are found a variety of horticultural practices. These range from houseplot gardens and simple swiddening systems to complex systems involving intensive labour input and significant alterations to the natural ecosystems. Most of New Guinea and half of its population fall into the less intensive class, where gardens depend upon long fallow periods during which the soil is naturally regenerated. Such gardens occur at a wide range of altitudes, and contain all the major crops at one place or another. All gardens are mixed, although one staple is usually dominant. Preparation of the ground is minimal; after clearing and burning crops are planted between fallen trunks. The gardens are untidy and quickly invaded by weeds, although they are normally fenced against the predatory pig.

In some areas gardens which remain essentially swidden gardens do exhibit greater intensification practices, particularly towards the production of a single crop or more intensive preparation of the ground, such as tillage and composting. Elsewhere more specific alterations may be noted. The Marind Anim of the south coast, for example, whose basic subsistence is derived from wild sago, construct elaborate high garden mounds on the edges of swamps for the growing of yams (Brookfield with Hart

Figure 52. Highland Papua New Guinea: paddle-shaped spade in use for yam plot *(photograph: R.J. Lampert).*

1971: 109).

More intensive gardening practices are confined for the most part to the highlands of New Guinea, where large areas of land have been transformed into tame ecosystems. Separate garden types can be recognized and normally high population densities are found in areas of arable land. Here deforested areas are maintained in frequent or constant use and the ground is prepared by complete tillage, grid-iron ditching or mound building. Slope retention practices are employed and drainage is practised by ditching and mounding. Crops are normally segregated as far as the staples are concerned although mixed gardens of subsidiary crops can be located. The epitome of these intensive agricultural practices is found amongst the Dani of what is now Irian Jaya. There on the floor of the Baliem Valley, island garden beds are maintained by a complex hydraulic system of dams and ditches with the outflow being eventually taken off into the river. Dry stone walling on the steep slopes is used as fencing and as a soil retention device (fig. 52).

To characterize this diversity in agricultural practices, Brookfield and Hart (1971: 94-116) have developed an intensity ranking which this brief résumé has followed and which is summarized in fig. 53. What are important here are two conclusions which these authors reached: firstly, that in New Guinea there is no simple correlation between agricultural intensity and population pressure or land shortage: 'We find intensive practices in situations where there is no population pressure, and extensive practices in areas where land is short' (ibid. :120). Secondly, that intensification is not a one-way process - that there has been in certain instances over the last century a retrogression to less intensive methods (ibid. :116-18). The point cannot be laboured here, but it would seem that both these situations occur because of a wide range of behavioural conditions applying which are not of immediate relevance to the food quest, but rather which impinge upon it because of a range of social and ritual considerations; for example some 60 per cent of sweet potato crops grown under intensive methods in the highlands are used to feed pigs, themselves not to be used primarily for food. 'The huge pig-exchange systems of the New Guinea highlands, the whole structure of intergroup and interpersonal exchange, security, prestige and power, is supported by production that is handsomely surplus to the basic subsistence needs of the population' (Brookfield with Hart 1971: 119). It is easy to see that fundamental alterations to agricultural procedure would probably occur under the development of this primarily ritual requirement, or indeed if it were now suddenly to cease.

This review has so far paid little attention to the collection of wild plants, and while details must be bypassed it must be re-emphasized that the collection and utilization of an enormous number of wild plants remains an important aspect of the food quest of New Guinea. Of these plants sago (Metroxylon spp.) is outstanding, and even though a wild plant, it is the staple for a large percentage of the lowland population, providing in some cases up to 90 per cent of the diet. Patricia Townsend working with the Sanio-Hiowe, an upper Sepik group, recorded that sago provides 85 per cent of the caloric value of the local diet, with a further 5 per cent coming from wild and domesticated vegetable foods such as bananas, tubers, breadfruit seeds, pandanus and green vegetables, and the final 10 per cent being meat from feral and domesticated pigs, small game, fish and insect larvae. Wild sago is abundant in the region; a single woman processing sago can provide 85 per cent of one day's caloric intake for 16-17 people in a day's work. Among these people it is the scarcity of the

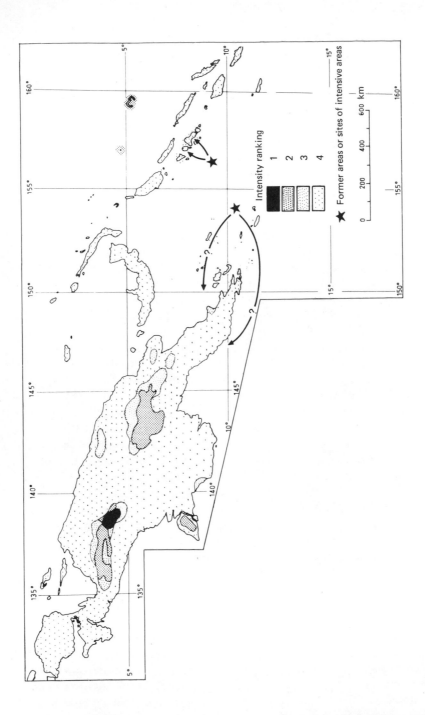

Figure 53. Papua New Guinea agricultural systems ranked according to the intensiveness of the systems as calculated by Brookfield and Hart (1971: 117, fig. 4.2). Classes 1 and 2 equate with Brookfield and Hart's 2A and 2B high intensity systems, and classes 3 and 4 with these authors' low intensity systems. For a full discussion of this classification see Brookfield with Hart 1971: 94-117.

remaining 15 per cent which is crucial. It not only prevents total sedentism but also restricts the birth rate (Townsend 1971). Variations in the pattern of adaptation of sago staple communities elsewhere in New Guinea appear to depend upon the sparsity or density of wild sago stands and the availability of the other elements of diet. Where sago stands are sparse and movement between stands is required, gardens may be limited to bananas or other crops which require little tending. Where stands are dense, a range of domesticated plants may be cultivated on a small scale. Elsewhere access to marine resources to supplement sago may provide conditions for larger and more sedentary settlement.

In view of the richness of New Guinea flora the role of indigenous wild animals in the food quest can only be regarded as minor. Compared with the characteristic large Asian fauna - rhinoceroses, elephants, deer, cattle, carnivores and monkeys - New Guinea's largest indigenous animals today are the cassowary and relatively small wallabies, the largest of which might average 20 kilos in weight. Adding to these other small marsupials, anteaters, rats, bats, flying-foxes, reptiles, birds and freshwater eels, and allowing for a scarcity of freshwater fish, it is reasonable to conclude that away from the coast, where shell and scale fish, turtle and dugong are plentiful, hunting for food is not a profitable year-round basis of existence even among groups whose economy can be considered to be essentially 'hunter-gatherer'. Despite eloquent tributes to the diversity and ingenuity of New Guinea hunters (R. Bulmer 1968 and 1976; Dwyer 1974), the spread of techniques and prey seem to reflect the stresses of a poor hunting situation as much as the ingenuity of the hunters.

Hard data on this question is poor, since specific studies of contemporary hunting are almost non-existent. Dwyer's recent study of the Komonku in the Eastern Highlands District would appear likely to be prejudiced by the fact that the area is both heavily populated and largely deforested, but even allowing for this returns were remarkably poor (Dwyer 1974). Nocturnal rain forest hunting for possum, cuscus and giant rats returned a yield of less than 20 kilos of meat for almost 500 man-hours of hunting, the food value of the yield being well below the estimated energy expended. Hunting flying-fox showed a collect of 32 kilos of these animals for 165 man-hours, in this case a slight energetic gain. Perhaps the best hunting situation recorded in the ethnographic literature comes from the Port Moresby savannah grasslands, where the Koita could take up to 500 wallabies, mainly *Macropus agilis,* in a single hunt (Romilly 1893:327). The figures here are not specific, but this might mean 800 man-hours for 7000 kilos bag weight, or about 9 kilos per man-hour - a return about 200 times greater than in the Komonku example above. But while this hunting is highly profitable in terms of energy return, it involves the organization of perhaps 100 men from five or ten different hamlets, and the use of fire-driving which is highly seasonal and limited to a few months of the year. At other times hunting individual animals by spear would be less profitable.

Most published anthropological studies in New Guinea pay little more than lip service to hunting for food, and even fewer have provided quantitative data or comment on hunting skills. Meggitt noted that the Western Highlands Enga recognized between 25 and 30 mammals and at least 100 sorts of bird which would be eaten if captured, but that only cassowaries, water fowl and pigeons would be hunted with enthusiasm for food, and that not withstanding the variety of animal food, it contributed negligible amounts of protein to the diet because most Enga are 'dismally inept bushmen and hunters' (Meggitt 1958:285).* Rappaport reported a similar situation among the Tsembaga, where although game is relatively plentiful in a number of ecological niches it contributes by weight only one per cent of the daily food intake. Unlike other Marin groups the Tsembaga do not raise many cassowaries from chicks, but these birds remain important as a trade item and a source of feathers for fighting headdresses. Despite this Rappaport recorded that in his 15-month field season the Tsembaga failed to catch any of these animals, and managed only six feral pig captures during the same period (Rappaport 1968 : 78-9).

Impressions gained from the available evidence are firstly that the modern suite of New Guinea fauna is not a viable basis for man's subsistence since it comprises small birds and animals which are predominantly non-gregarious and therefore more difficult to capture in sufficient quantities (Calaby 1971: 89), and secondly, that despite a diverse and ingenious range of hunting techniques, New Guineans as a whole may not be particularly proficient hunters. As a rationalization, the explanation of the growing unimportance of hunting and the loss of hunting skills as a consequence of increased gardening is only superficially attractive, for it is equally clear from the ethnography that hunting to produce a range of artifacts other than food, hunting for ritual and prestation purposes, hunting to acquire status, hunting as a pleasurable pastime, and hunting to obtain small but vital quantities of animal protein has remained of great importance. The loss of past skills in this activity seems doubtful.

The contrast between the potential of indigenous animal hunting and the potential for indigenous plant gathering in New Guinea appears more extreme than in some other places in the world, and clearly emphasizes Lee's remark that 'mammal hunting is the least reliable of the subsistence sources, and one would expect few societies to place primary dependence upon it' (1968: 42). In terms of both wild and domesticated foods New Guinea diet tends strongly towards the vegetarian, so much so indeed that nutritional studies suggest that average values for calorie and protein intake from the predominantly starchy diet are so far below what is considered 'normal' elsewhere as to indicate that metabolic pathways may also differ from accepted norms. New Guinean physical performances suggest that New Guineans are well adapted to this uneven diet (Powell, in press).

To summarize thus far, Papua New Guinea presents a patchwork quilt of subsistence strategies ranging from almost total dependence on wild foods to an equally great dependence on domesticated ones. Throughout the spectrum the importance of vegetable foods outweights that provided by animals. Gardening technology likewise ranges from simple houseplot horticulture and extensive swidden gardens to the labour-intensive, complex agricultural practices which have transformed natural ecosystems into artificial ones. Although the more intensive systems are largely confined to the highland valleys, there are no distinct gradings across the landscape. In 1936 F. E. Williams observed that the Garamundi of the Trans-Fly region depended almost entirely for subsistence on wild sago and wallaby hunting, while amongst their immediate neighbours hunting and gathering nowhere took precedence over gardening (Williams 1936: 221).

*This view may be prejudiced, however, since it is clear that Meggitt is measuring the Enga against Australian Aborigines with whom he had worked.

MAN

Faced with such an ethnographic picture archaeologists are hard pressed to try and apply their Old World models to the question of the development of agriculture in New Guinea. Studies such as Brookfield's and Hart's reinforce Harris's recent view that it may be more profitable to investigate how people altered the basis of their economy rather than why, which seems to have been the predominant question in latter years; indeed reasons may well be obviated by an understanding of processes (Harris 1972: 391).

Any present attempt to impose a model of adaptation levels upon the prehistory of New Guinea is fraught with difficulties because to date hard archaeological facts are few. The initial excavations by Susan Bulmer (1966) and White (1972) of a cluster of highlands rock shelters yielded artifactual sequences continuing from about 11,000 years ago almost to the present. These sequences lack any clear indication of change from a totally foraging to a predominantly food-producing economy, although one indirect suggestion is the presence of pig in several sites around 5-6,000 years ago. Presuming that pigs were introduced into the country by man it is likely that they would be fed by man and this would indicate that by this time horticulture probably existed somewhere on the island - probably, because pigs might also be fed on sago (Allen 1972: 186). Adding strength to the hypothesis was palynological evidence of forest clearing around the same time (Powell 1970). Since then, a change in the emphasis of archaeological enquiry from rock shelter to open site excavation strengthened the view that well before 5,000 years ago sophisticated forms of agriculture had reached highlands New Guinea (fig. 54).

Foremost amongst these sites is the Wahgi Valley swamp site of Kuk situated some 15km north-west of Mount Hagen township. An immense and complicated site (figs. 55 and 56), covering some 140 hectares (350 acres), Kuk has been the subject of an intense multidisciplinary project led by Jack Golson of the Australian National University over the past five years. Golson's current interpretation of the site varies in some degree from the most recent published account (Golson, in press), and I am grateful to him for permission to reproduce his most recent ideas.

The latest field season at Kuk has demonstrated that from before 5,000 years ago until about 1200 years ago the swamp was subjected to intensive agricultural activities involving complicated ditch drainage systems over large areas which operated continually throughout the period. In the absence of pollen or plant macrofossil evidence, the crop or crops grown can only be guessed, but taro is considered one likely candidate. Why the Kuk swamps were abandoned around 800 A.D. is not clear; the ditching systems appear to remain efficient, and in the absence of other indications, Golson invokes the arrival of the sweet potato at this time. With its greater cold tolerance this plant would enable gardens to be cultivated at higher altitudes than were favourable for taro or yam, and probably with greater and more frequent yields (W. Clarke, pers.comm.), and would thus relieve population pressure and reduce the need for intensive techniques on the valley floors. As we have seen above, the regression of intensive techniques to less intensive ones under similar impetus has taken place in Melanesia since European contact. Some 400 years ago the Kuk swamp systems were reactivated but had fallen out of use by about 100 years ago. Botanical evidence indicates that sweet potato was the staple grown during this period, but swamp management appears to have been less efficient than before.

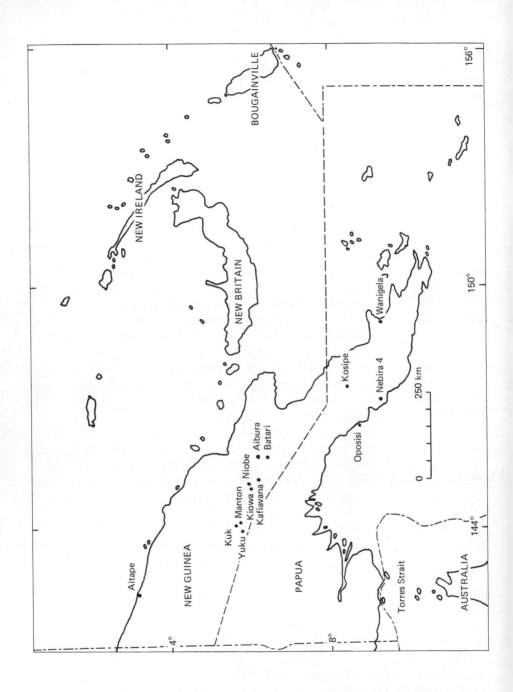

Figure 54. Papua New Guinea: distribution of archaeological sites.

Figure 55. Part of the Kuk swamp site near Mount Hagen. Modern drains carry water from the site, parts of which are currently planted under tea. As scale, the section of the road in the middle distance is approximately 300m long. Small prehistoric drains are visible in the foreground, and major prehistoric channels to take water from the site are arrowed. A modern grid-iron sweet potato garden in the distance is situated on rising ground at the margin of the swamp *(photograph: W. R. Ambrose)*.

Figure 56. A typical prehistoric ditch visible in the section of a modern drain. Long wooden spades (compare fig. 52), digging sticks and other artifacts have been retrieved from such ditches. Ranging pole in 20cm intervals *(photograph: J. Golson).*

By 250 years ago ditches in the centre of the swamp had silted up and were out of use, as gardens were forced to the margins of the swamp. It may be that, under the pressure of maintaining the system of clearing drains and mounding the silt between them the distinctive technique of sweet potato mounding seen today in the region on higher slopes was developed. The development of this technique aided the final move out of the swamps.

Recent work at Kuk has also uncovered other man-made structural alterations to the swamp reliably dated to between 9,000 and 10,000 years ago, but what they mean, if anything, in terms of horticultural practices must await further examination.

A singularly interesting tanged and shouldered flaked stone blade (fig. 57) had been recovered from non-archaeological trenching at Kuk in 1969. It was published and designated a stone hoe (Allen 1970; 1972: fig. 3), a functionally emotive description subsequently avoided by Susan Bulmer in her preliminary description of excavations at Wanlek, in the Kaironk Valley near Simbai (1974: *passim* and n.4). Work so far carried out suggests that Wanlek was an open village site dating between 5,500 and 3,000 years ago, and has yielded stratified evidence of house structures, the manufacture and use of polished axes and adzes, and a variety of tanged, waisted and concave slate implements of which several in general and one in particular is similar to the Kuk artifact (Bulmer S. 1974: 14, fig. 5d). A few similar surface finds from other parts of New Guinea (*ibid.*: 17) now suggest a range of tools which might be considered 'agricultural markers' of some sort, and Susan Bulmer is at present satisfied to ascribe the entire occupation at Wanlek to people who practised horticulture (1974: 13).*

Finally, a further review of the palynological evidence had recently led Golson (pers.comm.) to suggest that forest clearance of sufficient intensity to indicate probable gardening on hill slopes may now reasonably date to between 6,000 and 7,000 years ago.

In short, there is now respectable palynological and archaeological evidence for sedentism, forest clearance, agricultural stone tools, and water control techniques in the highlands valleys between 5,000 and 6,000 years ago, which indicate the development or adoption of sophisticated agriculture in New Guinea by this time, but which add little to the question of process in any fundamental sense. What can be said is that the evidence agrees remarkably on the fourth millennium B.C. for an elaboration of agricultural practices which strongly imply an increase in momentum at this time, without being able to suggest whether the dynamic involved is population increase, new technology, new plants, or a combination of these and/or other factors. If prior to about 7,000 years ago the occupants of highlands valleys were purely hunters and gatherers, with the sorts of social organization and group size normally attributed to this economic base, then the development of intensive agriculture in such a short time would seem to require the movement into the region of horticulturalists with their domesticated plants and probably at least the pig. Alternatively, while it is technically correct to describe such agriculture as intensive its archaeological manifestations are all too plainly slight, so that in seeking an

*This statement excludes consideration of a series of late Pleistocene dates from Wanlek which have recently become available, and for which the excavator has as yet published no statement concerning their cultural implications.

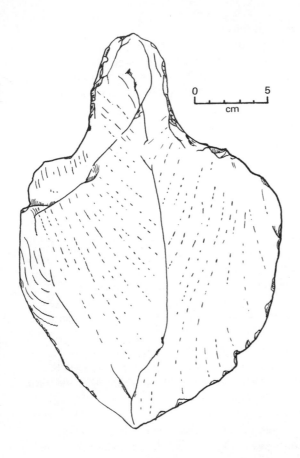

Figure 57. Kuk, New Guinea Highlands: tanged and shouldered flaked stone hoe blade
(drawing: W. I. Mumford).

alternative to a ready-made horticultural invasion we must perforce invoke earlier and simpler levels of indigenous cultivation which are so far archaeologically invisible, and may remain so in the future. The dilemma is thus that while in ethnographical and botanical-geographical studies sophisticated adaptation models are being delineated which challenge the simplicity of the commonly employed archaeological models, in the prehistoric context where the evidence will remain basically archaeological in nature, the question how may remain as speculative as the question why.

SPECULATIONS

To begin with the adoption of agriculture in the highlands of New Guinea, it has already been suggested that the rapid imposition of intensive practices as witnessed in the archaeological record would probably require an agricultural invasion to accomplish its establishment in such a short space of time. This invasion can be considered either in terms of a movement of agriculturalists arriving with their techniques, ideas and plants, or alternatively a diffusion of the techniques and plants alone. The hypothesis of a movement of people in sufficient numbers to achieve what is archaeologically recognizable lacks support in terms of archaeological evidence which could link New Guinea sites of relevant date to the South-East Asian islands to the west. Pottery, which had reached Timor between 4,000 and 5,000 years ago (Glover 1972: 360) and may have been in Sarawak 8,000 years ago (Golson 1971a: 137), has not been located in New Guinea earlier than the birth of Christ (although older dates should be expected eventually to come from the unexplored north coast), nor did the microlithic stone tools which entered Australia between 5,000 and 7,000 years ago (Mulvaney 1975: Ch.8) reach eastern New Guinea. Possible agricultural stone tools in New Guinea, such as the Kuk hoe, discussed above, may on the other hand have their antecedents in the widespread and much older Pleistocene 'waisted blades' found within the country (Allen 1972) (fig. 58). Without such indications it is difficult at present to postulate the arrival of agriculturalists from outside New Guinea at this time. (The further consideration, that they arrived in the highlands with a developed agricultural base from somewhere else in New Guinea, lacks evidence one way or the other, and is to some degree outside the present purpose of the discussion.) The second major consideration, of a diffusion of agriculture without its practitioners into a predominantly foraging community about 6,000 years ago, must account for the discrepancy between what are suggested as the most likely forms of organization and group size among tropical hunter-gatherers and that which we must postulate for a complex and labour-intensive agricultural situation like Kuk, even in its earliest stages.

Totally indigenous development of New Guinea agriculture is obviously denied by the foreign origin of present-day staples. Apart from Powell's recent paper (in press), the question of any indigenous beginnings of horticultural activity in New Guinea has only been considered indirectly by White (1972: 142-5) and directly by Yen (1971b: 6; 1973: *passim* and 73-5), who noted that the known timespan for man in New Guinea did allow for domestication of plants to become a complementary activity to hunting and gathering within the country and that such a situation was as equally likely as that local plants were domesticated under the influence of an already-introduced agriculture.

I have already listed above the range of local plant domestications, and while the

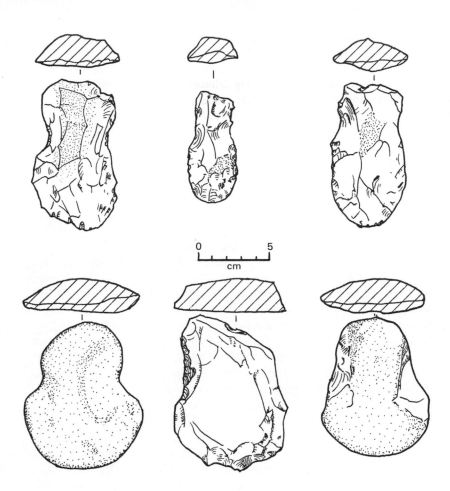

Figure 58. Flaked and polished waisted blades from New Britain (top row) and excavated examples from Yuku *(drawing: W. I. Mumford).*

list is perhaps a slender basis for arguing for an indigenous beginning to agriculture in New Guinea, alternatively it does not refute such a possibility. The extent to which these plants, which still remain in the garden repertoire, together with a wide range of valuable wild food plants, may have been manipulated and exploited in the past is today obscured by the dominance of imported tubers in much the same way as tuber cultivation has been overwhelmed by rice on the South-East Asian mainland. Thus while noting a 'New Guinea centre' of cultigen species (Yen 1971b: 4) the question remains an egg-and-chicken one: did the development of local plant manipulation develop the necessary social climate to allow the adoption of outside plants and possibly techniques, or were such plants manipulated to widen an introduced agriculture?

The Kuk evidence would seem to reflect what Harris has called ecosystem transformation (1972: 393-4), basically the creation of an artificial gardening environment, which he argues would be normally preceded by a long developmental period in which plants would be raised within the limits of the natural environment, this contrasting process being termed ecosystem manipulation. In the abstract Harris views the most likely entry into this pathway to tropical agriculture to be via an ecotone situation offering foraging bands a wide and seasonally diverse range of plants and animals which would promote sedentism, houseplot horticulture and on to succeeding levels of intensified agricultural activity. In the actual case of New Guinea the riparian situations favoured by Harris would appear less attractive because of the paucity of freshwater fish, but the montane forest/grassland ecotone, the lowland savanna/forest ecotone, the sago swamp/forest ecotone and the marine ecotone would for the most part fit the Harris model.

On the available evidence several assumptions can be made concerning the earliest arrivals of man in the New Guinea region. Current assessments of the antiquity of man in Australia, and by extension New Guinea, which was severed from the Australian landmass by post-Pleistocene rising sea levels, are around 40,000 years ago (Jones 1973). The oldest New Guinea date for man is c. 26,000 years ago for the Papuan highlands site of Kosipe (White et al.1970). Calaby has noted that when man first arrived in Australia he would have recognised many elements in the fauna, the principal exceptions being the large flightless birds and the Macropodidae (Calaby 1971: 88), and a similar situation can be postulated for the flora (Golson 1971b). Combining these indications with the previous discussion of modern floral and faunal suites suggests that the first human occupation of the New Guinea coastline may have been no difficult task, but that the largest of the modern fauna, the macropods and the cassowary, were probably strange. Here the role of the extinct Pleistocene megafauna is probably pertinent but somewhat obscure. Except for the southern Australian site of Keilor (Bowler, in press) and the New Guinea highlands site of Nombe (M.J. Mountain, pers.comm.), firm evidence of the relationship between man and the large extinct species is not yet forthcoming, and it can be assumed that whatever role man may have played in the extinction of the megafauna, the two did not share the landscape of greater Australia for any significant length of time.

If any long-term importance of the megafauna as a food source for early man in New Guinea is thus discounted, we must return to the question of whether the scanty modern suite of New Guinea animals may have hindered man's early colonization of inland New Guinea. In a recent paper Hope and Hope (in press) have argued for the presence of extensive montane grasslands during the Pleistocene and suggested that the ecotone between such grasslands and the forests below would have provided one excellent zone for hunter-gatherer occupation, but for New Guinea as a whole the question of hunter-gatherer prosperity may depend more abstractly upon whether the earliest colonizers were adapted to big game hunting or not, and thus whether the lack of such game in New Guinea may have created a stress situation calling for new adaptive strategies such as much more elaborate manipulation of the plant resources. On this point island South-East Asian evidence is vital but confused. As an indication, however, we may look at the food fauna recovered from the palaeolithic layers of Niah cave in Borneo, which include orang-utan, two-horned rhinoceros, elephant, wild buffalo, giant pig (*Sus gargantua*) and bearded pig, wild ox and three species of deer, as well as snake, frog, and riverine turtle and fish. Interestingly in the Niah deposit arboreal mammals are for the most part absent (Harrison 1959: 2). The extent to which the palaeolithic occupants at Niah were representative of the earliest colonizers of Australia and New Guinea remains unknown, and on first principles we might indeed assume that the colonizers were more likely culturally adapted to coastal exploitation. If they were not, the absence of large and/or gregarious game in New Guinea may have caused fundamental alterations to the inland food quest, but similarly if the first colonizers were coastal people, incursions into the New Guinea inland would probably have been hindered by the unavailability of such prey. Indeed, although in the archaeological record of New Guinea some sites can be regarded as specific hunting camp sites, the majority of the evidence so far fails to demonstrate that the scope for hunting as an economic basis ever existed there. The strong suggestion that man was visiting Kosipe, some 2,000m above sea level, to exploit indigenous montane species of pandanus some 26,000 years ago (White et al. 1970: 168-9) indicates both an acquired intimate knowledge of a local resource and perhaps a real need to exploit it. And finally, in view of the ethnographic evidence for sago exploitation, sedentism adjacent to sago stands may have developed as an adaptive strategy virtually from the time man arrived in New Guinea, and such localities present themselves as highly likely areas from which man could have launched himself into an agricultural pathway.

Australian Aborigines are today regarded as hunter/gatherers *par excellence,* but it is perhaps instructive that we can list a significant number of ecosystem manipulations among them. The use of fire is well known, but they also employ water control techniques to manipulate microenvironments, beekeeping, grub cultivation by placing branches of trees in salt water, steps towards the domestication of the dog and other animals for pets, if not food - and in one instance the tethering, taming and feeding of cassowaries for food. Aborigines have been recorded practising a variety of food preservation techniques including the smoking of flying-fox and kangaroo meat; preserving eggs; preserving the sap from the Salmon gum; and elaborate preservation of the nuts of *Cycas media,* one technique for which includes the digging of large grass-lined storage trenches. There are recorded instances of deliberate seed planting, and the habit of planting back portions of harvested yam is widespread (Harvey 1945; Campbell 1965; Irvine 1970). In view of Golson's recent demonstration of the similarities between food plants and their uses in Arnhem Land and Malaysia (Golson 1971b: passim and esp. table 15.14) it is intriguing to consider that some Aboriginal groups may have been for a long time poised a few steps along an agricultural pathway, or indeed may have regressed from further along such a pathway.

A priori, there is no reason to deny Pleistocene man in New Guinea the same or equivalent skills. The combined effect of New Guinea's suggested poor wild animal base and the range of domesticatable plants, together with suitable ecological situations which could have promoted early sedentism, may equally have promoted the emergence of simple forms of agriculture well back into the late Pleistocene, particularly in the lowland regions. The ramifications of such a development on group size, trade, warfare, and social and political organization can only be guessed. What is suggested here is the necessity for the growth of a social and economic situation sufficiently developed to be responsive to the diffusion of plants and animals from the west, and the possibility that it occurred.

Sahlins (1968: 29-32) has pointed to a number of common features found amongst forest agricultural groups. Given the amount of land required under a swidden system overall population density is low, frequently as little as 4 to the square kilometre. Similarly swidden agriculture has a centrifugal effect on the distribution of settlements, so that hamlets or quite small villages are normal. This in turn militates against political development, because tribes tend toward autonomous segmentary groups, and also hampers specialization of production, since similar tasks are performed in each group. On the other hand, exchange of locally unobtainable raw materials can go on over long distances, and warfare between groups is common, particularly where pressure on land resources exists. One can see many of these factors still in operation in New Guinea today, but there seems no way of commenting on their antiquity, except that by 9,000 years ago coastal shell was being traded to the central highlands (White 1972: 142).

Within the hypothetical model under consideration, one can assume that the taro, whenever it arrived, was of great importance. With its hydrophytic qualities it was ideally suited to the development of more intensive swidden agriculture within the lower altitude rain forests, particularly if coupled with a range of indigenous domesticated crops and perhaps pig, for which there is one tantalizing tooth 10,000 years ago at Kiowa (Bulmer 1974: 16-17). Alone taro may have altered the subsistence potential to one of greater carrying capacity and repeated centrifugal settlements. Once such a development reached the higher altitudes with their less humid climate and limitations on further upward expansion we might well expect the alterations and intensifications that we see at Kuk 6,000 years ago in terms of garden technology, or altered emphasis in the crop register, such as the greater exploitation of the dryer cropping yam. At present, however, it is difficult to point to lower altitude land shortage as the simple pressure behind the upward move. Alternatively less apparent factors such as sorcery or endemic diseases, and particularly malaria, may have to be invoked. While there is no immediately simple reason for the present population distribution in New Guinea, Brookfield (1971: 72-3) sees malaria as one very important limiting factor, and it has been noted that malaria and other insect-borne diseases did not reach catastrophic proportions until tree felling became sufficiently extensive to bring canopy-dwelling mosquitoes into contact with human populations. Alternatively and/or additionally, as Powell (in press) has pointed out, the New Guinea highlands climate was warmer between 5,000 and 8,000 years ago. Assuming that it also remained wet, the climate would have facilitated the expansion of the tropical tubers, bananas and sugar cane into the highlands at this time.

In keeping with many other commentators on man's early moves towards food production this paper has assumed that such moves in New Guinea were stress responses - in this particular case to a limited range of food animals in inland areas which created greater dependence upon plant resources. Nevertheless it may be too simple to argue that agriculture 'is irrelevant to a well-functioning hunting community' (Piggott 1965: 26). Within the more profound shifts of habit and behaviour which must have accompanied the initial colonization of New Guinea, man almost certainly was faced with circumstances which required adaptations to the food quest which varied considerably from place to place. Within the limits of the meagre evidence available to us one such adaptation could have been the early significant manipulation of food plants to levels which we might now call agricultural. We know now that in some highlands valleys intensive agriculture was practised by 5,000 years ago, but that even today in other more or less adjacent areas wild food sources have remained dominant. In New Guinea at least (and one suspects elsewhere as well) the archaeologist needs to develop frameworks which accommodate similar variations in the past, and ways to spot them in the fragmentary archaeological record. The New Guinea picture totally endorses the recent view of Higgs and Jarman that the development of agriculture now needs to be studied 'not as an invention or series of inventions designed to control man's environment, but as a continuously developing natural process of great selective value, in which adjustments to climatic and other ecological factors are visible up to the present day' (1972: 13).

REFERENCES

Allen, Jim, 1970. 'Prehistoric agricultural systems in the Wahgi Valley - a further note', *Mankind, 7(3),* 177-83.

Allen, Jim, 1972. 'The first decade in New Guinea archaeology', *Antiquity, 46,* 180-90.

Bowler, J.M. in press. 'Recent Developments in Reconstructing Late Quaternary Environments in Australia', in *The Origin of the Australians,* ed. R.L. Kirk and A.G. Thorne (Camberra).

Brookfield, H. with Hart, D., 1971. *Melanesia: A Geographical Interpretation of An Island World.*

Bulmer, R.N.H., 1968. 'The strategies of hunting in New Guinea', *Oceania, 38,* 302-18.

Bulmer, R.N.H., 1976. 'Selectivity in Hunting and in Disposal of Animal Bone by the Kalam of the New Guinea Highlands', in *Problems in Social and Economic Archaeology,* ed. G. de G. Sieveking, I.H.Longworth and K.E. Wilson, 1976, 169-86.

Bulmer, Susan, 1966. 'The Prehistory of the Australian New Guinea Highlands' (unpublished M.A. thesis, University of Auckland).

Bulmer, Susan, 1974. 'Settlement and Economy in Prehistoric Papua New Guinea', *Working Papers in Archaeology,* No.30 (Dept of Anthropology, University of Auckland).

Calaby, J.H., 1971. 'Man, Fauna, and Climate in Aboriginal Australia', in *Aboriginal Man and Environment in Australia,* ed. D.J. Mulvaney and J. Golson, 1971, (Canberra), 80-93

Campbell, Alastair H., 1965. 'Elementary food production by the Australian Aborigines', *Mankind, 6(5),* 206-11.

Dwyer, Peter D., 1974. 'The price of protein: five hundred hours of hunting in the New Guinea Highlands', *Oceania, 44(4),* 278-93.

Glover, Ian, 1972. 'Excavations in Timor: A Study of Economic Change and Cultural Continuity in Prehistory' (unpublished Ph.D. thesis, Australian National University).

Golson, Jack, 1971a. 'Both sides of the Wallace Line: Australia, New Guinea, and Asian prehistory', *Archaeology and Physical Anthropology in Oceania, 6(2),* 124-44.

Golson, Jack, 1971b. 'Australian Aboriginal Food Plants: Some Ecological and Culture-Historical Implications', in *Aboriginal Man and Environment in Australia,* ed. D.J. Mulvaney and J. Golson, 1971 (Canberra), 196-238.

Golson, Jack, in press. 'Recent Discoveries in the New Guinea Highlands: Simple Tools and Complex Technology'. Paper delivered to the Biennial Conference of the Australian Institute of Aboriginal Studies, Canberra, May 1974.

Harris, David R., 1972. 'The Prehistory of Tropical Agriculture: An Ethnoecological Model', in *The Explanation of Culture Change: Models in Prehistory,* ed. Colin Renfrew, 1972, 391-417.

Harrisson, Tom, 1959. 'New archaeological and ethnological results from Niah Caves, Sarawak', *Man. 59,* 1-8.

Harvey, Alison, 1945. 'Food preservation in Australian tribes', *Mankind, 3(7),* 191-2.

Hope, J.H. and Hope, G.S., in press. 'Palaeoenvironments for man in New Guinea', in *The Origin of the Australians,* ed. R.L. Kirk and A.G. Thorne, (Canberra).

Higgs, E.S. and Jarman, M.R., 1972. 'The Origins of Animal and Plant Husbandry', in *Papers in Economic Prehistory,* ed. E.S. Higgs, 1972, 3-13.

Irvine, F.R., 1970. 'Evidence of Change in the Vegetable Diet of Australian Aborigines', in *Diprotodon to Detribalization,* ed. A.R. Pilling and R.A. Waterman, 1970 (Michigan).

Jones, Rhys, 1973. 'Emerging picture of Pleistocene Australians', *Nature, 246(5431),* 278-81.

Lee, Richard B., 1968. 'What Hunters Do for a Living, or How to Make Out on Scarce Resources' in *Man The Hunter,* ed. Richard B. Lee and Irven DeVore, 1968 (Chicago), 30-48.

Meggitt, M.J., 1958. 'The Enga of the New Guinea Highlands: some preliminary observations', *Oceania 28(4),* 253-330.

Mulvaney, D.J., 1975. *The Prehistory of Australia* (rev. edn, Ringwood, Vic.).

Piggott, Stuart, 1965. *Ancient Europe.*

Powell, J.M., 1970. 'The Impact of Man on the Vegetation of the Mount Hagen Region, New Guinea', (unpublished Ph.D. thesis, Australian National University).

Powell, J.M. in press. 'Ethnobotany', in *The Vegetation of New Guinea,* ed. K. Paijmans, Ch.3.

Rappaport, Roy A., 1968. *Pigs For the Ancestors* (Yale).

Romilly, H.H., 1893. 'Letters from the Western Pacific and Mashonaland 1878-1891' (ed. S.H. Romilly).

Sahlins, Marshall D., 1968. *Tribesmen* (Englewood Cliffs, N.J.).

Townsend, Patricia K., 1971. 'New Guinea sago gatherers - a study of demography in relation to subsistence', *Ecology of Food and Nutrition, 1,* 19-24.

White, J. Peter, 1972. *Ol Tumbuna.* Terra Australis 2 (Dept of Prehistory, Australian National University).

White, J.Peter, Crook, K.A.W. and Ruxton, B.P., 1970. 'Kosipe: A late Pleistocene site in the Papuan Highlands', *Proc.Prehis.Soc., 36:* 152-70.

Williams, F.E., 1936. *Papuans of the Trans-Fly* (reprinted 1969).

Yen, D.E. 1971a. 'Construction of the Hypothesis for Distribution of the Sweet Potato', in *Man Across the Sea,* ed. C.L. Riley *et al.* 1971 (Austin, Texas), 328-42.

Yen, D.E., 1971b. 'The Development of Agriculture in Oceania', in *Studies in Oceanic Culture History 2,* ed. R.C. Green and M. Kelly,1971, 1-12.

Yen, D.E., 1973. 'The Origins of Oceanic Agriculture', *Archaeology and Physical Anthropology in Oceania, 8,* 68-85.

PETER GATHERCOLE

9 Man and environment in Polynesia

INTRODUCTORY NOTE

This short essay discusses some of the results of recent archaeological research in
Polynesia, in relation to the wider, more explicitly anthropological, theme of the
cultural adaptation of the Polynesian peoples to a variety of island environments.
This seems an appropriate way to introduce the area and its archaeological problems
to a reader familiar with neither, if only because, in the Pacific, the inherent
limitations of archaeology can be compensated to some extent by findings in
ethnography and social anthropology. Summaries of this kind inevitably distort by
compression and can also become unduly cluttered with references in the text. All
have therefore been excluded, but a note is added on the more pertinent and
accessible recent literature, where matters only touched on here are more fully
discussed.

The problems of the origins of the Polynesians have long fascinated a wide variety of
scholars. At various times, Egypt, Mesopotamia, and parts of India, South-East Asia
and the Americas have been nominated as the undoubted Polynesian homeland. This
was thought to be quite distinct from the homeland of the inhabitants of Melanesia
and Micronesia, the other major areas of Oceania, because of Polynesian differences
in body form and culture. These claims have always failed for want of convincing
evidence. Some continue to be held and new ones advanced, including even that of
settlement from outer space.
    Recent research in archaeology, linguistics, and anthropology, however, has
demonstrated the validity of a commonsense hypothesis. The Polynesians became

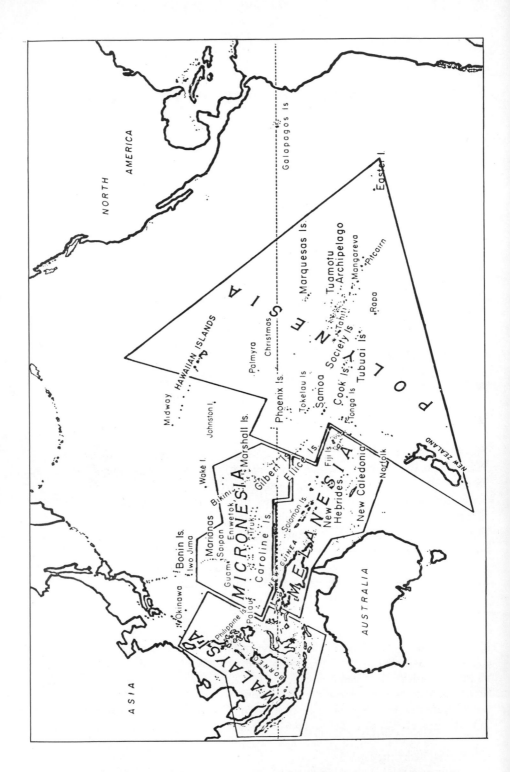

Figure 59. Map of the Pacific area *(reproduced by courtesy of the Pacific Science Information Centre, Bernice P. Bishop Museum, Honolulu, Hawaii).*

Polynesians within Polynesia. This process took place in the islands of Tonga and Samoa, immediately east of Fiji, between the latter part of the second and the middle of the first millennium B.C., when this area was first settled by groups from island Melanesia, i.e. the chain running eastwards from New Guinea to Fiji. The pottery, other items of material culture and probably the physical characteristics of these 'proto-Polynesians' suggest that they were a small section of an eastern Oceanic population that established itself in island Melanesia during the second millennium B.C. These people were mainly speakers of languages now called Austronesian. All of today's Polynesian languages have developed from this one linguistic stock. Archaeologically speaking, Polynesian cultures grew out of the earliest settlements in eastern Melanesia, possibly directly from Fiji, before the enormous variety of Melanesian cultures had developed. After a lengthy period of adaptation in western Polynesia groups by then recognizably Polynesian in language and culture began to spread into the more isolated islands of eastern Polynesia, hitherto uninhabited. On present evidence the Marquesas Islands appear to be the earliest settled in this area, by A.D. 300. Easter Island was inhabited by A.D. 500, Hawaii perhaps by A.D. 600, the Society Islands by A.D. 800, and the Cook Islands and New Zealand probably slightly later. Thereafter further exploration and settlement occurred within each major group. It now seems that the settlement of Polynesia, the last major area of the world to be occupied by pre-industrial man, was a process lasting some 2,500 years, undertaken by 'neolithic' seafarers whose ancestors had been exploring and colonizing many of the islands east of the South-East Asian mainland for many centuries. The emergence of Polynesia lasted from around the time of Stonehenge to the time of the Norman Conquest. But just as the Polynesians were not Celts, Saxons or Vikings, neither were they dynastic Egyptians, a lost tribe of Israel, Dravidians, the Children of Mu, or a 'pure' race from anywhere.

To reduce the question 'where did the Polynesians come from?' to something answerable in historical rather than speculative terms, as the archaeologists have done, does not deny the extent of Polynesian achievement. Archaeology has confirmed the extent of that achievement. After all, the high islands, coral islands, and atolls lying within the triangle formed by the Hawaiian chain in the north, Easter Island in the east, and New Zealand in the south-west are, with the exception of the latter, puny in size. New Zealand has an area of 268,686 square km. The remainder of Polynesia *together* amounts to only 25,803 square km. That these specks of land, the peaks of ancient volcanoes rising thousands of metres from the floor of the central Pacific Ocean, should have received human settlement at all is still a remarkable fact. When European voyagers 'discovered' Polynesia in the seventeenth and eighteenth centuries, they were amazed to find that all the high islands and many of the low coralline islands were, or had been inhabited. The inhabitants were sufficiently similar in physique, language, and culture to be grouped as one people. Captain Cook found that with some knowledge of the Tahitian language he could communicate reasonably well with the Maoris, Easter Islanders, Marquesans and Hawaiians, and, with more difficulty, with Tongans. He had little success with the darker and less amenable Melanesians encountered on the coasts of parts of the New Hebrides and New Caledonia.

Outside observers from Cook onwards have noted differences as well as likenesses between the Polynesian peoples. While differences are to be expected on general grounds, they are not always readily explicable, especially in view of the numerous common elements in the various environments and cultures. By comparison, even with Melanesia, the prehistoric environment of tropical Polynesia was a restricted one. The native flora was mainly an attenuated version of the Malaysian flora, the fauna was predominantly, where not wholly, marine and the plants and animals introduced by man were few. Major food crops observed in the eighteenth century were taro, yam, breadfruit, banana, coconut and sugar cane, all of South-East Asian and/or Malaysian origin, and the sweet potato, derived somehow (the mechanism is still not clear) from South America. There were only three animal domesticates, chicken, pig and dog, which were supplemented as food by the rat, and at times, by man himself. A much richer and more important food source was the sea, both the open ocean and, where they existed, the reef and the lagoon. From here came not only fish and shell fish, but also sea birds. All Polynesians were, to some extent, hunters and gatherers as well as horticulturalists, who appreciated the nutritive and economic value of many wild plants and animals, particularly when yields from domesticates were unavailable or low.

Plant and animal resources recognized as such by Polynesians were unevenly distributed between islands, particularly high islands and coral islands. A good example was the pandanus tree, which was tolerant of a wide range of conditions, but whose value was variably appreciated. On high islands it was usually considered important for its leaves, from which were made thatch, sails, mats and baskets. On coral islands it often provided food from its buds, fruit and seeds. Resources were also unevenly distributed and exploited among islands of similar character. Western Polynesia was richer in types of terrestrial plants and animals than was the east. Domesticates were variously spread, and exploited to different degrees. For example, dogs were a source of food in pre-historic western Polynesia, Hawaii and New Zealand (in the last place they were the sole domesticated animal). In the Marquesas they are recorded only as burials in early contexts, and were not present at the time of European contact.

It is probable, therefore, that each Polynesian habitat possessed a certain uniqueness from its time of settlement. The mechanism of colonization was itself a cultural filter, a process which archaeological research has helped to clarify. If we accept the view that the west to east primary settlement was one-way only, undertaken by very small groups of men and women who carried, perhaps in lone ocean-going canoes, very limited amounts of food, fresh water, animals, plants and small artifacts, then the drawn-out chronology of Polynesian discovery and settlement propounded by the archaeologists makes good sense. The evidence need not comprise a random scatter of traits reflecting an incoherent pattern lacking any cultural logic of its own. In addition, assuming that subsequent two-way, and therefore purposeful, voyaging between islands or groups was often limited to those lying not more than about 500km apart, the cultural differences apparent between various Polynesian peoples become understandable as the results of changes occurring within a definable but isolated area after settlement. Later one-way, long-distance landfalls by small groups on islands already occupied would have been unlikely to change the established culture to a very significant degree.

In sum, one might usefully isolate four main factors which determined the cultural possibilities of a particular Polynesian habitat. First, there were those aspects of the natural environment already familiar to the settlers from their previous experience, whether it was 'proto-', western or eastern Polynesian. Second, there were the peculiarly local, perhaps novel, features of the environment. Third, there were the cultural characteristics of the group of settlers arising from its history, including the specific circumstances in which it left its homeland, and the degree, therefore, to which it was equipped to undertake colonization. Fourth, there was the way each new environment was perceived and exploited by the settlers and their descendants. Taken together, these factors would have influenced, if not directly conditioned, the process of cultural localization in a new environment. Evidence of this process might not be readily apparent in the archaeological evidence. The results of cultural localization, however, are also recognizable in the ethnographic evidence observed after European contact. This could suggest ways in which particular island populations had retained traditional practices and beliefs, or developed new ones. Evidence from archaeology might then throw light on the chronology of these processes and their means of occurrence.

The ethnohistorical evidence from the late eighteenth and early nineteenth centuries shows that all Polynesian societies shared certain economic practices, had common forms of social organization based on the primacy of bilateral kinship affiliation, and possessed belief systems with many comparable features. But social and economic systems varied considerably in their details. Sometimes the social structure was markedly stratified, with clearly differentiated chiefs, commoners and even slaves. In Tonga, for example, existed a centralized society based on rank, ordered according to the individual's genealogical distance from the Tu'i Tonga, or highest chief. The economic system depended mainly on the careful cultivation of yam and taro - in 1773 the islands seemed a veritable picturesque garden to the visiting British. Tongan social stratification was of considerable complexity; there even existed an honorific language for addressing the chiefs. Cultural links were more with Samoa and Fiji rather than with eastern Polynesia. There are numerous references in Tongan tradition to contact, both peaceful and warlike, with the Lau Islands in the Fiji group, from where might come husbands for high ranking Tongan females. Eighteenth-century Tongan society can well be seen as the result of a lengthy process of local adaptation, where 'western' traits were developed from a 'proto-' Polynesian source, and from which, around the time of Christ, eastern Polynesian cultures were derived.

Other Polynesian groups did not follow the same forms of economic or social adaptation. Tongan society was not that of Tahiti or Hawaii or the New Zealand Maoris writ large. Tahitian society was also complex, but it possessed considerably different systems. The Tahitian islands were not unified under one chief in the 1770s; society was politically unstable, with several chiefly groups contending for power. Breadfruit cultivation appears to have been more important than that of root crops. Items of material culture were more similar to those in the other eastern islands than to those of Tonga. Some of the objects were very distinctive expressions of high status: for example, a mourning dress used in funerary rites for the chiefs, and helmets and breast gorgets worn by war chiefs. Warfare was no trivial institution. In April 1774 Cook witnessed a review of a fleet comprising 160 war canoes, gathered to attack the neighbouring island of Mo'orea.

Chiefly status was also important in Hawaii, elaborate visual symbols of which were the most sophisticated featherwork garments made in the whole of the Pacific. Manufacture was by specialists under the direction of chiefs. By the 1770s these *ali'i* had achieved a degree of control over the lives of commoners considerably different from elsewhere in Polynesia. There was extensive contact, including trade between the Hawaiian islands. Warfare was common, the most contentious issues being political prestige and control of land. Taro was the main food crop, cultivated in a range of local habitats both coastal and inland. Breadfruit cultivation was not particularly important. Although archaeology has not yet thrown much light on the development of political and religious institutions in Hawaii, it is elucidating the economic system which supported them. Both dry and irrigated forms of taro cultivation were used. Settlement patterns varied, ranging from nucleated villages on good-quality lands to dispersed huts on marginal lands.

The results of island localization were, in many respects, even more marked by the 1770s in Easter Island and New Zealand, which lie south of the tropics. To some extent, this can be attributed directly to environmental distinctions. For example, suitable trees for the making of bark cloth (*tapa*) were rare, so the few *tapa* objects existing at that time among Easter Islanders or Maoris had considerable prestige. Most authorities regard the archaeological data from Easter Island as evidence for a very individual and isolated cultural development from an early east Polynesian base, acting under severe environmental constraints, and producing unusual house forms, religious structures and stone carvings. Easter Island masonry techniques, and stone and wood sculpture, were much influenced by the nature and quantity of available raw materials. The overall style of the sculpture was unique, although there were analogues to some of its elements in the sculpture of the Marquesans, the Maoris and the Morioris, the prehistoric inhabitants of the Chatham Islands, lying about 800km east of New Zealand.

In New Zealand, eastern Polynesian culture had acquired numerous unusual features by the time of Cook. Maori social organization retained the Polynesian principle of recognizing affiliation by bilateral kinship, but residence and control of land was organized through tribes and sub-tribes. Chiefs did not possess the centralized political and religious powers often found in tropical Polynesia; their authority derived more from their influential status. Intertribal warfare had become common, particularly in the more heavily populated North Island. It seems that settlements were often widely dispersed and not permanently occupied. In part this reflected the size of the country and the dispersal of its economic resources. As many plants widely used in Polynesia, such as pandanus, coconut, paper mulberry and tropical species of cordyline, were either absent from, or poorly represented in, the New Zealand flora, the Maoris developed many local substitutes. The indigenous flax was commonly used to make clothes, mats, baskets, sails and cordage. The basis of Maori horticulture was the sweet potato, which, because of the extremities of the seasons, had to be stored during the winter months. In the South Island, the crop was not grown at all south of South Canterbury. Hunting and gathering were always important in the economy. The flightless moa (the word, incidentally, is Polynesian for chicken, absent in New Zealand) was one of a number of birds brought to extinction. An indigenous widely available fern root was regularly gathered, as was the root of the native cordyline.

New Zealand is geologically as well as climatically the most varied part of Polynesia. Maoris used a wide range of rocks for making tools, weapons, and ornaments, including nephrites found only in a few isolated localities in the South Island. In all Polynesian societies music, dance and the visual arts were characteristically innovative. This was particularly apparent in Maori sculpture, which used unique curvilinear decorative motifs. These were integral to the design and meaning of a large number of artifacts important in economic and social, as well as religious, contexts. The origin and development of Maori carving is still a largely unknown subject. Recently, New Zealand archaeologists have argued, on convincing evidence, that the culture recorded at the time of European contact developed from eastern Polynesian prototypes, without further settlement from the Society Islands' area in the fourteenth century, as claimed from certain traditions. The pattern and pace of that development is still unclear in many regions. The Maori retained in their imagery, perception and supernatural personification of their environment much traditional ideology from their tropical homeland, despite many novel elements in their culture. Their history is a good example of the process of cultural localization.

Although the archaeological evidence is patchy on many islands, reflecting the history of fieldwork as much as the distribution of known sites, it is generally consistent with the ethnographic evidence, in the sense that both derive from the same cultural tradition. They must be related. A major task is to establish the nature of that relationship in more detail within many island groups. In terms of the principle of cultural localization discussed above, evidence for local adaptation can be seen as a continuum, part of which is archaeological, part ethnographic. It is not only a matter of undertaking more fieldwork. It is also important to develop methods for expressing archaeological and ethnographic data in ways that are mutually consistent reflections of Polynesian cultural processes. This method of research is now developing in studies of Tongan, Tahitian and Maori ethnohistory.

It is not, I think, fanciful to recognize innovation (within limits set ultimately by the 'proto-Polynesian' habitat) as a characteristic feature present throughout Polynesian history. One of the tasks of the archaeologists has been to produce an outline prehistory for particular island groups within the 'west to east' framework which they have established. They have demonstrated that western and eastern Polynesia have had different, though related, histories. They have shown that, even in early times, the eastern Polynesians did not necessarily recapitulate western artifactual forms. These people stopped making pottery, found in the west in early layers. There are only a few, possibly locally-made, sherds in the earliest layers in the Marquesas, and none anywhere else in the east. Even the early eastern adzes, onepiece bait hooks and ornaments were innovations. At a later date, the *marae* used as a religious structure, and the stone food pounder, appear in eastern tropical islands. It is difficult, however, to pinpoint the place (or places) of origin and the migration patterns of their makers, because local forms might have developed too rapidly for that development to be recognizable in the archaeological evidence. The Marquesas may have been a major dispersal centre for all eastern Polynesia, despite the importance accorded to Tahiti in many island traditions. The relative richness of the archaeological information so far recovered from the Marquesas may reflect the existence of a habitat favourable to the emergence and development of this dispersal centre. On the other hand, the evidence may be skewed this way because the coastal topography of the Marquesas favours the preservation of sites, including early ones, whereas that of Tahiti and much of the Cook Islands does not.

Despite such difficulties, it may seem that archaeologists in Polynesia have a relatively easy task. They work within a short timespan of prehistory. The societies they study have a common origin and lacked, for much of their history, outside influences to complicate processes of cultural change. There also exists a large body of comparative ethnography, which contains much information pertinent to the elucidation of prehistoric economic, social and ideological systems. Unfortunately the situation is not quite so straightforward. The persistently adaptive nature of Polynesian societies can play havoc with conventional methods of research. Much of the ethnography thought to be traditional can be shown to be 'contaminated' by Western influences shortly after contact. The overall timespan of Polynesian history has been so brief and its cultural adaptation so rapid that the latter may have left little physical record which is recoverable, let alone classifiable within the Polynesian evidence. Similar artifacts and environments were sometimes used in such different ways that they produced very distinctive socio-economic results in islands of comparable type. For these and other reasons, 'diffusion' and 'independent invention' of cultural traits might be hard to distinguish. The difficulties can be multiplied and many are real ones.

Much, however, has been achieved, due primarily to the energetic work of a relatively small number of archaeologists. Another reason for the very considerable advance in knowledge in recent years is that archaeology is continually enriched by its links with anthropology, linguistics and other social sciences which have a common concern in the study of man in the Pacific, past and present.

SUGGESTIONS FOR FURTHER READING

An up-to-date summary account of the settlement of tropical Polynesia in relation to the rest of Oceania is included in Peter Bellwood's article, 'The Prehistory of Oceania', in *Curr. Anthrop., 16* (1975), 9-28. A valuable essay by Jack Golson, 'The Pacific Islands and their Prehistoric Inhabitants', in *Man in the Pacific Islands* (ed. R. Gerard Ward, 1972), examines the settlement of Oceania with particular attention to its environment. *The Pacific Islanders* by William Howells (1973) is a delightfully relaxed, scholarly and witty book, one of the virtues of which is that the author considers the evidence of physical anthropology and linguistics, as well as archaeology, concerning the origins of all Pacific peoples, including Australian aborigines. A briefer work recently available is *Oceanic Prehistory* by Richard and Mary Elizabeth Shutler (Menlo Park, Cal., 1975). Mainland and island South-East Asia, as well as Australia and Oceania proper, are included in this survey. The works by Bellwood and Howells mentioned above contain good bibliographies, which should be consulted for references to specific accounts of fieldwork and related topics.

Introductions to the archaeology of the major islands are directly or indirectly provided by many of the papers included in two recent symposia: 'Studies in Oceanic Culture History', 3 vols, ed. R.C. Green and M. Kelly (*Pacific Anthropological Records*, Nos. 11-13, Dept of Anthropology, Bernice P. Bishop Museum, Honolulu, Hawaii, 1970-1); and *Prehistoric Culture in Oceania*, ed. I. Yawata and Y.H. Sinoto (Bernice P. Bishop Museum, 1968). There is no recent book that brings together and discusses in satisfactory detail the major archaeological evidence from Polynesia as a whole.

The best introduction to the ethnography and post-contact history of Polynesia is still that contained in *The Pacific Islands* by Douglas L. Oliver (New York, rev. edn. 1961). This has a good, though naturally somewhat dated, bibliography.

The author is indebted to his colleague Dr Adrienne Kaeppler for critical comment of the text.

JOAN J. TAYLOR*

10 The earliest hunters, gatherers and farmers of North America

Man migrated across the Bering Strait into America some time before 20,000 years ago equipped with an advanced stone technology for hunting big game. His exact time of arrival is disputed as is the number of his sorties into the New World. Although dates on the Siberian side of the Bering Strait range from 15,000 to 10,000 BP, the dating for the Clovis projectile point industries in Canada and the United States ranges from 20,000 to 10,000 BP.

The likelihood that man arrived earlier than is indicated by the Siberian dates derives from numerous early North American dates, perhaps the most important being from Crow Flat on the Crow River in the Canadian Yukon, where a 'flesher' of caribou tibia was dated to 27,000 ±3,000 BP (Irving and Harrington 1973: 335). While some scholars claim satisfaction with dates as far back as 40,000 or even 50,000 BP (Bada and Helfman 1975; Berger 1975), no date prior to 24,000 BP has been universally accepted by American archaeologists. Geologically, the Bering Strait land bridge was present in the Pleistocene. Haag (1962: 18) estimates a corridor 700 miles in width was required for an extended period before plant migration could occur. Land bridges meeting these requirements would have existed but rarely. Both animals and plants crossed between the two continents during the Pleistocene period, but of particular interest to scholars of early man are the two last major periods of bridging: one between 50,000 and 40,000 BP and the other between 28,000 and 10,000 BP. It seems probable that the greatest migration would

*A paper on this subject was read at the conference in 1974 by Dr John Campbell of James Cook University, Queensland, Australia, who has kindly read this text; the views expressed within this chapter are of course entirely the responsibility of the author.

have occurred when milder climates on both the Siberian and American side permitted free flow, and as the climate worsened the animals would have been squeezed south on the American side to avoid the encroaching cold and narrowing corridor, the presumed route south being via the Mackenzie Gap and to the east of the Rocky Mountains. One would assume that the post-Glacial opening of the corridor would have been unpopular for migration because the climate of central Siberia was consistently milder throughout the major glaciations of America and the enticement to migrate into the colder American region would not have been great. It is necessary to find further reason for man to cross the land bridge after glacial maximum, although it is most likely that migrations took place during the earlier part of each major land bridge formation. Man, by over-killing, may have forced large game to migrate across the land bridge despite its Boreal climate. Compared with the extinction of big game in the Old World, the New World lost most of its mega-fauna abruptly between 10,000 and 5,000 BP, and the big kill-sites of the Palaeo-Indians range from slightly earlier throughout this period. The two events, migration and extinction, are probably inter-related (fig. 60).

There is difficulty over when the pre-projectile phase of pebble industries arrived in the New World. Some would have the industry brought by *Homo erectus* between 50,000 and 40,000 BP, others when the Mousterian flourished, and still others would have it arrive just prior to the projectile industries, if not fully contemporary with them. It is fair to say that studies of early man are still in their infancy in the New World and no reliable lithic parallels can be immediately brought to bear upon those found in America from the Siberian side of the Strait. Those who claim correspondence with Acheulian and Mousterian industries in Siberia and Russia are doing so on such general correlations that one could equally find the same parallels appearing as late as the neolithic. In other words, to presume an arrival of man over the land bridge around 40,000 BP on such parallels is indeed disputable, and the more so when one considered the physical evidence of man in the New World itself. These core industries, however, are accepted by MacNeish as earlier than the projectile industries on the evidence that he found in the Ayacucho valley of Peru, and through the dates of twelve excavations within the valley he has established an unbroken sequence ranging from 20,000 bc to ad 1500 (MacNeish 1972: 69-79; cf. here also the various contributions in Gorenstein 1975).

The main migration into the New World probably came when the widest corridor of perhaps 2,100 km was formed by the ice locking up water during the Wisconsin Glaciation, thereby reducing the depth of the strait by as much as 140m below that of today (Haag 1962: 15). No doubt with the strait often shallower than its present 55m, thereby exposing more land, migration over short distances of sea could have occurred at almost any time. Certainly the coastlines were visible to one looking across to the other side and the prospect of navigating these strong currents would not be daunting since land would never disappear from view. Therefore, migration of man into the New World might not have been restricted to times when only the land bridge was available. Penetration into the regions south of Alaska depended entirely upon a land corridor being open as well as access to Alaska across the Bering Strait being available. Even when this corridor, presumably closed at the Wisconsin Glaciation's greatest maximum and perhaps sporadically during other ice incursions, was open, the climate in the area was far from gentle.

Flint points out that the Japan Current would have ameliorated the weather of

Figure 60. General distribution of pre-projectile point and Palaeo-Indian complexes *(reproduced from Betty J. Meggers,* Prehistoric America, *Aldine Atherton, Chicago, 1972).* The land bridge is shown in black. The glacial maximum attained about 20,000 years ago and approximated by line a-a[1] created a barrier that isolated the New World for several thousand years. As the ice melted, a corridor opened in western Canada, and its position about 10,000 years ago is indicated by the lines b-b[1].

the Bering Plain when it rose above water between Alaska and Siberia, giving it a climate approximating to that of the Aleutian Chain today. The plain thickly covered with long, dense grass would have provided ideal fodder for herbivores in both summer and winter (Flint 1957: 474). Although the central area of Siberia was relatively free of glaciers due to lack of available water, the coastal regions did have glaciers at times which would have blocked access to the Bering Plain (Flint 1957: 415, 416 map). It seems that traffic over the Bering land bridge moved principally eastwards, as indicated by the cold-temperate and Boreal-living Asian species of bear, cat, elephant (only mammoths and mastodon), moose, caribou, antelope, cattle, sheep and musk oxen, while moving westwards across the bridge came camels, wolf and rodents. The Boreal climate of the bridge must have filtered out all but those animals who tolerated a rather cold climate, because many more warmth loving species on both continents never crossed the strait (Flint 1957: 474) (fig. 61).

Tundra, and further south, *Taiga* conditions would have exposed man to short, insect-infested, hot summers and bleak, frozen winters. His treeless environment would have failed to supply vital wood, raw material for implements, building and fuel. Cold might have restricted his stone working; however, bone would have been available to provide the solution to shortages of both wood and stone. His clothing would have resembled that of the Eskimo, a later population that occupied the same area. The principal supplies for his requirements would have come from the quarry he hunted on land and sea.

Although recent dating suggests some support for man's arrival in the New World prior to the last land bridge about 28,000 BP (Berger 1975), numerous paths of investigation still converge on a date about 15,000 BP as an important period for human migration. The extraordinary similarity of polymorphic traits throughout American Indian populations of both North and South America suggest one migration rather than a mingling of several groups coming into North America by diffuse means. *Polymorphic traits* receive great emphasis in physical studies because their appearance is the result of two or more genes coming together from the parents; in other words, the traits are inherited from previous populations, but the final outcome is open to change because more than one gene is involved. Such traits involve dental patterns, hair, facial features, stature, and so on, while single-gene traits such as the Diego factor or blood group A_1 carry less weight in an argument because only one gene is involved. Geographical distances impose great strain on the continuity of polymorphic traits because small, closed breeding populations can evolve independently from the more general pattern. The point here is that the American Indians, despite their dispersal throughout the New World, still retain greater continuity in these polymorphic traits than any other population over a similar area in the world. No other population has remained so uniform and scholars are unanimous that they show less diversity between themselves than is commonly found in indigenous populations of comparable area in Europe and Africa (Laughlin 1967: 415; Stewart 1960: 262). Further, although there is no evidence incompatible with a time-lapse of only 15,000 years, this does not exclude older populations arriving, but rather suggests no evidence for a longer population history (Laughlin 1967: 417). No pockets of population displaying traits other than those consistent with the American Indian have ever been detected, apart from the Eskimo, who will be discussed shortly. It is apparent that should an older population be identified in the future, one can now say that it could not have played a major role in the

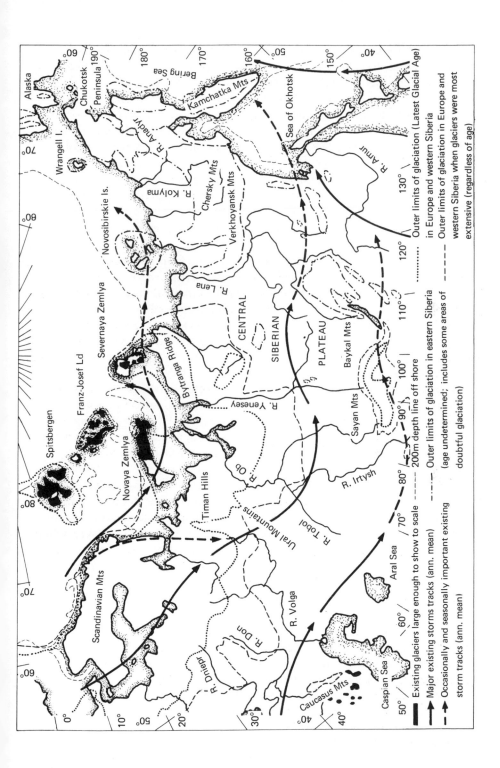

Figure 61. Northern Eurasia showing existing and former glaciers *(after Flint 1957).*

development of the American Indian, and one could be bold enough to presume at this point in time that such a population would have died out before it could interact with the ancestors of the present population.

A convenient check on this evidence lies in the very distinctive Eskimo/Aleut populations, which agree most closely with the modern Asiatic or 'Mongolian' populations of the Siberian area, and differ from the indigenous American Indian populations to their south. The American Indian seems to derive from a 'proto-Mongolian' population of Asia, which W.W. Howells suggests can be traced in three crania from the Upper Cave of Chou-kou-t'ien, among others, in China. This seems more than likely because one must accept that a living population undergoes continuous change, not least of which occurs through the mechanism of polymorphism, and the Asian and American populations would continue to diverge from their common ancestor.

Support lies again in the mechanism of the body to adapt to its environment. Laughlin aptly points out that the polymorphic similarities are so close that the time-span is very short, and the lack of increased pigment in the skins of tribes living near the Equator in the New World, unlike the increase in pigmentation in Africa, supports this short elapse of time (Laughin 1967: 416). Equally, the Eskimo, equipped with extra fat pads over his cheek bones, a compact bodybuild and short appendages such as fingers and toes, is admirably suited to the region which can only be assessed as an extreme marginal environment unsuitable for any other population of people. The circumpolar peoples adapted over a long period of time and had no reason to follow their less adapted distant cousins, the Palaeo-Indians, south when the land bridge broke up. Laughlin suspects two routes of migration across the land bridge. One, a coastal route, was less of a route than an area settled out of preference by the ancestors to the Aleuts and Eskimo populations, who became isolated into their present distribution at least by 3,000 B.C; the other was an interior route used by the migrating 'proto-Mongolians', who must have appeared very like the modern native American populations today. The question of whether blood groups A and B were absent from the earliest populations, or were selected out by natural evolutionary processes, is a moot point. There are three very definite areas which suggest early differences were regionally retained: O in South America; A_1 and O in North America; and B, A_1 and O in the Aleut and Eskimo populations. Further, the presence of the Diego factor in American Indians and in many Asiatic Mongoloids while it is absent in the Eskimos suggests the coastal inhabitants who were the forebears of the Eskimo were by-passed by the ancestors of the American Indians who moved through the interior of the land bridge (Laughlin 1967: 516). It is interesting that Laughlin feels the Eskimos migrated along the coastal regions of the land bridge and indeed inhabited them until rising water isolated them in Alaska, while the Aleuts remained in the Bering land bridge area, thereby occupying islands that once formed part of this bridge. Linguistically, the Aleuts and Eskimos are linked in their past and the idea of their adapting to their respective environments seems a plausible theory supported by this evidence, although Laughlin cautions us that much more work needs to be done (Laughlin 1967: 447).

The evidence therefore strongly supports the arrival of an intact population moving as one migration across the land bridge about 15,000 BP. The suggestion that previous peoples crossed the 40,000 BP land bridge is less likely, and if they did they probably died out before they contributed to the peoples who were directly ancestral to the modern indigenous populations of America.

To return to the lithic industries that are identified as periods within American prehistory. MacNeish would have four traditions: *Core Tool; Flake and Bone Tool; Blade, Burin and Leaf-Point; and Specialized Point* (MacNeish 1972: 79). It is apparent that correlation between early man sites in the Old World and those in the New suffer from the types of site excavated. As Coles and Higgs (1969: 421-2) point out, most of the American sites are kill-sites or transit sites in the grassland areas, while the basis for the European succession is on home-base cave sites.

There have been several attempts to link the New World lithic industries with those of the Old World. The latest has been Müller-Beck's two-prong influence into the New World of first a 'Mousteroid' and then an 'Aurignacoid' industrial phase (1967: 373-408). The Mousterian influence he sees in the early Llano development and the Aurignacian influence he can pin to about 15,000 BP on the Siberian Plain. The separation of the two as they are absorbed into the Southern area of North America is the result of the isolation each from the other by the coalescing of glaciers with the Rocky Mountains (Müller-Beck 1967: 403). This theory has severe problems; the general parallels in Asia are so general that they could belong to any industry, and the time-span involved for these industries must be telescoped on the Siberian side only to be extended on the American side almost simultaneously. Not very sophisticated New World bifaces seem so general that their connection with any specific Old World assemblage is very tenuous. Laughlin also disagrees with Müller-Beck over the presence of *burins,* which Müller-Beck emphasizes would fit into any Aurignacoid complex and were present in the Levi Rockshelter level dated to 10,000 ±175BP (Müller-Beck 1967: 395). Laughlin notes that the 'burins' from Anangula functioned not as graving tools but as scraping tools that were produced from flakes or blade fragments off which smaller flakes have been removed transversely and slightly ventrally (Laughlin 1967: 433). Here the argument revolves around function rather than appearance, again diluting the argument that favours fully-developed industries being carried into the New World from the Old. Müller-Beck's argument must be considered, although it is weakened when he acknowledges the extremely poor case he tries to make for man's arrival across the land bridge of more than 40,000 BP, and there is little doubt that he cannot resolve the situation of both the Mousteroid and the Aurignacoid industries arriving over the same land bridge at approximately the same time. At this moment, the argument for a major migration over the last land bridge is supported both by the physical and archaeological evidence.

MacNeish in his studies of the Tehuacan and Ayacucho valleys has endeavoured to study the entire ecology of the two areas and in doing so has included the winter camp sites, repeatedly visited, of the people he studies. Therefore, from only these two valley areas, Tehuacan in Mexico for the early agricultural periods of man and Ayacucho in Peru for the early development of man in that region, do we have studies that enable correlation with the type of early site most studied in the Old World. As is discussed in the following chapter, it is generally thought that man followed his game across the land bridge in conditions that favoured the migration of both animals and man. If man indeed followed his game across in the 40,000 BP period, the interpretation that he had an unspecialized industry that restricted him to hunting in small bands similar to the late Lower Palaeolithic or Middle Palaeolithic of the Old World may be right. But surely, the unspecialized nature of this

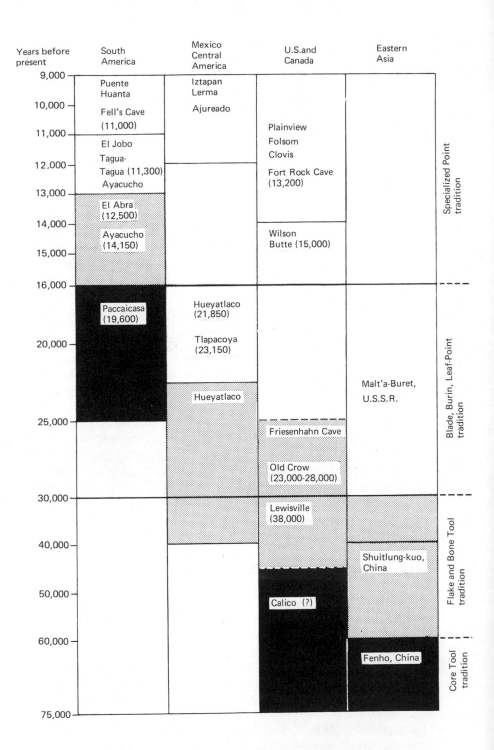

Figure 62. Suggested Old World sources of the four earliest prehistoric traditions in the New World *(after MacNeish)*.

pre-projectile industry is cruder than that of the Mousterian and yet the game man is expected to bring down in the New World is a challenge to even the more specialized Mousterian hunter with equipment such as hand spears, traps, and a social organization that would have given substantial group hunting support. At present, the distribution of the Palaeo-Indian sites seems to be restricted to very open environments of grasslands, desert, and away from wooded areas, but these are perhaps the result of archaeological field emphasis rather than true distributions. Controversial also is the dating of the pre-projectile phase, which ranges between 37,000 BP for Lewisville, Texas and $14,150 \pm 180$ BP for Pikimachay (Flea Cave), Peru (Meggers 1972: 9-11).

The detailed argument favouring man's arrival prior to the last land bridge and, therefore, via the previous one of between 50,000 and 40,000 BP, runs as follows. MacNeish believes there is a case for this early arrival in the evidence found in the Ayacucho valley of Peru. He has three pre-projectile traditions: *Core Tool; Flake and Bone Tool; Blade, Burin and Leaf-Point.* The *Core Tool Tradition* of Paccaicasa in Peru is the earliest. The industry contains large corelike choppers, large side-scrapers and spoke shaves, and what he terms 'heavy denticulate implements' (MacNeish 1972: 77). In South America, these industries range from 25,000 to 15,000 BP, but MacNeish again feels that the much disputed Calico site in the Mojave desert north of Barstow, California, might possibly represent this tradition in North America (MacNeish 1972: 77) (fig. 63).

There are two more intervening traditions before the projectile point phase in MacNeish's Ayacucho series. The *Flake and Bone Tool Tradition* found at Ayacucho has a reduced number of core tools from that of the previous industry and more implements made from flakes, among which are projectile points, knives, side scrapers, gravers, burins, spoke shaves, and again, 'denticulate' tools. The bone implements consist of projectile points, awls and scrapers. Again in South America, the range of dates lies between 15,000 and 12,000 BP, while accurate dating of the North American sites is lacking (MacNeish 1972: 78, fig., maps).

The last stage before the *Specialized Bifacial Point Tradition,* which in North America includes *Clovis* and *Old Cordilleran,* is the *Blade, Burin and Leaf-Point Tradition.* It is characterized by double-ended points, blades, burins, core-like scrapers, and is associated with extinct animals. The dates range from 14,000 to 10,000 BP and MacNeish (1972: 78) feels that the dates in North America are earlier, but again supporting evidence is not available.

There is little to support MacNeish for his theory of man's early arrival across the 40,000 BP land bridge - no dates; the fauna, doomed to extinction about 10,000 to 5,000 BP, could have existed across the New World in an ecological balance until man's arrival over the land bridge which existed between 28,000 and 10,000 BP. The dates, after all, are principally within this latter range. Flint points out that the Rancholabrean fauna of camels, horses, ground sloth, two species of musk ox, peccaries, pronghorns, and all but one specie of bison as well as the giant bison, a giant beaver-like animal, stag moose, and several kinds of large cat became extinct rather rapidly between 10,000 and 5,000 BP. In the Old World the animals took rather longer than 5,000 years to die out, and such generously-sized animals as the Columbian mammoth, Imperial mammoth, mastodon, and woolly mammoth also vanished. Man, according to Flint (1957: 468-70), must be the culprit! It is likely that the wasteful driving of large herds of these giant animals to their death would

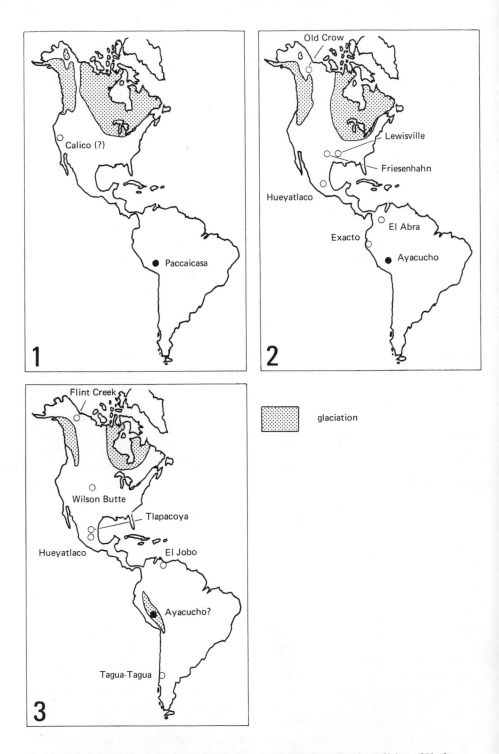

Figure 63. Distribution in the New World of (1) the Core Tool tradition, (2) the Flake and Bone tradition, and (3) the Blade, Burin and Leaf-Point tradition *(after MacNeish).*

have speeded their extinction. This too is reflected in the industrial development of man's lithic equipment.

Most experts seem in agreement that the projectile point tradition had appeared by about 12,000 BC. At the same time arrive the Palaeo-Indians of East Asian physical type, and indeed the only form of man identified as populating the New World before European arrival. Although there is no question that the projectile point industries were a vast improvement in bringing down the game over the unspecialized traditions named by MacNeish, there is dispute over whether the hunter was assisted in propelling his spear with the spear-thrower (atlatl), which served to extend his arm, thereby giving greater force and accuracy to his throw. The points of this stage were considered too heavy to have been propelled by the bow.

The principal concentration of the Clovis tradition lies on the Llano Estacado (Staked Plains) region of Texas and New Mexico near the town of Clovis. The fluted or channelled Clovis points range from 7-12cm in length and 3-4cm across the base. The edges near the base are ground, presumably to keep from cutting their binding. The production of these points was by percussion with only the occasional pressure retouching along the edge (Willey 1966: 38-9). Willey feels that the presence of lanceolate and fluted blades in America associated with a specialized hunting economy must have arrived with its rudiments already developed and could be best linked to that of the Levallois-Mousterian complex in Central Siberia (Willey 1966: 37). It is implied that the specialization occurred later and the Clovis or 'Llano complex' of points, scrapers, flakes and bone artifacts was concentrated first in the Llano Estado region before the Clovis points spread throughout the United States and northern Mexico; adaptations of this point have been found as far south as the Tierra del Fuego. The hunting tradition lends itself to a grassland or plains environment, and interpretation of this preference receives further support from the concentration of kill-sites being exclusively on the North American Plains area.

The standard designation by American archaeologists for this phase is 'Big-Game Hunting Tradition', which is characterized by a specific series of specialized lanceolate projectile points, notably *Clovis, Folsom* with its related forms, the single-shouldered *Sandia* point, and several types best classified as 'Plano' points and associated with lithic and bone remains. 'Big-Game Hunting' was eclipsed about 8,000 to 7,000 BC when warmer, drier conditions theoretically caused many large animals to become extinct; yet climate cannot be blamed as their sole cause of extinction. Man initiated the unbalancing of Nature's equilibrium in this area, no doubt he also perpetuated it, and climate merely gave the *coup de grâce*. There was, however, a persistence of the 'Plano' point in some areas until about 4,000 BC. There is also a warning from many American archaeologists that the emphasis on 'Big-Game' kill-sites may be a false emphasis because these are the sites excavated at present, but with different emphasis in the future, the story may change.

The site of Blackwater Draw No.1, which was a kill-site of camel, horse, bison and mammoth and may also have been a camp site, provides stratigraphy for the Clovis or 'Llano Complex' below that of the Folsom Fluted points and Midland points associated with bison bones. Above this level, Plano points thought to be of the Agate Basin period were also found. Other 'Plano' points found in this upper occupation strata have not been fully dated by radiocarbon. Dates unrecalibrated for this site are given as mean radiocarbon dates:

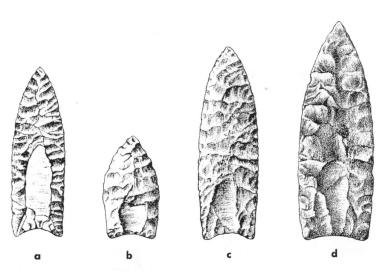

Figure 64. Clovis projectile points: a-c. Lehner site, Arizona; d. Blackwater Draw, New Mexico *(reproduced from Gordon R. Willey,* An Introduction to American Archaeology, vol.1, *Prentice-Hall Inc., Englewood Cliffs, N.J., 1966).*

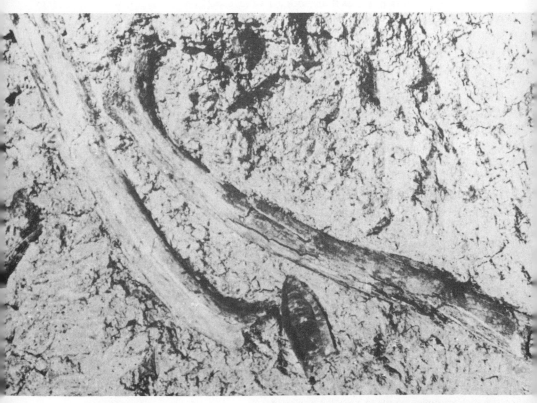

Figure 65. Folsom, New Mexico: Folsom point embedded in bison rib *(photograph: courtesy Denver Museum of Natural History).*

Clovis point level	=	9220 bc
Folsom-Midland point level	=	8340 bc
Agate Basin Plano point level	=	7840 bc

It is thought by comparisons alone that the subsequent 'Plano' complexes equate best with the Frederick level, which would date within the range of 6,000-5000 bc (Willey 1966: 40). Other sites, especially that of Dent, near the modern city of Denver, Colorado, have Clovis points associated with mammoth remains, suggesting that these hunters preferred mammoth to any other game. There is a radiocarbon date for Dent about 9200 bc. Lehner, Arizona, has a similar date for Clovis points with mammoth remains. Clovis points found in Eastern North America are equally old, being dated between 10,000-9,000 bc. Vance Haynes Jr, inspired by E.S. Deevey Jr's work on demography, calculated that a single band of Clovis hunters, comprised of about 30 individuals or approximately five families, passing down the corridor opened by the Two Creeks interval, might over the course of the next five hundred years sire a population numbering between 800 and 12,500 people, who would have produced between two million and 14 million Clovis points during the course of their evolution. He believes the Clovis hunters could easily have spread across the North American continent from coast to coast during this short time, as well as extinguishing the mammoth by 9,000 bc, leaving the Folsom hunters with nothing more than bison to hunt (Haynes: 1966: 52).

Perhaps earlier than, or at least as early as, the Clovis hunters is a related industry of percussion-flaked lanceolate points called Sandia points, named after the Sandia Cave in the Sandia Mountains of central New Mexico. No reliable radiocarbon dates have been forthcoming for either the Folsom or Sandia levels in the Sandia Cave. These would help to resolve the controversy of whether the Sandia point level is earlier than that of Folsom or merely the product of burrowing animal activity (Willey 1966: 40-1).

Folsom points developed from the Clovis fluted form. It is appropriate here to warn the reader that in all of the assemblages so far mentioned there is a proportion of the industry that is made up of unfluted projectile points. It is the fluted form, however, that is diagnostic of the Palaeo-Indian series from Clovis on to the Archaic period. For both the Clovis and the Folsom points, the knapper would rough out the general shape and bevel the base; he then detached a long flake leaving a channel about a third of the point's length. The fluting might be one or both sides. Because of the blunting of the edges either side of the channel, it seems likely that the function of the channel was not for blood letting, but to stop the binding from fraying while holding the split end of a wooden shaft in its purpose-built channel (Haynes 1966: 45). The Folsom points were lighter in construction, smaller in size, and more delicately made than the Clovis points. The channel usually ran almost the full length of the point. The distribution of this point was more limited than that of Clovis points. The best site for the Folsom complex is the Lindenmeier kill- and camp site in north-eastern Colorado. The arroyos contained a heap of extinct bison bones. From that part of the site, and from the camp a quarter of a mile distant, came the fluted points, thin unfluted points of similar shape, knives with channelling, other knives made from the channel flakes, leaf-shaped knives, core choppers, and a variety of scrapers, including the thick 'snub-nosed' scraper, small 'thumb-nail' scrapers, 'turtle-back' scrapers and concave-edged 'spokeshaves' (Willey 1966: 43).

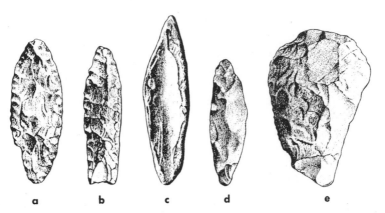

Figure 66. Stone and bone implements from Sandia Cave, New Mexico: a. Sandia Type 1; b. Sandia Type 2; c. bone point; d. leaf-shaped point; e. snub-nosed scraper *(reproduced from Gordon R. Willey,* An introduction to American Archaeology, vol.1, *Prentice-Hall Inc., Englewood Cliffs, N.J., 1966).*

Figure 67. Folsom point *(reproduced from Gordon R. Willey,* An Introduction to American Archaeology, vol.1, *Prentice-Hall Inc., Englewood Cliffs, N.J., 1966).*

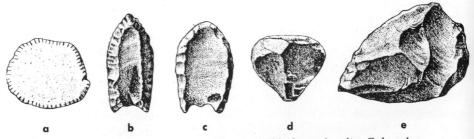

Figure 68. Stone and bone implements from the Lindenmeier site, Colorado: a. decorated bone disc; b-c.   Folsom-type projectile points ; d. snub-nosed scraper; e. side scraper *(reproduced from Gordon R. Willey,* An Introduction to American Archaeology, vol.1, *Prentice-Hall Inc., Englewood Cliffs, N.J., 1966).*

Work on these early Big-Game Hunters has advanced little in reconstructing their society since F.H.H. Roberts Jr dug Lindenmeier in the 1930s. Joe Ben Wheat attempts to reconstruct the hunting pattern and butchering preferences of the later Scottsbluff Milnesand and Eden Point hunters who destroyed a herd of *Bison occidentalis* in an arroyo 16 miles south of Kit Carson, Colorado. This is informative work, but must be matched at numerous and varied sites before we gain any ground in defining the Palaeo-Indian's pattern of life. Even with Joe Ben Wheat's laborious work at Olsen-Chubbuck, we are little more informed about the hunting practices of about 6500 BC than we concluded from ethnographic parallels of the living Plains Buffalo hunters (figs. 71-2). The bison were purposely stampeded and their escape routes covered by hunters stationed at appropriate points along their predicted path of flight. Some 200 animals were killed as they crashed into the arroyo sometime in late May or early June, as deduced from the bones of young calves only a few days old (Wheat 1967: 85). Here careful excavation permitted a reconstruction of 'butchering units', which is of considerable interest, while other valuable information obtained was the range of projectile point and its variations that occur in a single hunting group: a warning to typologists! These points all qualify as variants of the 'Plano' point series which may have developed from the Clovis and Folsom forms, although they are unfluted and lanceolate in shape. Equally, they could be derived from the Sandia form. They are pressure flaked and finely done. Radiocarbon dates for these points range from 7800-5100 bc and their distribution ranges from the Canadian Plains into Mexico (Willey 1966: 45-6). The Horner site near Cody, Wyoming, is the type of site for these Plano or parallel-flaked projectile points. Frequently referred to in the literature as the Cody complex, it is a site of extensive butchering of modern bison, and possibly a habitation. The Eden and Scottsbluff points are found together, as is the asymmetrical 'Cody' knife, some scrapers, knives, perforators, choppers, pounders and rubbing stones (Willey 1966: 48). The appearance of rubbing and grinding stones is important as it emphasizes the coming of increasing dependence on plant life to supplement the meat diet of these Big-Game Hunters.

In the Pacific North-West, a willow-leaf, bi-point projectile point seems to have had a very early use and the phase of which it is characteristic is called the *Old Cordilleran* complex. The assemblage of this complex includes knives of a similar leaf-shaped form, oval knives and cobbles (Willey 1966: 51-2). The complex is thought to be the remains of a relatively unspecialized group of hunters, gatherers and fishers. This is the group that MacNeish believes is part of the *Specialized Bifacial Point Tradition,* which follows his *Blade, Burin and Leaf-Point Tradition* (MacNeish 1972: 78-9). In some ways, MacNeish jumbles Clovis, Sandia, Folsom, Plano points and the Old Cordilleran into the general category of *Specialized Bifacial Point Tradition,* but for his purposes this is not unjustifiable because what he is really distinguishing is the major economic change signalled by these points in the life of the hunter and gatherer. Here are people exploiting a bountiful meat supply by gaining superior control over herds of animals, probably with the use of the throwing spear; something man had never before achieved in the New World. Yet, is it fair for MacNeish to lump the variables of the Projectile Point phase into one category, when he so carefully had three separate traditions at Ayacucho that he labelled Pre-Projectile Point Tradition? He puts forward the date of 13,200 years BP for the earliest known specialized projectile points found at Fort Rock Cave in

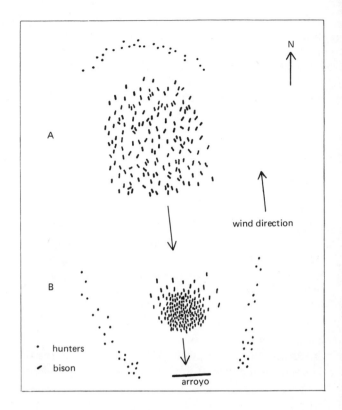

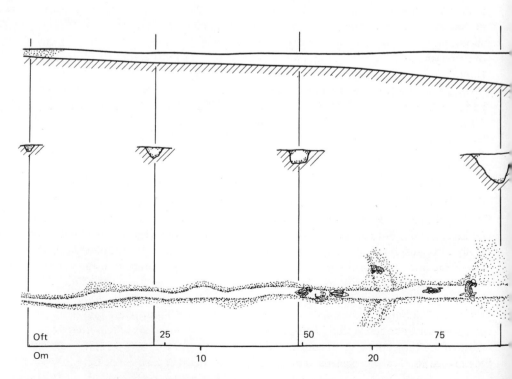

Figure 69. Schematic plan of (a) pattern of Palaeo-Indian hunters' stalking of grazing bison and (b) subsequent driving of herd to eventual kill-site in arroyo *(after Wheat)*.

Figure 70. Olsen-Chubbuck kill-site, Colorado. Sections and plan showing excavated remains of dead and butchered bison *(after Wheat)*.

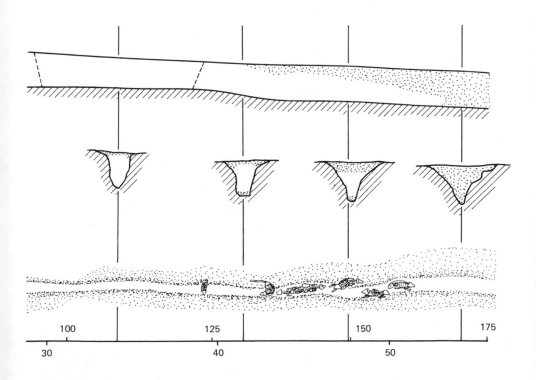

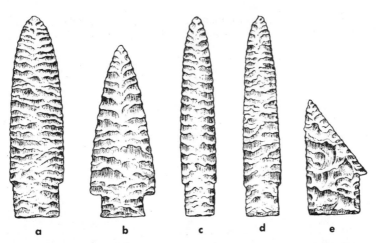

Figure 71. Lanceolate projectile point types: a. Scottsbluff Type 1; b. Scottsbluff Type 2; c. Eden collateral-flaked point; d. Eden transverse-flaked point; e. Cody knife *(reproduced from Gordon R. Willey,* An Introduction to American Archaeology, *Prentice-Hall Inc., Englewood Cliffs, N.J., 1966).*

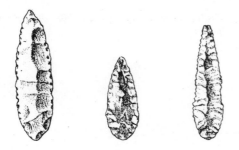

Figure 72. Old Cordilleran tradition: cascade points *(reproduced from Gordon R. Willey,* An Introduction to American Archaeology, vol.1, *Prentice-Hall Inc., Englewood Cliffs, N.J., 1966).*

Figure 73. North and Mesoamerica: main culture areas *(after Willey)*.

Oregon (MacNeish 1972: 78-9). Willey seems to overlook or disagree with this as he puts the Fort Rock Cave as later. In the lowest levels were found not only leaf-shaped points of the Old Cordilleran tradition, but also basketry, cordage, sandals and notched points more in keeping with the Desert cultural tradition, which has a range of dates about 8000 to 7000 bc (Willey 1966: 53, 56). It seems that there is a confusion or an agreement to disagree about what the Old Cordilleran tradition represents. There appears to be agreement, however, in the interpretation of the tradition as an unspecialized one. Dates range from 9000 bc to 5000 bc, but with a strong clustering in the middle periods. One school of thought suggests that the Old Cordilleran is a response to the area it occupies rather than a chronological stage in the development of the Palaeo-Indian. How it relates to the *Desert Tradition* is unresolved at present, but in the semi-arid Great Basin area, the Old Cordilleran shares its preference for basketry, matting, and netting with that of the Desert Tradition.

The Desert Tradition persisted into historic times, shown by superb preservation on prehistoric sites as well as ethnographic studies of such marginal gatherers as the Northern Paiute of Utah. Archaeologically the evidence obtained from the Desert Tradition sites show that these people pursued a gathering existence rather than one with its emphasis on hunting. Found in association with their milling stones and basketry were a series of chipped-stone projectile points. These points tended to be broader and smaller than either the Big-Game Hunting or Old Cordilleran traditions, and it can only be assumed that they were used as throwing-stick dart tips (Willey 1966: 56). The fauna associated with their sites was modern, and therefore smaller than that hunted by the Big-Game Hunters. The origins of the Old Cordilleran and the Desert traditions are at present unknown, but there is general agreement that the two are linked, if not in their ancestry then in their chronological sequence. What does seem apparent is that they existed in an overlapping chronology with the Big-Game Hunters, and after that tradition ceased they were able to continue because of their total adaption to a gathering economy (fig. 74).

It is apparent that man first made a resounding impact on the North American continent in the Palaeo-Indian Big-Game Hunting period, when he over-killed his food supply and ultimately forced himself into a more varied and severe economy that relied heavily upon the plant food resources and much less on animal products. The Archaic period of American Indian development is a demotion to subsistence won from small-game hunting, fishing, and plant collecting. A similar demotion occurred in the Mesolithic period of Europe, and one can only imagine that the New World imposed a harsher environment in the Plains area than any experienced in Europe. It forced the population to occupy the kinder woodland areas and with it came the polished tools better adapted to woodworking. It seems logical to suppose that at this time the American Indian first practiced elementary agriculture by planting sun-flower and other easy food sources. The response which resulted in the Mesolithic in Europe and the Archaic in the New World might be excused by some as imposed on man by climatic change, which indeed did take place in both areas, but there was more of an element of over-kill in the New World. This may come as a surprise to some, as frequently the Indian is referred to as the first conservationist, who was praised for utilizing all of the animal he killed. Unfortunately, the kill-sites disabuse this myth, and we see man in the Archaic period learning too late that he must alter and adapt his living to a new environment. Positive contributions come

Figure 74. Paiute woman of northern Utah making a basket outside shelter, photographed near Grand Canyon during the 1871-5 Colorado River Expedition of Major John Wesley Powell *(photograph: courtesy Office of Anthropology, Smithsonian Institution).*

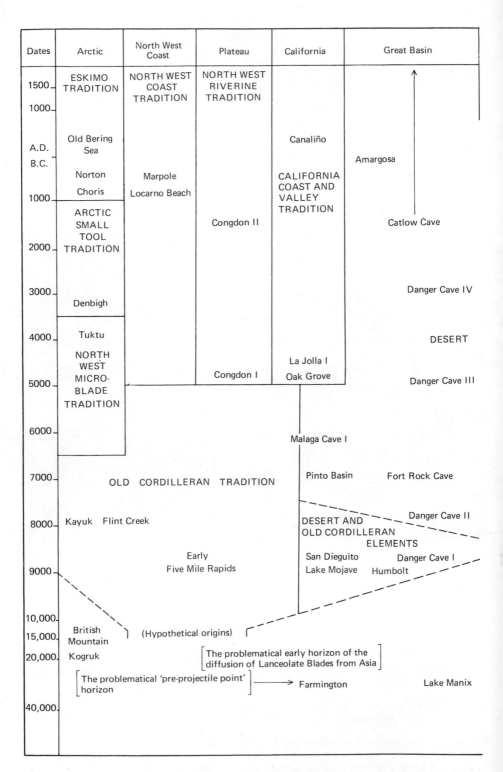

Figure 75. North America: early cultures, phases and traditions *(after Willey).*

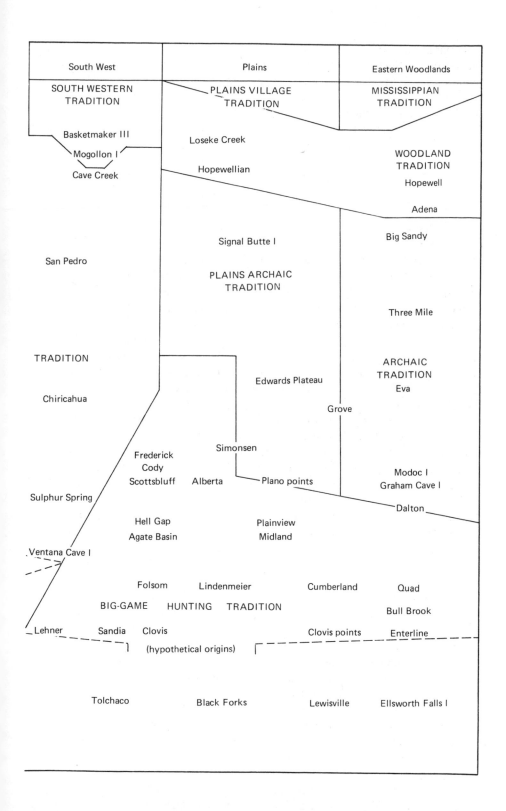

South West	Plains	Eastern Woodlands
SOUTH WESTERN TRADITION	PLAINS VILLAGE TRADITION	MISSISSIPPIAN TRADITION

Basketmaker III

Loseke Creek

WOODLAND TRADITION

Mogollon I

Hopewellian

Cave Creek

Hopewell

Adena

Big Sandy

Signal Butte I

San Pedro

PLAINS ARCHAIC TRADITION

Three Mile

TRADITION

ARCHAIC TRADITION

Edwards Plateau

Eva

Chiricahua

Grove

Simonsen

Frederick
Cody

Modoc I

Scottsbluff   Alberta   Plano points

Graham Cave I

Sulphur Spring

Dalton

Hell Gap

Plainview

Agate Basin

Midland

Ventana Cave I

Folsom   Lindenmeier   Cumberland   Quad

BIG-GAME   HUNTING   TRADITION

Bull Brook

Lehner   Sandia   Clovis   Clovis points   Enterline

(hypothetical origins)

Tolchaco   Black Forks   Lewisville   Ellsworth Falls I

from this harder existence. Agriculture, for which man had no earlier need, now became useful. Some chose to practise it to the extent that it led them to a settled economy, while others never did more than plant and return to harvest. The Penobscot Indians of Maine pursued this type of economy. One might consider them Big-Game Hunters in the winter when they hunted the moose, but their best achievement was canoe building, and in the summer as they passed down river to the coast, they would plant maize on the river islands, and continue. Their subsistence existence on the coast resembled that of a shell-midden-based economy, but on their return to winter hunting grounds, the maize would be harvested in the journey up river. The Penobscot only functioned in tribal concentration in the summer, while in the winter they broke up into family units, with allocated family hunting rights. Not precisely the same pattern, but a similar one of the tribe breaking into smaller units during periods of seasonal hardship, was noted by MacNeish in the study he conducted on the valley of Tehuacan, where between 6800 and 5000 bc the natural exploitation of plant and animal life became more regularized into groups practising agriculture (see Chapter 11). But the criteria with which one judges the level of man's achievement in what is termed the Neolithic of the Old World, that is animal domestication, agricultural control, pottery, settled towns, trade, and so forth, simply do not apply to the American Indian. There remained in North America a much more diverse population of varying achievement right up to the arrival of Europeans. Here man seemed to resist settlement economy and retain his hunting ties even while living in village complexes such as those of the Eastern Woodland Indians (fig. 75).

To conclude: man arrived as an experienced hunter of big-game in the New World from Asia to exploit a mega-fauna that was easily put out of its natural balance. This fauna was abused by man, who hunted principally by stampeding herds into fatal situations such as running them over abrupt edges of arroyos or into marshy areas, where they were at a disadvantage. This mass slaughtering was unnecessarily wasteful of these large animals who probably had long gestation periods. The mammoth, like its cousin the elephant, probably took two years to produce an offspring. The final *coup de grâce* to this style of hunting was the change of climate to a warmer, drier environment. Although there is controversy about the arrival of a pre-projectile man in the New World, which some would argue occurred during the 50,000 to 40,000 BP land bridge period, it seems unlikely that the mega-fauna would not begin to show consequent signs of diminishing during this period. Instead, the fauna of the Rancholabrean period goes into marked decline about 10,000 BP. The Big-Game Hunters appear in force in North America about 13,000 BP, which suggests they are the cause of the animal decline. Certainly by 7,000 BP but possibly earlier, there is another group, the Old Cordilleran-Desert group, who have adapted to an environment of hunting, gathering and fishing, which enables them to continue into the historic period, whereas the Big-Game Hunters must have given up their hunting practices and adapted to new ones by about 5,000 BP. These new practices probably resulted in the diverse groups seen as the Archaic traditions. Rudimentary agriculture developed, with more sophisticated agricultural advances in Mexico. The Mexican achievements ultimately were shared with groups north and south. With the triumvirate of squash, bean, and maize, the pattern of the American Indians' exploitation settled down to remain more or less the same within regional patterns, with only the occasional addition of such things as pottery making or weaving until the European arrival.

REFERENCES

Bada, Jeffrey L. and Helfman, Patricia M., 1975. 'Amino acid racemization dating of fossil bones', *World Archaeology, 7(2),* 160-73.

Bandi, Hans-Georg, 1969. *Eskimo Prehistory.*

Berger, R., 1975. 'Advances and results in radiocarbon dating: early man in America', *World Archaeology, 7(2),* 1974-84.

Coles, J.M. and Higgs, E.S., 1969. *The Archaeology of Early Man.*

Farb, Peter, 1971. *Man's Rise to Civilisation.*

Fitting, James, De Visscher, Jerry, and Wahla, Edward J. 1966. 'The Paleo-Indian Occupation of Holcombe Beach', *University of Michigan Museum of Anthropology, Anthropological Papers* No.27.

Flint, R.F., 1957 (3rd edn 1963). *Glacial and Pleistocene Geology* (New York).

Flint, R.F., 1971. *Glacial and Quaternary Geology* (New York).

Gorenstein, Shirley (ed.), 1975, *North America* (New York).

Hagg, W.G., 1962. 'The Bering Strait land bridge', in MacNeish 1972, 11-18.

Harry, Emil W., Saylor, E.B., and Wasley, W.W., 1959. 'The Lehner mammoth site, southwestern Arizona', *American Antiquity, 25,* 2-30.

Haynes, C. Vance, 1966. 'Elephant-Hunting in North America', in MacNeish 1972, 44-52.

Haynes, C. Vance, and Agogins, George, 1964. 'Geological significance of a new radiocarbon date from the Lindenmeier site', *Denver Museum of National History, Proceedings, No. 9.*

Hopkins, David (ed.), 1967. *The Bering Land Bridge* (Stanford, Cal.).

Howells, W.W., 1959. *Mankind in the Making: the story of human evolution* (New York).

Hrdlicka, Ales, 1925. 'The origin and antiquity of the American Indians', *Smithsonian Annual Report for 1923,* 481-95.

Hrdlicka, Ales, 1930. 'Anthropological Survey in Alaska', U.S. Bureau of American Ethnology, Forty-Sixth Annual Report (1928-9), 21-654.

Hrdlicka, Ales, 1932. 'The coming of man from Asia in the light of recent discoveries', *Proceedings American Philosophical Society, 71,* 393-402.

Hrdlicka, Ales, 1945. 'The Aleutian and Commander Islands and their Inhabitants', The Wistar Institute of Anatomy and Biology, Philadelphia, 630.

Irving and Harrington, 1973. *Science, 179,* 335.

Laughlin, W.S., 1967. 'Human Migration and Permanent Occupation in the Bering Sea Area', in Hopkins 1967.

MacDonald, George, 1968. 'Debert: A Paleo-Indian campsite in central Nova Scotia', National Museum of Canada, Anthropology Papers, No.16.

MacNeish, Richard S., 1972. 'Early Man in the Andes', in R.S. MacNeish (ed.), *Readings from Scientific American: Early Man in America,* 69-79 (San Francisco).

Meggers, Betty J., 1972. *Prehistoric America* (Chicago).

Müller-Beck, Hansjürgen, 1967. 'On Migrations of Hunters Across the Bering Land Bridge in the Upper Pleistocene', in Hopkins 1967.

Roberts, Frank H.H. Jr, 1935. 'A Folsom Complex: Preliminary report on investigations at the Lindenmeier site in northern Colorado', *Smithsonian Miscellaneous Collections, 94,* 4.

Roberts, Frank H.H. Jr, 1936. 'Additional Information on the Folsom Complex', *Smithsonian Miscellaneous Collections, 95,* 10.

Roberts, Frank H.H. Jr, 1940. 'Excavations at the Lindenmeier site contribute new information on the Folsom Complex', *Explorations and Field Work of the Smithsonian Institution in 1939,* 87-92.

Roberts, Frank H.H. Jr, 1951. 'The Early Americans', in MacNeish 1972, 39-43.

Stewart, T.D., 1960. 'A physical anthropologist's view of the peopling of the New World' *Southwest Journal of Anthropology, 16,* 259-73 (Albuquerque, New Mexico).

Wheat, Joe Ben, 1967. 'A Paleo-Indian Bison Kill', in MacNeish 1972, 80-8.

Willey, Gordon R., 1966. *An Introduction to American Archaeology, Volume One: North and Middle America* (New Jersey).

Wilmsen, Edwin N., 1974. *Lindenmeier: A Pleistocene Hunting Society* (New York).

Wormington, H. Marie, 1957. *Ancient Man in North America,* Denver Museum of Natural History, Popular Series, No.4.

WARWICK BRAY

11 From foraging to farming in early Mexico

To search for 'the first domestic plant' is to search for an event; it is poor strategy, it encourages bitter rivalry rather than cooperation, and it is probably fruitless. We should instead search for the processes by which agriculture began.
(Flannery 1973: 308)

In studying the development of agriculture in the New World, the problem of independent invention versus diffusion does not arise. With the possible exception of the bottle gourd, for which no wild ancestor has yet been recognized in the Americas (Heiser 1973; Lathrap 1973), native American farming was based on indigenous plants and animals, and on a technology which owes nothing to contacts with Europe or Asia. In Mesoamerica (the area with which this paper is concerned), the only domestic animals were the dog, the turkey and the stingless bee, none of which played a significant role in the agricultural cycle. The complex inter-relationship between livestock and crops, which is such a standard feature of Old World farming, was never an important factor in the western hemisphere, except in parts of the high Andes of South America where some communities relied heavily on herds of llamas and alpacas, and where the dung from these animals provided an essential fertilizer for the potato crop (Thomas R.B. 1973: 114-16).

Mexico had no such herd animals, and in this area farming is virtually synonymous with plant cultivation. In compensation for the lack of domestic animals, the plant foods of Mexico were numerous and varied. The staples were maize and beans, supplemented by squashes (plants of the pumpkin family), by seed crops such as amaranth and setaria, and by many kinds of fruits, vegetables and cactus products. The combination of maize and beans is especially important from the dietary point of view, maize being rich in starch but deficient both in total protein and, more particularly, in the essential amino acids lysine and tryptophane. Beans are not only high in protein, but are also rich in the very amino acids lacking in maize (Kaplan 1965; 1967: 202).

Figure 76 shows the range of cultivated plants attested archaeologically in the

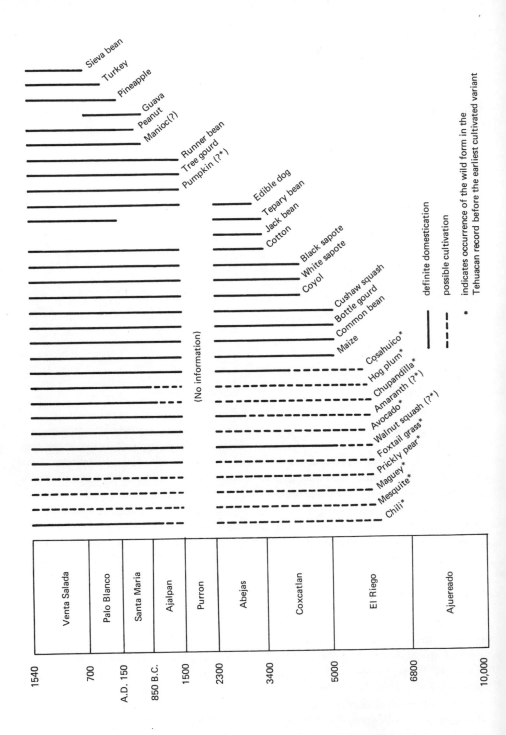

Figure 76. Plant and animal domestication in the Tehuacan Valley.

Tehuacan Valley of central Mexico, but the list does not include such crops as tobacco, tomato and *salvia* (a small-seeded annual), which are recorded in documentary sources but were not recovered in the excavations. In coastal and lowland regions of Mesoamerica, manioc tubers may have been a major source of food, but the evidence for this is circumstantial rather than direct, and is still the subject of controversy (Green and Lowe 1967: 58-60; Davis 1975; Flannery 1973: 273; Lathrap 1973).

Organic materials are not usually preserved in the humid tropics of America. For anything approaching a complete picture we must turn to excavations in rock shelters and village sites throughout the arid highlands of Mexico, where archaeologists have unearthed plant remains, coprolites, wooden tools, and objects of cloth, leather and fibre, which allow us to study the gradual changeover from foraging to farming. In some of these regions the archaeological sequence is almost unbroken from the end of the Pleistocene until the Spanish Conquest. The evidence on which the later sections of this paper are based comes mainly from three such areas: Tamaulipas (in north-east Mexico close to the Texas border), the Tehuacan Valley (in the central Mexican state of Puebla), and the Valley of Oaxaca in southern Mexico.

Although the *nature* of Mesoamerican agriculture is so different from that of Eurasia, the study of how, and why, Mexican foragers transformed themselves into farmers raises theoretical issues which apply equally to the development of agriculture in the Old World.

THE PRE-AGRICULTURAL BACKGROUND IN MEXICO

Any attempt to understand what happened during the transition from foraging to farming must take as its base the subsistence pattern of the early post-Pleistocene, at the time when the first experiments with agriculture were taking place.

In the terminal Pleistocene period, both Oaxaca and Tehuacan were slightly cooler and drier than they are today, but the transition from Pleistocene to modern conditions does not seem to have been accompanied by any major climatic change (Schoenwetter 1974; Byers 1967a, ch.4; Flannery 1967). Although, as has been seen in the previous chapter, mammoth kill-sites dating to the eighth millennium B.C. are fairly common in the Basin of Mexico (Aveleyra 1964), the evidence from caves and rock shelters of the same date suggests a pattern of broad-range exploitation in which small animals and wild plants played a more important part than big game.

During the Early Ajuereado phase in Tehuacan (pre-7000 B.C.) the animals brought back to the rock shelters included the occasional horse and pronghorn antelope, but 55 per cent of the individual animals were rabbits. Most of the other bones were from small game (fox, skunk, coyote, ground squirrel, birds, turtle, lizards and rodents). As part of the annual cycle, edible seeds and pods were harvested from the wild mesquite trees of the valley floor, and bunches of grass were collected. By 6500 B.C. (the Late Ajuereado phase) the horse was extinct and the antelope had disappeared from the valley. In the new, post-Pleistocene, environment, the Tehuacan fauna was of present-day type, and there is evidence for the consumption of several wild plants (setaria, amaranth, prickly pear, avocado and chupandilla fruits - Smith 1967).

In Oaxaca the most complete evidence comes from the earliest occupation

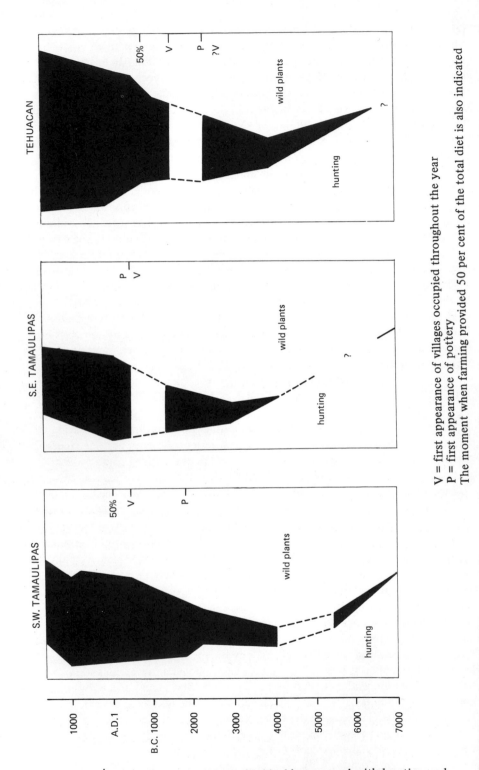

Figure 77. The importance of agriculture (in black) compared with hunting and plant-collecting in the diet of three areas of Mexico.

floors in the rock shelter of Guilá Naquitz, with radiocarbon dates ranging from 8750 to 6910 B.C. The pollen analysis suggests a somewhat cooler and drier climate than at present, though all the plants which are native to the valley today would have been available in the past (Schoenwetter 1974).The archaeological evidence indicates seasonal occupation by small groups of people who hunted rabbits and deer, collected mud turtles, and harvested acorns, pinyon, *susí* nuts, mesquite, maguey, prickly pear, runner beans, wild onions, several kinds of fruits and berries, and a squash whose seeds resembled those of the pumpkin *Cucurbita pepo* (Flannery MS.). The pollen data show that a second species of squash (with pollen grains resembling those of *C. moschata* or *C. mixta)* was eaten at the site, as well as a plant closely related to, or perhaps ancestral to, maize. Of the plants on this list, pumpkin, runner bean and the maize-like species may have been in a very early stage of domestication, though the balance of probabilities is against this view (Schoenwetter 1974; Flannery 1973: 300).

LIFE IN THE PERIOD OF INCIPIENT AGRICULTURE

For reasons which will become apparent, this pattern of broad-spectrum hunting and collecting did not suddenly change with the planting of the first seed. Cultivated plants at first played only a minimal role in the economy, and there is no sharp transition from 'pre-agricultural' to 'agricultural' life (fig. 77). The time between the first experimental planting and the emergence of full-time village farming sometime around 2000 B.C. has been called the Period of Incipient Agriculture - a convenient term, though not a very satisfactory one.

Tamaulipas, Tehuacan and Oaxaca share a number of features in common. All three are arid or semi-arid highland regions with broken topography and close juxtaposition of several ecological zones (or microenvironments), each of which offers it own individual set of resources to farmers and foragers alike. Rainfall is seasonal, and fluctuates unpredictably from one year to the next. Because many of the wild staples are available only at certain times of year, and occur only in restricted localities, the little bands of foragers and incipient cultivators followed an annual round from one microenvironment to another, eating whatever was in season.

The reconstruction which follows is firmly based upon the archaeological evidence, but owes a great debt to ethnography. Some information is available on the historic hunter-gatherer groups of Tamaulipas (Saldívar 1943; MacNeish 1958: 14-17), but the most influential studies have been those by Julian Steward of the early nineteenth-century Shoshoni Indians of the Great Basin of western North America (Steward 1934, 1955: 101-21; Thomas 1973). When the Europeans first met them, the Shoshoni were broad-spectrum hunter-gatherers in an arid highland environment not unlike that of Tehuacan. Archaeological evidence (Willey 1966: 342-56) and the contents of dessicated prehistoric faeces (Heizer and Napton 1969) demonstrate that, despite minor changes, the Desert Culture pattern in the Great Basin is at least 5000 years old and may be more ancient still. The Shoshonean-speakers, therefore, provide a useful ethnographic analogy for the Mexicans of the Period of Incipient Cultivation, and (used with caution) the analogy can help us to visualize the real people behind the archaeological data.

Flannery (1968) has reconstructed the yearly cycle for the Valley of Oaxaca, and MacNeish (1971, 1972, 1973) has done the same for Tehuacan. During the dry

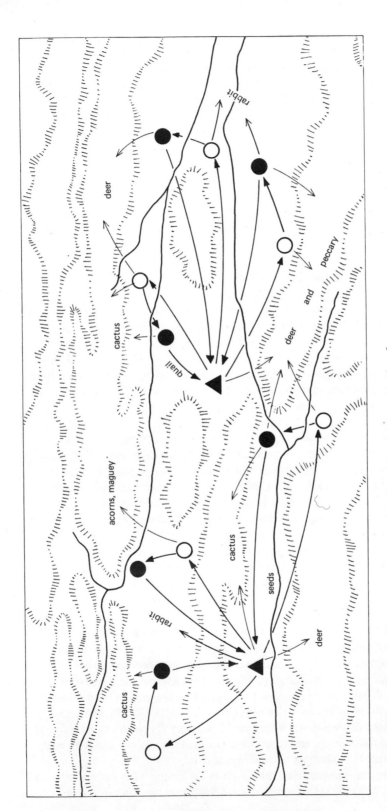

Figure 78. Reconstruction of the annual subsistence cycle in the Tehuacan basin of highland Mexico between about 6800 and 5000 B.C., based on food remains and the location of archaeological sites. In the wet season when foods were abundant, families camped together (triangles); when the dry season came and food was scarcer, they split up into small groups and moved to exploit more dispersed resources (open circles); as the dry season progressed, camp would be moved again (black circles). Finally groups would meet up again at the beginning of the wet season and the cycle begin anew (after Meggers).

season, the time of scarcity when food was hard to come by, the community split up into 'microbands' consisting of a few families, no more than 15 people in all. The archaeological campsites are small, lack permanent structures, and have only two or three hearths. The food remains consist principally of deer bones and such plant products as cactus leaves and the bulbous roots of the pochote tree (*Ceiba parvifolia*), which are available throughout the year. In the wet season, a time of temporary abundance, the scattered microbands came together, forming communities of up to 100 people. Camp sites occupied during the rainy months are in the zones richest in seasonal foods, and are larger than those of the dry period. The food debris reflect these easier conditions. The proportion of deer bones is reduced, there is an increase in rabbits and small animals trapped close to the camp site, and the unappetizing starvation diet of leaves and roots is replaced by one based on seeds, pods, nuts and berries. When the harvest of wild plants was over, the rainy-season 'macrobands' split up again, and the cycle began anew (fig. 78).

Ignoring for the moment minor regional or temporal variations, the archaeological evidence allows us to build up a fairly detailed picture of life in the Period of Incipient Cultivation (MacNeish 1964). Medium-sized animals such as deer and peccary were stalked by hunters who used stone-tipped darts hurled with the aid of a spear-thrower. Small game was snared (Tehuacan) or taken in wooden spring traps (Tamaulipas). Rabbits may also have been obtained in communal drives carried out by men armed with nets, sticks and clubs, as in the Great Basin. The bones of large animals were smashed to extract the marrow, and bits of charred flesh in the coprolites show that meat was roasted. Fire-cracked stones suggest one method of cooking.

Plant foods were collected in nets and baskets. Seeds were crushed in stone mortars, or ground on milling stones, and fibrous plants were cut up and crushed by means of stone choppers and scrapers. Beans were at first eaten young and green, sometimes in the pod; later they were eaten mature, and after soaking. The early races of pumpkin had bitter and stringy flesh, so the plant was first grown for its seeds, which were roasted; later, with the emergence under cultivation of juicier and sweeter races, crushed pumpkin flesh begins to appear in faeces. Young maize cobs were originally sucked and chewed, or else roasted whole, but by the third millennium B.C. the kernels were also ground into flour. Some plants required elaborate processing to make them palatable at all. The leaves of the maguey cactus were roasted in pits for up to five days, and then chewed as fibrous quids (Flannery 1968: 70), while acorns had to be leached in water to remove the tannic acid (Flannery 1973: 287).

Bones of small reptiles, rodents and birds were present throughout the Tehuacan sequence (Flannery 1967), but it is the coprolite evidence which really brings home the nature of broad-spectrum foraging long after the first experiments with cultivation. Besides food plants, the Tehuacan faeces contained pieces of charred snail shell, bones of mice, lizards, snakes and birds, as well as feathers and fragments of egg shell (Callen 1967). In the Sierra de Tamaulipas, as late as the third millennium B.C., the coprolites included bits of uncooked grasshopper and the shells of snails which had been eaten raw (MacNeish 1958: 146; Callen 1963). The similarity between the Mexican diet and that of the prehistoric and nineteenth-century foragers of the Great Basin is striking (Steward 1934: 255; Heizer and Napton 1969).

The tool kit during the Period of Incipient Agriculture accurately reflects the way of life, and is rich in artifacts of perishable materials (MacNeish 1964; Byers 1967b). Wood was employed for tool handles, digging sticks, dart shafts, flutes, fire drills, wedges, traps, rabbit clubs and the tongs used for picking spiny cactus fruits. Hides were dressed with the aid of chipped stone scrapers, and bone needles were used for sewing. Bast and cactus fibres were rolled by hand into a yarn which was used to make nets, tumplines, cordage and kilts. Other perishable objects from the dry caves include gourd containers, woven baskets, hand-twined textiles (made without the help of a loom), and bags and sleeping mats made from split palm leaves.

THE PROBLEM OF RECOGNIZING EARLY AGRICULTURE

Since domestication can only be recognized some time after the process has started, when the plants have been so modified under human selection that they are morphologically distinct from their wild relatives, we shall never know precisely where or when the first experiments were made. But one thing we can be sure of: the first 'cultivated' plants would have been, to all appearances, 'wild'. Except where an agricultural economy is introduced ready-made from outside, 'cultivation' (i.e. the tending of wild plants) will precede 'domestication' (which implies human intervention in the breeding process).

Although separated by 7000 years from the Incipient Cultivators of Mexico, the Shoshoneans once again provide the best ethnographic analogy for the early experimental stage of cultivation without domestication. All the Shoshoni groups lived primarily by hunting and gathering, but some groups deliberately sowed the seeds of edible grasses, and other groups expended considerable effort on building dams and canals to irrigate natural stands of bulb- and seed-bearing plants (Steward 1934: 242-50). This tending of wild plants was not accompanied by any conscious selection, and did not lead to the energence of high-yield domesticated varieties (Harris 1973b).

When, in an archaeological situation, the botanical difficulty of distinguishing between wild and cultivated plants is compounded by small samples and by conflicting prejudices about the way in which agriculture ought to have developed, there is bound to be controversy.

Some of these problems can be illustrated from the early stages of the Tehuacan sequence (fig. 76) where the evidence for cultivation during the El Riego phase is, at best, ambiguous and is interpreted in different ways by the specialists attached to the project (contrast Smith 1967 with MacNeish, Ch.15 in the same volume, Byers 1967a). Certain plants, notably tree crops and those which are vegetatively propagated, change only slowly, if at all, under cultivation. Smith notes that maguey, prickly pear and mesquite are commonly planted in the Valley today, but show no signs of modification from the wild forms. Although botanical proof is lacking, he believes that these were among the earliest cultigens in Tehuacan.

The botanical status of the other plants has been summed up by Barbara Pickersgill, and her sceptical comment is worth quoting in full:

In discussing the Mesoamerican sequence one must beware of circular arguments. The statement that plants were being cultivated (the first step towards domestication and agriculture) by about 5,000 B.C. rests mainly on the presence in the archaeological record of plants grown as crops by later cultures. Because a plant was a cultigen at the time of the European Conquest, it does not follow that it was a cultigen at the time of its first appearance in the archaeological record. Other criteria must be satisfied also. Does the morphology of the archaeological specimen indicate unequivocally that it was a domesticate? If not, does the species occur in quantities too great to be derived from exploitation of wild plants, or occur outside the range of its wild relatives (including the possibility of trade)? We still do not know the ancestry of the cultivated bottle gourd, squashes and pumpkins, and human selection has not established in these species characters clearly deleterious in the wild. It is therefore difficult if not impossible to tell whether most early records of cucurbits represent domesticated plants or not. For chili pepper and avocado the earliest specimens are seeds, which fall within the size range of modern wild forms. On the basis of seed size, avocados were domesticated by about 1,500 B.C. and chilis by about 1,000 B.C. - later than is generally supposed and probably much later than the first experiments in cultivating these plants (Pickersgill 1975: 3).

There are similar ambiguities in the evidence from Oaxaca (Schoenwetter 1974).

For Tehuacan, the extent of this uncertainty is indicated in fig. 76. Solid lines indicate *proof* of domestication (i.e. morphological change away from the wild types), while broken lines indicate *presumptive* cultivation (based on ecological criteria) of plants which are still indistinguishable from their wild forms.

Another important botanical controversy, and one which is still far from settled, concerns the origins of domesticated maize. On the one hand are those who maintain that the cultivated forms arose from an ancestral form of wild maize, that is now extinct; on the other side are those botanists and geneticists who believe that maize *(Zea mays)* is descended from its closest wild relative, a weedy grass called teosinte *(Zea mexicana)*. The argument is conveniently summarized by Flannery (1973: 290-6) and Beadle (1973). The implications of this controversy are considerable. Apart from colouring one's view of the entire history of maize evolution, it reopens the question of where maize was first domesticated and casts doubt on the status of the oldest cobs from the Tehuacan excavations. These tiny cobs are clearly maize rather than teosinte, but what exactly does this mean? They were originally published as wild maize (Mangelsdorf et al. in Byers 1967a), with 'cultivated' maize appearing archaeologically around 3000 B.C., but - if teosinte is accepted as the ancestor of all domesticated maize - the smallest and earliest of the Tehuacan cobs are already some distance along the evolutionary road. Beadle (quoted in Lathrap, Collier and Chandra 1975: 14, 20) believes that the Tehuacan maize has already undergone 1000 to 2000 years of development under primitive cultivation, and that its centre of origin may lie in the state of Guerrero where there are dense stands of wild teosinte.

Admitting, then, that the very early stages of domestication are still hidden in a grey fog of uncertainty, all one can say is that rudimentary agriculture *may have been* practised in Mexico before 5000 B.C., and undoubtedly *was* practised soon after that date.

THE NATURE AND RATE OF AGRICULTURAL EVOLUTION

Within Mesoamerica, the order in which the various cultigens appeared in the archaeological record was different in each local sequence (Bray 1976), though it is difficult to assess how much of this may be due to a sampling bias combined with incomplete preservation. Nevertheless, and irrespective of local differences, the general course of agricultural evolution was similar wherever there is adequate evidence. From a comparison of all the available Mesoamerican sequences the following general points emerge:

1. Agriculture was adopted only slowly, and the hunter-gatherer communities showed a marked reluctance to give up their foraging life and to take a commitment to farming (fig. 77).

2. The increasing importance of cultivated foods in the diet can be correlated with (a) genetic improvements leading to more productive races of certain plants which eventually became staple foods, and (b) a progressive intensification of farming, with the adoption, where practicable, of irrigation, drainage, terracing, land-reclamation etc.

3. These changes took place against a background of climatic fluctuation, though this was never extreme enough to determine the course of agricultural evolution.

4. Increasing commitment to farming was accompanied by population growth.

5. Side by side with the changes listed above, were changes in social organization and in those institutions connected with the emergence of settled life, the growth of political states, and the eventual achievement of civilization.

I have carefully avoided phrasing any of these statements in cause-and-effect form. They constitute a series of linked phenomena which are best explained by some kind of systems model, in which climate, population, natural resources, technology and social organization mutually influenced each other, and no individual factor can be singled out as the primary stimulus for change (Bray 1976).

This kind of model seems to hold good for all areas of the world where agriculture developed in situ. Slow and very gradual commitment to farming seems such a general feature that it is worth asking why.

In part, the slowness to take up farming was due to the need to develop high-yield races of plants that could support full-time agricultural life. The rate and nature of genetic change are governed by several inter-related factors, three of which are particularly important for the present study: 1. the genetic potential of the plant itself, 2. the environment, which exerts selective pressure on the genotype, and 3. the way in which the plant is propagated and harvested (Harris 1973b; Pickersgill and Heiser 1977).

The genetic history of each individual species is a story unto itself, and only the most general trends can be discussed in this paper. Selection by man introduces a new dimension into the process of genetic evolution, and variants which in nature would be eliminated may now survive, and even be at a selective advantage. In some cases, natural and human selection favour completely opposed qualities. In a fluctuating and unpredictable environment (such as highland Mexico) selection in wild plants tends to favour small seeds or fruits, irregular and staggered germination, and an effective mechanism for seed dispersal. In contrast, the cultivator selects for large seeds or fruits which, for ease of harvesting, all come to maturity at the same time and have a reduced natural capacity for seed dispersal.

By a process of unconscious selection, the loss or reduction of natural seed dispersal mechanisms has independently taken place in many of the world's principal crop plants. In those cereal crops (maize, wheat, barley, rye and rice) which are harvested by removing the entire seed head, this takes the form of selection for non-shattering varieties. The wild forms of these plants have a brittle rachis (the axial 'stalk' of the seed head), which disintegrates piecemeal to shed the seeds one by one over a period of time. But among a population of wild grasses there will be some mutant forms in which the rachis is of tough, non-shattering type, which would be selected *against* in the wild because it hinders efficient seed dispersal. A plant-collector harvesting by hand or with a sickle will inevitably collect a disproportionate number of non-shattering mutants. If the collector is also a farmer, keeping back a portion of the yield for seed, each generation of the crop will tend to include a higher percentage of non-shattering varieties until, in the course of time, the mutant comes to replace the original wild form (Flannery 1973: 279 ; Beadle 1973; Harris 1973b). In extreme cases (and maize is one) the end product is a plant which has not its natural capacity for seed dispersal and is dependent on man for its very survival.

Similar 'unnatural' changes took place in several other Mesoamerican cultigens. Some chili peppers have changed from deciduous to non-deciduous fruits, and have lost their natural means of seed dispersal by birds (Pickersgill 1971); domesticated beans no longer have pods which twist and explode to expel the seeds (Kaplan 1967: 204); manioc, after millennia of vegetative propagation, has all but lost its capacity to produce viable seeds (Lathrap 1970: 48).

Qualitative changes (such as those affecting seed-dispersal, flavour, colour etc.) are usually determined by one or a few major genes, and show relatively simple patterns of inheritance. These features appear early in the archaeological record. On the other hand, *quantitative* changes (such as those which produce larger seeds and fruits in edible plants, or the thicker fibres of domesticated cotton) are normally controlled by several genes (Pickersgill and Heiser 1977). The process of developing and then stabilizing a more productive race is inevitably a slow one, but it was this increased productivity which, more than anything else, allowed foragers to become village farmers, and which was a necessary precondition for the emergence of civilization.

Agriculture in Mexico means primarily the cultivation of maize as the staple of life, and the maize yield can therefore be employed as a rough indicator of agricultural success. Using this as an index, the effects of selection for larger size can be seen to affect patterns of nutrition, population statistics, land use, and socio-political organization.

The best illustration of this point comes from research carried out by Anne Kirkby (1973: 123-46) in the Valley of Oaxaca (fig.79). Her studies indicate that modern Zapotec Indians do not consider it worthwhile, in terms of effort and nutrition, to grow maize on land which yields less than 200 kilos of shelled kernels per hectare. With modern, high-yield races of maize a good deal of the valley is suitable for farming, but the picture changes dramatically when we substitute the primitive maizes found in the caves of Oaxaca and the Tehuacan Valley. The earliest cultivated maize of the 5th millennium B.C. bore cobs about the size of a thumb joint and gave a yield of no more than 60-80 kilos per hectare (roughly the same as wild teosinte, Flannery 1973: 297). By 3000 B.C., cobs were bigger and the yield can be estimated at 90-120 kilos per hectare. Even on the best land, these figures do not allow a commitment to full-time agriculture, and (disregarding nutritional differences) make maize cultivation less productive than the collection of pods from the groves of wild mesquite trees which formed the natural vegetation of the floodplain (Flannery 1973: 298). The critical threshold of 200 kilos of maize per hectare was not crossed until about 2000 or 1500 B.C. From that time onwards, maize was better value than wild foods. It became worth while to clear mesquite from the valley floor and to replace it with maize fields. Settled agriculture became feasible on the best land, and it is at just this time that villages were first occupied on a year-round basis in the highlands. In this area, sedentary life had to wait upon the development of high-yield plant species and an efficient agricultural technology.

Selection for increased size continued after 1500 B.C., and the cumulative effects of this process on the landscape of Oaxaca are shown in fig. 79. At first, only prime floodplain land could provide the minimal 200 kilos per hectare, but, as cobs became larger, second-quality land could be brought into production and the area under maize was gradually expanded. This was merely the start of a chain reaction, and the maps also show a correlation between genetic improvements in maize and (1) an increase in the area of land suitable for settled farming, (2) a progressive replacement of the natural vegetation cover by crop plants, and (3) an increase in the number of people which the valley could support. Item (3) is a notional figure, and the archaeological evidence suggests that the actual population at no time came near the theoretical maximum, though the overall increase and expansion are well documented.

DRIFT OR PUSH? ALTERNATIVE MODELS FOR AGRICULTURAL ORIGINS

The productivity figures quoted above do much more than show how big was the nutritional gap between agriculture as an occasional subsidiary activity and agriculture as a full-time way of life. They lead naturally to the next key question: why bother with farming at all?

Anthropological fashions change, and as part of the new ecological consciousness the once-despised hunter-gatherers are being reassessed. The new picture - perhaps an overreaction against the old view - portrays them as 'The Original Affluent Society' (Sahlins 1972), enjoying a varied and nutritious diet, obtaining their food with very little effort (certainly less than the farmer expends), and living at a low population density with no risk of over-exploiting the environment. We may be witnessing the growth of a new myth, the Myth of the Happy Hunter, which ignores the evidence that modern foraging bands sometimes suffer starvation and hardship, and that what seems a low population in an average year may be the most that can be sustained in a bad one (Allen 1974: 317; Hayden 1975). Nevertheless, the general impression remains that hunter-gatherer economies are finely balanced and are at least as well adapted as those of the later farmers. Why, then, take up agriculture?

Most of the explanations popular at the moment share two assumptions: first, that the changeover to agriculture was the result of a conscious desire on man's part, and second, that the stimulus for this change was the need to increase, or at least to maintain, the supply of food. What all such hypotheses have in common is a conviction that only some kind of pressure or stress could have induced man to take up farming (Meyers 1971; Bender 1975: Ch.2).

I am sceptical of any theory which seeks to explain the development of farming in terms of calories alone. In the early experimental stages, as we have already seen, cultivation was no more productive than the collecting of wild plants, nor was there

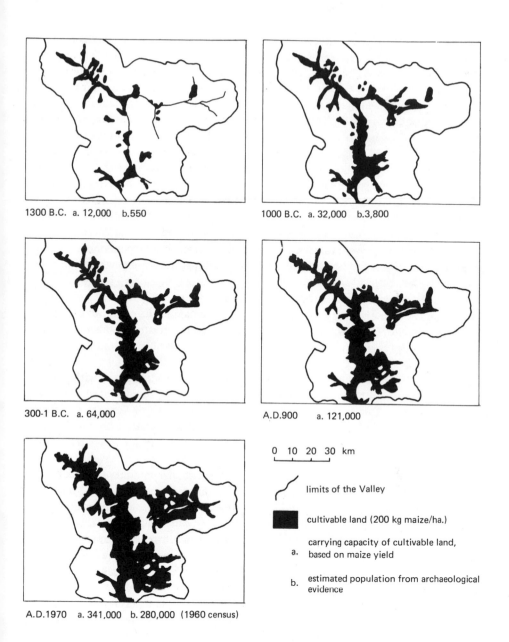

1300 B.C. a. 12,000 b.550

1000 B.C. a. 32,000 b.3,800

300-1 B.C. a. 64,000

A.D.900 a. 121,000

0 10 20 30 km

limits of the Valley

cultivable land (200 kg maize/ha.)

a. carrying capacity of cultivable land, based on maize yield

b. estimated population from archaeological evidence

A.D.1970 a. 341,000 b. 280,000 (1960 census)

Figure 79. The relationship between maize yield, land use and population size in the Valley of Oaxaca *(after Kirkby)*.

anything in the early cultigens (pea-sized chilis, maize/teosinte cobs less than 3cm long) to hint at what they would become after generations of selection. There is also the problem of identifying the stress which acted as the initial trigger. Neither severe climatic change nor sudden and massive population growth can be recognized in the Mesoamerican archaeological record (Bray 1976), and the very slowness of change argues against any stress explanation. The minimal contribution of cultivated plants, no more than 25 per cent of the total diet after at least 2000 years of agricultural effort (fig. 77), shows a lack of urgency which in turn implies either the absence of any great stress or else a completely inadequate response to it.

At this point one is left with the conclusion that the Mexican hunter-gatherers were not pushed into agriculture at all, but drifted into it by accident. This view has much to recommend it. I have argued elsewhere (Bray 1973, 1976) that biological evolution provides a useful analogy for cultural change, and that the 'Neolithic Revolution' fits very well into this general model. What we are examining is, in fact, the evolution of one food-producing system (broad-spectrum foraging) into another (specialized agriculture).

It is a characteristic of biological evolution that it does not plan ahead. Changes which improve the efficiency or viability of the organism in the conditions of the moment are selected for without regard for the long-term future. In practice, most of the small, beneficial changes which are the substance of both biological and cultural evolution consist of marginally improved ways of doing what is already being done. Evolution is in many ways a conservative process, concerned not with innovation but with maintaining successful existing patterns of adaptation (Maynard Smith 1966: 40). This principle is implicit in what has come to be known as Romer's Rule: *The initial survival value of an innovation is conservative, in that it renders possible the maintenance of a traditional way of life in the face of changed circumstances* (Hockett and Ascher 1964: 137). When, as seems to have been the case in the early post-Pleistocene, there was no great change in either the biophysical or the social environment, the need for readaptation would be small, and a massive or sudden change in the mode of food-procurement would do more harm than good (Bray 1976).

Applying these arguments to the study of early agriculture, the prediction is that a well-adapted hunter-gatherer community will make only small and gradual modifications to its resource-procurement system, and that these changes will be directed towards increasing the efficiency of the existing mode of exploitation - i.e. towards increasing the variety and accessibility of useful plants. This preserves the strategic advantages of broad-spectrum exploitation, but cuts down the time needed to search out wild plants. The primary aim is not to increase the food supply (unnecessary if the existing economy is already working effectively), but rather to ensure that a few examples of *all* useful plants are available close to the camp site. It has already been demonstrated that the first experimental cultivation was carried out in a setting of generalized *multi-purpose* plant exploitation, and there is no reason to assume that the first attempts at planting were concerned exclusively with food.

Smith (1967), Harris (1973a) and Lathrap (1973) have already argued that farming began with small, permanent, fixed plots similar to the 'house gardens' of many present-day Indian communities. In his analysis of cultivation practices among the Shipibo of the Peruvian tropical forest, Lathrap draws attention to the conceptual distinction between two kinds of plot: the *chacra* (a swidden field in which are grown the few species which provide the bulk of the food supply) and the *house garden* (a permanent plot containing 50-100 useful species, each represented by only a few individuals). The plants in the house garden are chosen to provide a whole range of useful products: food, fibres, dyes, containers, coca and hallucinatory snuffs, fish poisons, condiments, perfumes and medicines, tobacco etc. In addition, 'The house garden functioned as an experimental plot. New species of plants brought in from the forest or received through contact with other ethnic groups would be introduced into the house garden in a conscious effort to evaluate their potential as a useful cultigen' (Lathrap 1973: 33). Most of the house garden plants are morphologically 'wild'. The characteristics of tropical forest house garden cultivation may be summed up as diversity, experimentation, and the deliberate transplantation both of wild species and of cultigens borrowed from elsewhere.

The same pattern extends to Panama, where Covich and Nickerson (1966) have studied Choco Indian house gardens, and northwards to Mesoamerica where one of the first - and still the most quotable - studies of a house garden was made by Edgar Anderson at Santa Lucia, in the maize-growing region of highland Guatemala.

What appeared at first sight to be a riotous and haphazard growth turned out to be a sophisticated garden plot containing no noxious weeds and giving a high return per man-hour of effort. Like the Shipibo and Choco gardens, the one at Santa Lucia was organized on the 'little of each' principle, and it contained 28 useful plant varieties. These included staple foods (two kinds of maize, beans, chayote and two species of squash), herbs (rosemary and rue), ornamental flowers (poinsettia and dahlia), maguey and cacti with edible fruits, one stimulant (coffee), and a wide variety of native and European fruit trees, the whole surrounded by a hedge of maize stalks and chichicaste shrub, which has medicinal qualities as well as painful leaves.

In Anderson's words,

the garden was a vegetable garden, an orchard, a medicinal garden, a dump heap, a compost heap, and a beeyard. There was no problem of erosion though it was at the top of a steep slope; the soil surface was practically all covered and apparently would be during much of the year. Humidity would be kept up during the dry season and plants of the same sort were so isolated from one another by intervening vegetation that pests and diseases could not readily spread from plant to plant. The fertility was being conserved; in addition to the waste from the house, mature plants were being buried between the rows when their usefulness was over....The garden was in continuous production but was taking only a little effort at any one time; a few weeds pulled out when one came down to pick the squashes, corn and bean plants dug in between the rows when the last of the climbing beans were picked, and a new crop of something else planted above them a few weeks later (Anderson 1952: 140).

Similar garden plots, rarely more than an acre in extent, have been observed in the Tehuacan valley at the present day (Smith 1967: 221).

As Harris (1969, 1973a) has pointed out, a house garden of this type constitutes a generalized ecosystem, characterized by a wide variety of species (trees, shrubs, climbers, root crops and herbs), each represented by only a few individuals. A generalized, 'palaeotechnic' system of this kind is both productive and stable, coming 'closer to simulating the structure, functional dynamics and equilibrium of the natural ecosystem than any other agricultural system man has devised' (Harris 1969: 6). Wild species are replaced by useful equivalents, but there is no large-scale transformation of the landscape. Harris also argues that, with improved races of plants and a more sophisticated agricultural technology, a generalized 'palaeotechnic' system of this kind may gradually evolve into a specialized 'neotechnic' one which concentrates efforts on a few very productive species. The Shipibo *chacra* represents a step in that direction, as do the maize fields of the modern highland Indians of Mexico.

There is no conflict between this model and the 'rubbish heap' explanation advanced by many botanists (e.g. Anderson 1952; Hawkes 1969). In the process of bringing man and plants into closer association, either party may take the initiative; man may seek out useful plants, or the plants may, in a sense, seek out man. The ancestors of most of the cultivated food species, with the exception of tree crops, were marked by a tendency towards 'weediness' - the ability to colonize open or disturbed habitats with thin soil. Such plants are also vulnerable to competition from other vegetation.

In many ways these plants were pre-adapted for agriculture. The clearings and rubbish heaps around dwelling places offered both open ground and a reduced competition from other species, and the rubbish heaps also provided the kind of nitrogen-rich conditions preferred by many potential crop plants (Harris 1973a: 400). Flannery and his collaborators have shown that, in the thorn forest of the highland Mexican state of Guerrero, abandoned fields and clearings are invaded by teosinte, wild runner beans and wild squashes - the ancestral forms of the maize-beans-squash triumverate which is the basis of Mesoamerican agriculture (Flannery 1973: 291). A foraging band, returning to last year's campsite as part of an annual cycle, would find these proto-cultigens already established.

THE ROLE OF TRANSPLANTATION

The previous section has introduced the theme of transplantation, the removal of a species from its natural habitat to a new environment where it may never before have grown, and to which it may be ill-adapted. In Mexico, with its broken and mountainous topography, the old habitat and the new one may be separated by only a few kilometres linear distance or a few hundred metres of altitude - and both habitats may lie within the annual foraging range of a single hunter-gatherer band.

Conceptually, the idea of deliberate transplantation represents 'agriculture', as opposed to opportunistic 'tending' of wild plants (Flannery 1973: 282). Biologically, the altered circumstances provide a powerful stimulus towards genetic change and, under human selection, towards the eventual emergence of high-yield crops which are the basis of full-time farming.

Different patterns of seasonality, or changes in day length, temperature and rainfall, create new selective pressures, favouring not the varieties which did best in the old habitat, but rather those most fitted to the new one. The genetic effects of removing a plant from its parent population have been discussed by Hawkes (1970: 70), Harris (1973a: 400), and by Pickersgill and Heiser (1977). In a cross-fertilizing species, such as maize or teosinte, transplantation and subsequent isolation from the parent population reduces opportunities for inter-crossing between the potential cultigen and its wild relatives, thus simultaneously removing a major brake on the speed of evolution and permitting more rapid fixation of characteristics desired by man. Galinat (1974) has already pointed out that the most extreme varieties of maize did not develop until the plant had spread beyond the range of wild teosinte. At the same time, transfer of a cultigen to a new habitat, where a different set of wild varieties is available to hybridize with it, encourages genetic recombination and the emergence of further useful varieties. If such hybridization takes place between cultivated and wild species of different genomes, then polyploidy is liable to result, bringing a new dimension of variability into the cultivated species. In the artificial, man-made environment of a garden, varieties which in nature would be eliminated are permitted to survive, and even thrive, at the expense of the ancestral forms.

THE ARCHAEOLOGICAL EVIDENCE FROM THE TEHUACAN VALLEY

With these points in mind, we can now test the theoretical arguments against the archaeological evidence.

The Tehuacan Valley during the early post-Pleistocene was inhabited by semi-nomadic bands of broad-spectrum hunters and collectors who had a detailed knowledge of wild plants and of how these could be most effectively exploited. Combining data from all periods, between 70 and 80 different plant species have been recovered from excavations in the valley (Smith 1967: table 26). Fig. 76 shows only those which were eventually domesticated. The others are morphologically wild, though there is a strong suspicion that several of them (in particular, maguey, prickly pear and mesquite) were planted and tended as dooryard crops from earliest times, just as they are today (Smith 1967).

The tending of a great variety of useful plants, both wild and cultivated, is, as we have seen, a characteristic of house garden horticulture. Can this pattern be projected back into the past, and does it (as Harris and Lathrap have suggested) represent the earliest form of 'proto-agriculture' in tropical America?

MacNeish (in Byers 1967a: 306) has attempted to reconstruct the changing pattern of agriculture in the Tehuacan Valley from the sixth millennium B.C. until the Spanish Conquest. His earliest types of agriculture, which he places in the El Riego period (though see p.232), are *barranca horticulture* ('the planting of individual hardy cultivars in the barrancas [stream gullies] near the cave sites') and *hydro-horticulture* ('individual domesticates - avocado trees and chili plants - were planted beside springs or along the flanks of the Rio Salado where they received a steady year-round supply of water'). Whether these plants were grown in actual house gardens is, of course, unknown. Later, the Coxcatlan phase saw 'the planting of such grains as corn [maize] and amaranth in fields (albeit in this phase very small) in the arroyo bottoms, or on low terraces next to arroyos or barrancas where they would receive a supply of moisture from runoff during the rainy season'. With the development of high-yield races of maize, and of improved tree fruits, the later stages show increasing dependence on a few staple foods grown in irrigated fields and orchards. MacNeish's developmental sequence involves a good deal of speculation, but it fits the prediction that agriculture began with small permanent gardens rather than with swidden cultivation.

Earlier sections of this paper have emphasized the role of experimental transplantation (of both wild and cultivated plants) in the creation of garden plots and the subsequent genetic modification of certain key species. Looked at from this point of view, the order in which the various domesticates appear in the Tehuacan record takes on considerable significance (fig. 76).

The cultivated plants from the Tehuacan sequence can be grouped into four categories:

1. Plants native to the valley bottom and the lower slopes
This is the zone in which the rock shelters and villages are located. The prevailing vegetation below the 1800m contour is short grass steppe, thorn forest and cactus scrub, with more luxurious growth around the El Riego springs and along the stream gullies. Mesquite is common throughout the valley; maguey, prickly pear and other edible cacti grow in the thorn-cactus zone; amaranth and setaria form stands in the moist areas along stream courses. Of the fruit trees, chupandilla (*Cyrtocarpa procera*) occurs in the thorn scrub and barranca forest, and cosahuico (*Sideroxylon cf. tempisque*) is native to the watercourse margins.

2. Plants native to the upper slopes of the valley
This zone consists of oak-pine forest which, at about 2500m, gives way to montane forest. It also includes the upper reaches of the barrancas. Rainfall is higher than that of the valley bottom and the lower hills. The upper slopes and barrancas seem to have been little exploited, but they are the natural habitat of the avocado. Ciruela, or hog plum (*Spondias mombin*), is also reported from the eastern slopes and the barranca forest (Flannery 1967: 138; Byers 1967a: 291). Smith (1967: 288) has suggested that wild chili peppers may have grown on the upper valley slopes, and that runner beans could have been raised in this zone, though the late arrival of this plant in Tehuacan argues that it was brought into domestication somewhere outside the valley altogether (Kaplan 1967: 205; Flannery 1973: 300).

3. Plants native to other parts of highland Mesoamerica
These are species whose wild forms do not grow anywhere in the Tehuacan valley, and could not have grown there under the climatic conditions of the last 8000 years. Their centres of origin (and of domestication) lie in various areas of highland Mesoamerica, some of them close to Tehuacan, others more distant. The list of outsiders includes the crops which later became staple foods: teosinte (the putative ancestor of maize), all the varieties of bean, and all the squashes except perhaps *Cucurbita mixta*. To these must be added the coyol palm (*Acrocomia mexicana*) and two other tree fruits: white sapote (*Casimiroa edulis*) and black zapote (*Diospyros digyna*).

4. Plants originating outside highland Mexico
These are all late arrivals that took thousands of years to diffuse northwards to Mexico. Manioc (a tentative identification based on faecal material) is a lowland tropical plant whose centre of origin is probably lowland South America. Peanut, guava and pineapple are undoubtedly South American, though this last may never have been cultivated in Tehuacan and is best explained by trade with other regions of Mexico (Callen 1967: 276). The sieva bean was probably introduced into Mexico via the Gulf Coast lowlands (Kaplan 1967).

Although the picture is imperfect, and the status of individual plants open to argument, the overall tendency is clear. The first experiments in cultivation were made with plants which were already exploited by the hunter-gatherer population of the valley and were available close to the home base (Category 1) or within foraging distance of it (Category 2). As might be expected, the wild forms of these species appear in the Tehuacan archaeological record before their domesticated forms (fig. 76). Besides food plants, fibre-yielding species such as sotolin (*Beaucarnia gracilis*) and palmetto (*Brahea dulcis*) were collected from locations more than a day's walk from the caves. Trade contacts with more distant regions, outside the valley altogether, are attested as early as the El Riego phase by the presence of imported obsidian and marine shell (Byers 1967b: 78, 147).

The next arrivals (Category 3) were complete outsiders, transplanted as fully-fledged domesticates from nearby areas with which the Tehuacan people were already in contact. This, in turn, implies multiple centres of domestication within highland Mesoamerica, the sequence in each region beginning with those species which were locally available (for archaeological confirmation see Flannery 1973, Pickersgill and Heiser 1973, Bray 1976). Maize, beans and squashes had already undergone some selection in their centres of origin before being introduced to Tehuacan, but some other species (notably tree crops) were - and remained - indistinguishable from their wild forms. Fruit trees, garden crops par excellence, are notoriously slow to change under human selection. (Smith 1967, 1968). Like the tropical forest horticulturalists described by Lathrap, the Tehuacan farmers continued to be receptive to new crops, adopting South American species once these had reached Mexico (Category 4). The final stage in the borrowing process is represented by the European plants which grow, side by side with the oldest indigenous crops, in Tehuacan house gardens today.

WHAT IS A FARMING SOCIETY?

Thus far, I have argued that the development of early American agriculture proceeded by a series of infinitesimally small steps and with no intention to create an agricultural society, still less with a long-term plan to achieve a state of civilization. In the absence of sudden change, this raises a question of definition and terminology. What is a 'Neolithic community' or an 'agricultural society', and how can the archaeologist recognize it?

Becoming 'Neolithic' is one of those transformations which - like falling in love or getting drunk - is easy enough to recognize after the event but not always apparent at the time. The exact moment of transition from one state to another is ill-defined, and there is no clear critical threshold between the two conditions. The problem of definition, of where to draw the line between non-agricultural and agricultural societies, is one which archaeologists have tended to shirk, concentrating their attentions on the question of the origin of farming. This gets the priorities wrong. The critical moment was not the planting of the first seed, or the taming of the first animal, but the achievement of a fully effective system of agriculture and of dependence upon cultivated foods.

The quantitative evidence from three regions of Mexico is given in fig. 77, though the percentages must be regarded as gross approximations only (see Cohen 1975 on the problems of calculating quantitative data from midden material). Tehuacan, even though it is not one of the most favoured regions of Mesoamerica, eventually supported an urban civilization, and MacNeish's figures suggest that by the fifteenth century most of the valley's food was produced by its farmers. Tamaulipas, on the other hand, is a marginal area for farming, and lies on the northern edge of civilized Mesoamerica. In south-west Tamaulipas the contribution of cultivated foods to the total diet barely rose above 50 per cent, and in south-east Tamaulipas it never at any time reached that figure - though at certain periods both these areas supported settled villages with temple pyramids and some of the trappings of civilization.

Most people would accept that fifteenth-century Tehuacan was a farming society, but what about fifteenth-century Tamaulipas? And at what point in the development of the Tehuacan Valley did the transition from experimental to effective farming take place?

The easy way out of the dilemma is to choose some arbitrary figure and to define an agricultural society as one which obtains, say, 50 per cent of its total calorie intake from farming (cf. Smith and Young 1972: 58 on the definition of incipient cultivation). This approach may be useful for purposes of classification and description, but it does not necessarily correspond with the realities of life. Why calculate on the basis of food energy rather than, for example, the relative amounts of time and/or effort spent on obtaining different kinds of food? And why pick on 50 per cent rather than 30 per cent or 70 per cent? As the diagram shows, there is no very close correlation between any fixed percentage for cultivated food in the diet and the appearance of such phenomena as sedentism or changes in tool kits. What is needed is a definition which can be consistently applied but which takes local circumstances into account.

Rather than employ arbitrary figures, I would prefer to introduce a more flexible definition based on the idea of *dependence,* i.e. that an agricultural society (whatever the proportion of its diet derived from farming) is one which has reached a stage of dependence on cultivated foods. Consciously or not, such a society has arrived at the point of no return: hunters and gatherers have become, and must remain, farmers.

There is a rather simple criterion for this state of dependence or commitment; it is irreversible. The community, no matter how little cultivated food it consumes, can no longer revert to a hunting and gathering existence without suffering a loss of population through death or migration. In effect, this means that the stage of commitment has been reached as soon as the number of part-time farmers becomes greater than the number of people which the area could support under a purely hunting and gathering regime, or when the landscape has been so modified (for instance, by removal of the natural vegetation) that a return to the former way of life is no longer feasible.

This definition avoids the tyranny of arbitrary percentages and allows each local case to be considered on its own merits. In practical terms, the enquiry is narrowed down to the study of two variables: *population size* and *carrying capacity.* Carrying capacity is here defined as the largest number of people who can be indefinitely supported from the resources of a particular area under a specified system of food-procurement, without causing permanent or accumulating damage to the environment. This upper limit is largely conditioned by the available food supply, though other factors may also be involved (Bray 1976). Population size and carrying capacity can both be expressed in quantitative terms, though I have to admit that they are two of the most difficult things for an archaeologist to measure.

The nature of this relationship is shown diagrammatically in fig. 80, in which x represents the number of people in a given region at the moment when the first experiments with cultivation are about to be made, and f is the factor by which this

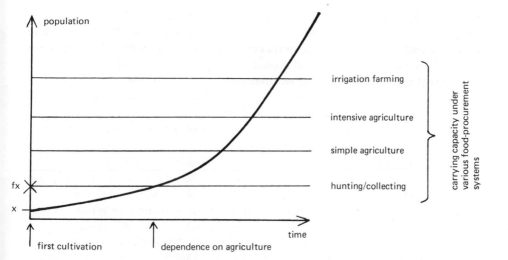

Figure 80. The relationship between population size and carrying capacity under various systems of food-procurement.

population figure would have to be multiplied before it exceeded the carrying capacity of the area under a hunting and gathering economy. Thus, if a population of size x was at 25 per cent of carrying capacity (towards the lower end of the range for present day hunter-gatherers), f would equal 4. The original population could quadruple during the period of incipient agriculture before reaching the stage of irreversible dependence on cultivated foods. If population growth was slow, as seems to have been the case during the early post-Pleistocene, a long time would elapse before the population of incipient farmers reached, and eventually passed, the carrying capacity under a foraging economy.

In other words, the critical point which I have taken as the moment of commitment, the transition to agriculture as the essential way of life, does not come until long after the first experiments with cultivation. The actual figures will differ from one region to another, but until this critical point is reached the process of becoming 'Neolithic' is still reversible.

The same principle can be applied at higher levels of development, for example in defining that much misused term 'irrigation society'. Dependence on irrigation begins not with the first tentative attempts at water control but when population size has risen beyond that which could be supported by dry farming alone.

In fig. 80 we can therefore begin to talk about a farming society from the time when the curve of population growth crosses the horizontal line marking the carrying capacity under hunting and gathering. By this time, if the economy has been properly managed, agriculture will have begun to make a significant contribution to the food supply. Better techniques of cultivation, plus improved races of plants, will have raised the productivity of the region to a new and higher level so that population size and carrying capacity increase together, the former always remaining safely below the latter. Archaeological evidence suggests that this was the case in pre-hispanic Oaxaca (Kirkby 1973: 146).

If the actual population always remains less than the theoretical maximum in the conditions of the moment, the growth curve may be a smooth one as in fig. 80. If it happens that productivity (i.e. carrying capacity) does not keep ahead of population growth, the process of steady increase will be interrupted whenever a temporary limit is reached, and the population curve will have the appearance of a series of steps (Higgs and Jarman 1975: 6). In both cases, however, the population curve will eventually rise above the level of the original hunter-gatherer carrying capacity, and will define the start of the period of agricultural dependence.

This model, so neat in theory, is difficult to operate in practice. Ethnographers working with present-day foraging communities are only just beginning to appreciate the complex relationship between population and resources, and many cherished assumptions may turn out to be invalid. The belief that hunter-gatherers always stabilize below carrying capacity is coming under attack (Hayden 1975), as is the assumption that these people provide an appropriate analogy for the hunter-gatherers of the past. The problems of estimating the size of prehistoric populations are all too familiar, and we have still no satisfactory way of accurately measuring prehistoric carrying capacity. Attempts based on direct observation of food resources (e.g. Baumhoff 1963) or on dubious calculations from the total biomass (Zubrow 1971, 1975), contain too many uncertainties, and make no attempt to tackle the problem of annual and seasonal fluctuations (Hayden 1975).

In highland Mexico the critical factor is rainfall, which varies unpredictably from one year to another. In Oaxaca and Tehuacan the maximum recorded rainfall is more than four times that of the driest year (Kirkby 1973: 158; Byers 1967a, Ch.4; for Tamaulipas, see MacNeish 1958: 10-14). Since it is primarily the rainfall pattern which determines the annual crop of both wild and cultivated plants, the carrying capacity will not be the same every year. To encompass the range of variability resulting from these climatic fluctuations, the horizontal lines of fig. 80 could be more accurately shown as thick horizontal bands. Nevertheless, it remains true that, as long as population and agricultural productivity increase together, the number of people will eventually exceed that which the region could support on the basis of hunting and gathering in even the most favourable year.

These, and many other, problems of measurement are still unresolved. My aim in this final section has not been to offer easy solutions, but to pose certain questions and to indicate where research effort might usefully be invested.

REFERENCES

Allen, H., 1974. 'The Bagundji of the Darling Basin: cereal gatherers in an uncertain environment', *World Archaeology, 5(3)*, 309-22.
Anderson, E., 1952. *Plants, Man and Life* (Boston, Mass.).
Aveleyra Arroyo de Anda, L., 1964. 'The Primitive Hunters', in *Handbook of Middle American Indians*, gen.ed. R. Wauchope, vol.1, 1964, 384-412 (Austin, Texas).
Baumhoff, M.A., 1963. 'Ecological Determinants of Aboriginal California Populations', *University of California Publications in American Archaeology and Ethnology, 49(2)*, 155-236.
Beadle, G.W., 1973. 'The Origin of Zea Mays'. Paper presented to the ICAES Symposium on 'The Origins of Agriculture', Chicago, August 1973. To appear in C.A. Reed (ed.), *The Origins of Agriculture* (The Hague).
Bender, B., 1975. *Farming in Prehistory: from hunter-gatherer to food-producer.*
Bray, W., 1973. 'The biological basis of culture', in *The Explanation of Culture Change: Models in Prehistory*, ed. C. Renfrew, 1973, 73-92.
Bray, W., 1976. 'From Predation to Production: The Nature of Agricultural Evolution in Mexico and Peru', in *Problems in Economic and Social Archaeology*, ed. G. de G. Sieveking, T.H. Longworth and K.E. Wilson, 1976, 73-95.
Byers, D.S. (gen.ed.), 1967a. *The Prehistory of the Tehuacan Valley: Vol.1, Environment and Subsistence* (Austin, Texas).
Byers, D.S. (gen.ed.), 1967b. *The Prehistory of the Tehuacan Valley: Vol.2, The Non-Ceramic Artifacts* (Austin, Texas).
Callen, E.O., 1963. 'Diet as Revealed by Coprolites', in *Science in Archaeology*, ed. D. Brothwell and E. Higgs, 1963, 186-94.
Callen, E.O., 1967. 'Analysis of the Tehuacan Coprolites', in Byers 1967a, 261-89.
Casteel, R.W., 1972. 'Two static maximum population-density models for hunter-gatherers: a first approximation', *World Archaeology, 4(1)*, 19-39.
Cohen, M.N., 1975 'Some problems in the quantitative analysis of vegetable refuse illustrated by a Late Horizon site on the Peruvian coast', *Ñawpa Pacha, 10-12*, 49-60.
Covich, A.P. and Nickerson, N.H., 1966. 'Studies of cultivated plants in Choco dwelling clearings', *Economic Botany, 20(3)*, 285-301.
Davis, D.D., 1975. 'Patterns of early formative subsistence in southern Mesoamerica 1500-1000 B.C.', *Man.N.S. 10(1)*, 41-59.
Flannery, K.V., 1967. 'The Vertebrate Fauna and Hunting Patterns' in Byers 1967a, 132-77.
Flannery, K.V., 1968. 'Archeological Systems Theory and Early Mesoamerica', in *Anthropological Archeology in the Americas*, ed. B.J. Meggers, 1968, 67-87 (Anthropological Society of Washington).
Flannery, K.V., 1973. 'The origins of agriculture', *Annual Review of Anthropology, 2*, 271-310.
Flannery, K.V., manuscript 'Preliminary Archaeological Investigations in the Valley of Oaxaca, Mexico, 1966-69'. Report presented to the National Science Foundation and the Instituto Nacional de Antropología e Historia, Mexico.
Galinat, W.C., 1974. 'The domestication and genetic erosion of maize', *Economic Botany, 28*, 31-7.
Green, D.F. and Lowe, G.W., 1967. 'Altamira and Padre Piedra, Early Preclassic Sites in Chiapas, Mexico'. *Papers of the New World Archaeological Foundation, No.20*, Pub. 15.
Harris, D.R., 1969. 'Agricultural systems, ecosystems and the origins of agriculture', in *The Domestication and Exploitation of Plants and Animals*, ed. P.J. Ucko and G.W. Dimbleby, 1969, 3-15.
Harris, D.R., 1973a. 'The prehistory of tropical agriculture: an ethnoecological model', in *The Explanation of Culture Change: Models in Prehistory*, ed. C. Renfrew, 1973, 391-417.
Harris, D.R., 1973b. 'Alternative Pathways towards Agriculture'. Paper presented to

the ICAES Symposium on 'The Origins of Agriculture', Chicago, August 1973. To appear in C.A. Reed (ed.), *The Origins of Agriculture* (The Hague).

Hawkes, J.G., 1969. 'The ecological background of plant domestication', in *The Domestication and Exploitation of Plants and Animals,* ed. P.J. Ucko and G.W.Dimbleby, 1969, 17-29.

Hawkes, J.G., 1970. 'The Taxonomy of Cultivated Plants', in *Genetic Resources in Plants - Their Exploration and Conservation,* ed. O.H. Frankel and E. Bennett, 1970, 69-85.

Hayden, B., 1975. 'The Carrying Capacity Dilemma', in *Population Studies in Archaeology and Biological Anthropology: A Symposium,* ed. A.C. Swedlund, *American Antiquity, 40(2),* Pt 2, Memoir 30: 11-21.

Heiser, C.B., 1973. 'Variation in the Bottle Gourd', in *Tropical Forest Ecosystems in Africa and South America: A Comparative Review,* ed. B.J. Meggers, E.S. Ayensu and W.D. Duckworth, 1973, 121-28 (Washington).

Heizer, R.F. and Napton, L.K., 1969. 'Biological and cultural evidence from prehistoric human coprolites', *Science, 165,* 563-68.

Higgs, E.S. and Jarman, M.R., 1975. 'Palaeoeconomy', in *Palaeoeconomy,* ed. E.S. Higgs, 1975, 1-7.

Hockett, C.F. and Ascher, R., 1964. 'The human revolution', *Curr.Anthrop., 5,* 135-47.

Kaplan, L., 1965. 'Archaeology and domestication in American *Phaseolus* beans', *Economic Botany, 19,* 356-68.

Kaplan, L., 1967. 'Archaeological Phaseolus from Tehuacan', in Byers 1967a, 201-11.

Kirkby, A.V.T., 1973. 'The Use of Land and Water Resources in the Past and Present Valley of Oaxaca, Mexico', *Memoirs of the Museum of Anthropology, University of Michigan, 5.*

Lathrap, D.W., 1970. *The Upper Amazon.*

Lathrap, D.W., 1973. 'Our Father the Cayman, Our Mother the Gourd: Spinden Revisited, or a Unitary Model for the Emergence of Agriculture in the New World'. Paper presented at the ICAES Symposium on 'The Origins of Agriculture', Chicago, August 1973. To appear in C.A. Reed (ed.), *The Origins of Agriculture* (The Hague).

Lathrap, D.W., Collier, D. and Chandra, H., 1975. *Ancient Ecuador: Culture, Clay and Creativity 3000-300 B.C.* (Chicago: Field Museum of National History).

MacNeish, R.S., 1958. 'Preliminary archaeological investigations in the Sierra de Tamaulipas, Mexico', *Transactions of the American Philosophical Society,* N.S. 48(6).

MacNeish, R.S., 1964. 'The Food-gathering and Incipient Agriculture Stage of Prehistoric Middle America', in *Handbook of Middle American Indians,* gen.ed. R. Wauchope, Vol.1, 1964, 413-26 (Austin, Texas).

MacNeish, R.S., 1971. 'Speculation about how and why food production and village life developed in the Tehuacan Valley, Mexico', *Archaeology, 24(4),* 307-15.

MacNeish, R.S., 1972. 'The Evolution of Community Patterns in the Tehuacan Valley of Mexico, and Speculations about Cultural Processes', in *Man, Settlement and Urbanism,* ed. P.J. Ucko, R.Tringham and G.W. Dimbleby, 1972, 67-93.

MacNeish, R.S., 1973. 'The Scheduling Factor in the Development of Effective Food Production in the Tehuacan Valley', in *Variation in Anthropology: Essays in Honor of John C.McGregor,* ed. D.W. Lathrap and J. Douglas, 1973, 75-89 (Urbana: Illinois Archaeological Survey).

Maynard Smith, J., 1966. *The Theory of Evolution* (Penguin, 2nd edn).

Meggers, B.J., 1972. *Prehistoric America* (Chicago).

Meyers, J.T., 1971. 'The Origins of Agriculture: An Evaluation of Three Hypotheses', in *Prehistoric Agriculture,* ed. S. Struever, 1971, 101-21 (Garden City, New York).

Pickersgill, B., 1971. 'Relationships between weedy and cultivated forms in some species of chili peppers (Genus *Capsicum)', Evolution, 25(4),* 683-91.

Pickersgill, B., 1975. 'Agricultural origins in the Americas: independence or interdependence?' Paper delivered to the Research Seminar in Archaeology and

Related Subjects, London, 25 March 1975.

Pickersgill, B. and Heiser, C.B., 1973. 'Origin and Distribution of Plants Domesticated in the New World Tropics'. Paper presented to the ICAES Symposium on 'The Origins of Agriculture', Chicago, August 1973. To appear in C.A. Reed (ed.), *The Origins of Agriculture* (The Hague).

Pickersgill, B. and Heiser, C.B., 1975. 'Cytogenetics and evolutionary change under domestication', in *The Early History of Agriculture*, ed. Sir Joseph Hutchinson *et al.*, 1977, 55-67.

Sahlins, M., 1972. *Stone Age Economics* (Chicago and New York).

Saldívar, G. 1943. 'Los Indios de Tamaulipas', *Instituto Panamericano de Geografía e Historia, Mexico*, Pub. 70.

Schoenwetter, J., 1974. 'Pollen records of Guila Naquitz Cave', *American Antiquity, 39(2)*, Pt 1, 292-303.

Smith, C.E., 1967. 'Plant Remains' in Byers 1967a, 220-55.

Smith C.E., 1968. 'Archaeological evidence for selection of chupandilla and cosahuico under cultivation in Mexico', *Economic Botany, 22(2)*, 140-8.

Smith, P.E.L. and Young, J.C., 1972. 'The Evolution of Early Agriculture and Culture in Greater Mesopotamia: A Trial Model', in *Population Growth: Anthropological Implications*, ed. B. Spooner, 1972, 1-59 (Cambridge, Mass.).

Steward, J.H., 1934. 'Ethnography of the Owens Valley Paiute', *University of California Publications in American Archaeology and Ethnology, 33*, 233-350.

Steward, J.H., 1955. *Theory of Culture Change: the methodology of multilinear evolution* (Urbana, Ill.).

Thomas, D.H., 1973. 'An empirical test for Steward's model of Great Basin settlement patterns', *American Antiquity, 38(2)*, 155-76.

Thomas, R.B., 1973. 'Human Adaptation to a High Andean Energy Flow System', *Occasional Papers in Anthropology*, 7 (Pennsylvania State University).

Willey, G.R., 1966. *An Introduction to American Archaeology: Vol.1, North and Middle America* (Englewood Cliffs).

Zubrow, E.B.W., 1971. 'Carrying capacity and the dynamic equilibrium in the Prehistoric Southwest', *American Antiquity, 36(2)*, 127-38.

Zubrow, E.B.W., 1975. *Prehistoric Carrying Capacity: A Model.* (Menlo Park).

Index

Abetifi, 83, *88, 89*
Abyssinia, 96
Acacus, 107
Adamgarh, *132,* 142
Adrar Bous, 99, 102, 107
Adwuku, 77
Aeta, 153
Afghanistan, 139
Afikpo, 83
Africa, 16, 20, 32, 34, 116-17; 'Aquatic
    Civilisation of Middle Africa', 11, *113;*
    Late Stone Age, 111, 112, 115:
    population, 202; Middle Stone Age:
    see Industries, Levallois-Mousterian;
    East, 15, 71, 74, 109-10, 116; North,
    109; North-East, 93; South, 37, 109;
    South-West, 109; Sub-Saharan, 111,
    115-18; West, 12, 32, 69-118, *94-5,*
    100-1: Late Stone Age, 74, 93; yam
    and oil palm agriculture, *104,* 114
African cereals, 96-106, *113;* African or
    'false' banana, 102
Agate Basin period
Ahar, 135
Ain Mallaha, 56, 60, 61, 63, 65
Ainu, 16, *18,* 20
Air, 102, 107
Ajureado phase, 227
Akreijit phase, 77
Alaska, 200, 204
Aleutian Chain, 202; Aleuts, 204
Algeria, 107

Ali Khosh, 54, 55
Amazon Basin, 33; lowlands, 32
Americas, 34, 103, 189: *see also* New
    World; Central, 35, 115: *see also*
    Mesoamerica; North, 25, 28, 31, 32,
    35, 149, 199-222, *217, 220;* Pacific
    Coast, 43, 46; South, 25, 31, 35, 36,
    149, 202, 204, 207, 225, 242;
    tropical, 241
American Indians, 20, 43, 46, 202, 204:
    see also Palaeo-Indians
Amri, 131
Anangula, 205
Anatolia, 52, 93, 107
Andaman Islands, 16, 148, 149, 153, 155
Andes, 225
Andhra Pradesh, 135
Angola, 110
Annam, 148
Arabia, 99
Aravalli hills, 127, 128
Archaic period, 218
Arizona, *210,* 211
Arnhem Land, 184
Asia, 16, 20, 32-5, 97; Central, 127;
    Minor, 117; Northern, 25; South, 12,
    15, 111, 127-43; South-East, 12, 15,
    16, 20, 33, 34, 117, 127, 128, 145-63,
    189; agriculture, 155-63; hunters-
    gatherers, 149-55; South-West, 11,
    107, 110, 115, 117; West, 93, 127
Asiatic Mongoloids, 204

Assam, 127, 148
Atakora hills, 71
Aurés mountains, 107
Australasia, 16
Australia, 11, 15, 22, 25, 28, 32, 35, 36, 63, 149, 181, 183; Australian Aborigines, 16, *19,* 174, 184
Austronesian languages, 191
Ayacucho valley, 200, 205, 207, 213
Ayios Epikitos, 56

Bagor, 142
Baiga, 136
Baliem Valley, 171
Baluchistan, 142
Bambandyanalo, 109
Bangladesh, 135
Banjara, 140
Banyan Valley, 149, 158
Bardwal, *130,* 138
Barstow, 207
Bauchi Plateau, 71, 74
Beidha, 54, 59
Bengal, 127, 135
Benin, 118
Bering land bridge area, 204; Plain, 202; Straits, 20, 199, 200
Bhils, 136
Bhutan, 127
Big Game Hunters, 218, 222
Blackwater Draw, 209, *210*
Blandé, 83
Bomagai-Angoiang, *45*
Bombay, 128, 138
Borneo, 15, 148, 149, 155, 184
Bornu, 83
Britain, 56
British Academy Major Research Project in the Early History of Agriculture, 11
Burma, 148, 149
Bus Mordeh, 54, *55*
Bushmen, 149

Calico site, 207
California, 207
Cambodia, 148, 149, *152,* 158
Cameroon Mountain, *72*
Cameroun, 93
Canadian Plains, 213; Yukon, 199
Candy, 136
Cape, the, 110
Catabatu province, 149
Ceylon, 136
Chalcolithic cities, 131, 139; settlements, 133, 135, *141,* 142; stone-blade industry, *140*
Chandoli, 140
Chatham Islands, 194
Chenchu, 136
Childe, V. Gordon, 11, 12, 37, 65
China, 15, 20, 22, 33, 34, 115, 127, 128, 148, 156, 163, 204
Clovis tradition, 207, 209, *210,* 211, 213
Cody, 213; knife, *216*

Colani, 148
Colorado, 211; Colorado River Expedition (1871-5), *219*
Conakry, 77, 83
Congress of Prehistorians of the Far East, First, 145
Cook, Captain James, 191, 193, 194
Cook Islands, 191
Coxcatlan phase, 241
Crete, 107
Crow Flat and River, 199
Cutch, 135
Cyprus, 56
Cyrenaica, 83, 110

Dafal, 153
Dakar, 83
Daima, 83
Dani, 171
Deccan, 128, 136, 139
De Chardin, Teilhard, 148
Desert Culture, 229
Desert tradition: *see* Tradition
Dent, 211
Denver, 211
Dhar Tichitt, 77, 83, 110, 102, 107
Diego factor, 202, 204
Djambi, 153
Drakensberg mountains, 109
Dwarf Shorthorn Breeds, Ndama and West African, 107
Dynasty, Third, 110

Easter Island, 191, 194
Eastern Woodland Indians, 222
Eden Points, *216;* hunters, 213
Egypt, 93, 97, 106, 108, 110, 111, 115, 117, 127, 189
El Riego phase, 232, 241, 243
El Wad, 59, 60, 61, 64
Enga, Western Highlands, 173, 174
Ennedi, 107
Epipalaeolithic cultures, 53, 83
Eskimos, *45,* 202, 204: *see also* Netsilik
Ethiopia, 32, 96, 99, 102, 103, 106, 111
Eurasia, *203*
Europe, 15, 31, 46, 71, 83, 93, 127, 202; Europeans, 168
Eyasi population, 15

Fayum, 110
Fernando Po, 83
Fiji, 191, 193; Fijians, 16
Folsom complex, *210,* 211, *212*
Fort Rock Cave, 213, 218
Fouta Djallon, 71, 102
Frontier, moving, 25-38, (tables) 29, 30, 34

Galilee, Upper, 56
Gambia, River, 102
Gangaget, 77
Garamundi, 174

Ghana, 71, 77, 83, *84, 88, 89, 92,* 106, 110, 118
Ghats, 128, 136
Glaciation, 200, 201; Wisconsin, 200; Würm, 64
Golson, Jack, 175, 179, 184
Great Basin (North America), 229, 231
Greece, 107, 111
Grotte Capeletti, 107
Grotte de Kakimbon, 77, 83
Gua Kechil, 149, 162
Guerrero, 233, 240
Guinea, Republic of, 77, 83, 99, 102
Guita Naquitz, 229
Gujarat, 102, 128, *130,* 135, 138

Hadza, *44,* 118, 149, 153
Hamites, 96
Hanoi, 145
Harappa, Harappan culture, 117, 131, 133, *134,* 135; stone-blade industry, 140
Haua Fteah, 110
Hausa States, 118
Hawaii, 191-4
Hayonim, 59, 60, 61
Heve, 171
Himalayas, 127
Hindu Kush, 127
Hoabinhian culture, 145-63, *146, 147, 150*
Hoggar highlands, 102, 107, 110
Holocene period, 16, 22, 64; populations of, *17*
Horner site, 213
Hwang-Ho Valley, 117

Iban longhouse, *44*
India, 99, 117, 127, *129,* 131, 135, 139, 142, 163, 189; Central, 34; Northern, 33; Southern, 16, 34: *see also* Asia, South; Indian Stone Age, 131
Indians: Choco, 239; Eastern Woodland, 222; Penobscot, 222; Shoshoni, 229, 232; Zapotec, 235; *see also* American Indians
Indonesia, 34, 103, 148
Indus, River, 93, 97, 115, 131
Industries: Acheulian, 74, 200; Aurignacoid, 205; Levallois-Mousterian, 74; Lungshanoid, 157; Mousterian, 128, 131, 200, 205, 207; pre-projectile, projectile, 200 *and see* Traditions; *see also* Harappan, Hoabinhian, Mesolithic, Neolithic, Palaeolithic, Pleistocene
Inter-Tropical Convergence Zone, 115
Iraq, 52, 93
Iran, 52, 93; Iranian Plateau, 117
Irian Jaya, 171
Iron Age, 109, 136
Ivory Coast, 93
Iwo Elero, 77, 83

Jamuna, River, 135
Japan, 16, *18,* 20, 34; Japan Current, 200
Java, 15, 148, 160
Jebba, *72*
Jebel Kafzeh, 15
Jebel Moya, 107
Jebel Qeili, *98*
Jebel Tomat, 99
Jericho, 58, 59, 61, 62, 63

Kalibangan, 131
Kaironk Valley, 179
Kamabai, 83
Kanem/Bornu, 118
Kanjera, 15
Karkarichinkat, 83
Kathiawar, 135
Kebarah, 59-61; Kebaran culture, 53, 54, 62, 64
Keilor, 183
Keniaba, 77
Kenya, 110
Kerala, 128
Kets, 20
Kharga Oasis, 107
Khartoum, 99, 102
Khimiya, 83
Khoikhoi, 109
Khon Pa, 149
Kindia, 83
Kintampo, 83, 92, 106, 107, 110
Kiowa, 185
Koita, 173
Kokosu, 83
Komonku, 173
Kosipe, 183-4
Kot-Diji, 131
Kotoko, 102
Koumi, 77
Kourounkorokale, 77, *80-1,* 83, *85, 86-7*
Kubus, 149, 153
Kuchi, 139
Kuk, 175, *177,* 179, *180,* 183, 185
!Kung Bushmen, 42, 43, 153
Kwangsi, 148

Laang Spean, 149, *150-1, 152,* 158
Lake Chad, 99, 102
Lake Mungo, 15
Langhnaj, *132, 141*
Laos, 148
Lau Islands, 193
Lehner, *210,* 211
Leicester symposium, 25
Leopard's Kopje Culture, 109
Levallois-Mousterian, 209; *see also* Industries
Levant, the, 107
Levi Rockshelter level, 205
Lewisville, 207
Liberia, 83
Limpopo, 109

Lindenmeier site, 211, *212,* 213
Llano Estado region, 209
Lungshanoid, *see* Industries

Mackenzie Gap, 200
Macropodidae, 183
Madagascar, 103, 116
Maharastra, 128, 135
Maine, 222
Malacca Strait, 148
Malawi, 99, 102
Malaya, 148, 149, 153, 155, 158;
    Malay Aboriginal, 149, 153; Malay
    Peninsula, 84
Malaysia, 184, 192
Mali, 77, *80-1,* 83, *85, 86-7,* 118
Mansuy, 148
Maori, 191, 194; ethnohistory, 195
Mapa, 15
Marind Anim, 169
Marquesas Islands, 191; Marquesans, 191,
    194
Mauretania, 77, 102, 107, 110
Mediterranean, 128, 163; coastlands, 32
Megiddo, 60, 61
Mejiro Cave, 77, *78*
Melanesia, 12, 169, 175, 189, 191, 192;
    Melanesians, 167
Meroe, 99, 111; Meroitic period, 97
Mesoamerica, 11, 12, 31, 32, 43, *217,*
    225, 227, 233, 234, 235, 239, 240,
    242, 243; *see also* America, Central
Mesolithic culture, 131; deposits, 56;
    European, 22, 218; economy, 52;
    hunting people, 136; industries, 58;
    levels, 142; population, 62;
    settlements, 59, 63; sites, 56, 59, 139,
    141; South-West Asian, 22
Mesopotamia, 189; Mesopotamian
    desert, 127
Mexico, 225-47; Period of Incipient
    Agriculture in, 229, 232; Period of
    Incipient Cultivation in, 229, 231;
    Mexicans, 232, 238, 240
Micronesia, 189
Middle Niger Delta region, 102
Mindanao, 149, 155
Mohenjo Daro, 135
Mojave desert, 207
Mo'orea, 193
Morioris, 194
Mount Carmel, 61, 64
Mount Hagen, 175, 177
Mousterian; *see* industries
Mrabri, 149
Mrbrai forest collectors, 155
Munhatta, 58
Mysore, 135, 142

Nahal Oren, 53, 54, *55,* 56, *57,* 58-62,
    64
Nam Wa Valley, 153
Narosura, 110
Natufian, culture, 53; sites, 59-61, 63

Neanderthalers, European, 15; South-
    East Asian, 16
Near Eastern Stocks, 22
Negritos, 16, 149, 153
Negros, 96
Nepal, 127
Neolithic, 83; Aceramic, 54, 56, *57,*
    58-64; Ceramic, 56, *57;* communities,
    243, 246; cultures, 131, 136;
    economy, 52; Kenyon's Pre-Pottery,
    53; of the Old World, 222; Pottery,
    61, Pre-Pottery, 63: *see also*
    Aceramic; Neolithic Revolution, 41;
    Sahara, 83, 93; settlements, 133, *141;*
    sites, 56, 139; technology, 51
Netsilik Eskimo, 42
Nevasa, *140*
New Britain, *182*
New Guinea: *see* Papua New Guinea;
    Highlands, 156
New Mexico, 209, *210,* 211
New Todzi, 77
New World, 20, 22, 63, 200, 202,
    204-5, *206,* 207, 218
New Zealand, 168, 191, 192, 194
Nhampasseré, 83
Niah cave, 15, 184
Niamey Est, 77
Niger, 77; River, *72,* 96, 97
Nigeria, 71, *75-6,* 77, *78-9,* 83, *89, 92,*
    93, 99, 106 107, 115, 116
Nile, River, 93, 97, 99, 107, 110, 111,
    117, 127
Nombe, 183
North Luzon, 148
Ntereso, 83, *84*
Nubia, Egyptian, 97
'Nuclear Mande' series, 96-7

Oaxaca, Valley of, 227, 229, 233,
    235-6, *237,* 246-7
Old Cordilleran complex, 213, *216,* 218
Old Oyo, 77, *78*
Old World, 16, 110, 200, 205, *206,* 207,
    222, 225
Olsen-Chubbuck kill-site, 213, *214-15*
Omo, 15
Ongba Cave, 149
Orang Batin, 149
Oregon, 218
Oudia, 83
Outer Banda Archipelago, 160
Oyo, 118

Paccaicasa, 207
Pacific, 20, 28, 168, 169, *190;* islands
    of western Pacific, 157
Padah-Lin, 149
Paiute, 218, *219*
Pakistan, 127, 131, 135, 139
Palaeo-Indians, 20, 22, 200, *201,* 204,
    209, 211, 213, 218
Palaeolithic, Lower, 59, 128, 205;
    Middle, 61, 62, 128, 131, 205; Upper,

16, 20, 42, 53, 54, 59, 61; industries, 131
Palembang, 153
Palestine, 53, 58, 59, 60, 62
Pamirs, 128
Panama, 239
Papua New Guinea, 34, *45*, 167-86, *170, 172*, 174, *176;* Papuan man, *18*
Penan, 149, 153
Peru, 11, 200, 207
Phi Tong Luang, 149
Philippines, 34, 148, 149, 153, *154*
Pikimachay, 207
Pita, 83
'Plano' complex, 209, 211
Pleistocene, late, 16, 20, 22, 64, 65, 158, 160; man, 185; Middle, 15; period, *17*, 52, 109, 180, 184, 199, 227; Post-, 148, 157, 162, 227, 238, 241, 246; Pleistocene-Recent boundary, 149; terminal, 227; tools, 18; Upper, 15, 16, 22
Polynesia, 189-96
Port Moresby, 167, 173
Puebla, 227
Punan, 149,153
Punjab, 135
Pushkar Raj, 138, 139
Pygmies, 118, 149

Quafsah, 60, 61, 64

Rajasthan, 102, 128, 135, 138, 142; Rajasthan Nilgai, 135
Rakafet, 59 -62, 64
Rancholabrean period, 222
Recent period, early, 158; Mid-, 160, 162
Red Sea, 96
Rhodesia, 15, 99, 102, 109, 110
Rigveda, 138
Rim, 77
Rio Salado, 241
Rocky Mountains, 200, 205
Romans, 11
Romer's Rule, 238
Rop, 77, 83, *89*
Rufisque, 83
Russia, South, 128

Sahara, 15, 32, 69, 71, 77, 99, 102, 106, 111, 112, 115, 127
Sahul shelf, *159*
Saldaha population, 15
Samoa, 191, 193
San (Bushmen), 118
Sandia Cave, 211, *212*
Sangoan tools, 74
Santa Lucia, 239
Sarawak, 181
Scottsbluff Milnesand hunters, 213; point types, *216*
Semang, 153, 162
Senegal, 74, 93
Senoi, 149, 153

Shaheinab, 102, 106, 110
Shanidar, 54
Shang Dynasty, 115
Sheik' Ali, 60-1
Shipibo, 238-40
Shuqbah, 60-1
Siberia, 20, 200, 202, 205, 209
Sierra Leone, 77, *82*, 83, *84*
Simbai, 179
Sind, 135, 139
Skhul, 15
Society Islands, 191, 195
Solo, 15
Songhai, 118
Sopie, 83
Spanish Conquest, 227, 241
Spirit Cave, 149, 157, 158, 162
Sri Lanka, *18*, 127, *137*
'Stone Bowl' folk, 109; Stone Bowl site, 110
Suberde, 52, 53
Sudan, 15, 97, 99, 106, 107
Sukajadi Kec., 147
Sulawesi, 149
Sumatra, *147*, 148, 149, 153, 155, 160
Sunda shelf, *159*, 160, *161*
Swazi tribe, *18*
Syria, 58, 62

Tahiti, 193, 195
Taiwan, 157
Tamaulipas, 227, 229, 231, 243, 244
Tamil plain, 128
Tanzania, 99
Tapi estuary, 135
Tasaday, 149, 153, *154*, 162
Tassili, 107
Tchad, Republic of, 93
Tehuacan Valley, 205, 222, *226*, 229, *230*, 231-3, 235, 239, 241-3, 247; sequence, 231
Tell Abu Hureyra, 56, *57*, 58-9, 62, 63
Tell Gezer, 54, 56
Tell Mureybit, 58, 59, 62, 63
Tepe Guran, 54, *55*
Texas, 207, 209, 227
Thailand, 148-9, 153, 155, 158, 162
Thai-Laos border, 155
Thar desert, 127, 135
Tibesti, 107
Tiemassas, 74
Tierra del Fuego, 209
Tigris/Euphrates, 93, 97, 127
Timor, 181
Tiwi, 42
Toala, 149, 153
Toda woman, *18*
Togo hills, 71
Tonga, 191, 193; Tongan ethnohistory, 195
Tonkin, 148, 162
Traditions, Blade, Burin and Leaf-point, 207, *208*, 213; Core Tool, 207, *208;* Desert, 218; Flake and Bone Tool,

207, *208;* Specialized Bifacial Point, 207, 213
Trans-Fly region, 174
Tsembaga, 168, 174
Tu'i Tonga, 193
'Tumbian', 83
Tunisia, 107
Turkey, 53
Turner, Frederick Jackson, 25: *see also* Frontier, moving

Uganda, 111, 116
Upper Volta, 77
'Upper Yengeman', 83
Utah, 218, *219*
Uttar Pradesh, 135

Van Niekerk ruins, 99

Vavilov, 96
Veddas, 136, *137*
Vietnam, 148, 149, 158

Wahgi Valley, 175
Wanlek, 179
Wanyanga, 107
'Wave Front' theory, 33
Wyoming, 213

Yagala, 83
Yangtze River, 156
Yengema, 77, *82, 84*
Yuku, *190*

Zambezi, 109
Zambia, 99, 109, 110
Zulus, *47*

9936